DATE DUE

~~NO 8 00~~			
AP 2 '02			
~~MR~~ 22 06			

BORDER HEALTH

GARLAND REFERENCE LIBRARY OF SOCIAL SCIENCE
VOLUME 909

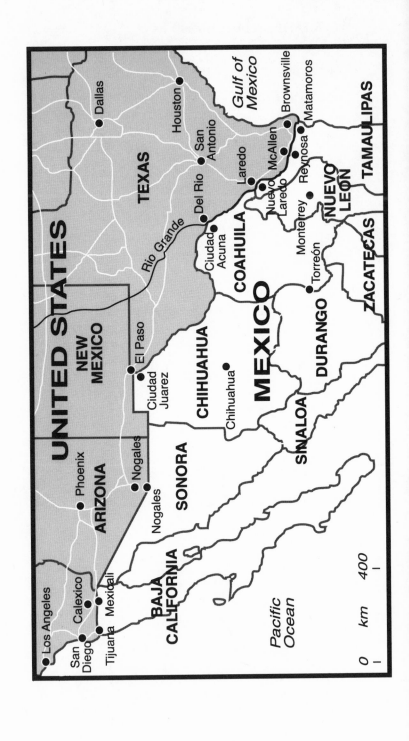

BORDER HEALTH
CHALLENGES FOR THE
UNITED STATES AND MEXICO

EDITED BY
JOHN G. BRUHN AND
JEFFREY E. BRANDON

GARLAND PUBLISHING, INC.
NEW YORK AND LONDON
1997

Copyright © 1997 by John G. Bruhn and Jeffrey E. Brandon
All rights reserved

Library of Congress Cataloging-in-Publication Data

Border health : challenges for the United States and Mexico / edited by John G.
    Bruhn and Jeffrey E. Brandon.
            p.   cm. — (Garland reference library of social science ; v. 909)
        Includes bibliographical references and index.
        ISBN 0-8153-1386-1 (alk. paper)
        1. Public health—Mexican-American Border Region.   I. Bruhn, John
    G., 1934– . II. Brandon, Jeffrey E.   III. Series.
    RA446.5.M49B665   1997
    362.1'0972'1—dc21   97-1984
                                                                             CIP

Printed on acid-free, 250-year-life paper
Manufactured in the United States of America

CONTENTS

Foreword

Enemies in war, allies in war, trading partners, and economic competitors—these are a few of the many relationships that Mexico and the United States have shared during their history. Their futures are inextricably codependent due, among other things, to the 2,000 mile border they share.

I was born and raised along the U.S.-Mexico border. I had the opportunity to live on both sides of the border and know first-hand how interrelated their actions are. Along much of the border, the citizens of both countries rely on the Rio Grande as a recipient of their sewage and as the source of their drinking water. If one country pollutes the air and the other does not, they both inhale polluted air. An infectious disease outbreak in one country quickly makes its presence known in the other. Citizens of each country eat in the other country's restaurants, and food is one of the many commodities that are constantly imported and exported across the border. In addition, an economic downturn in one country quickly makes its presence known in the economy of the other, in many cases impacting on the populations' financial access to medical care.

Despite their interdependent future, the U.S. and Mexican sides of the border are sometimes separated by language and cultural differences—differences in the supply, training, and orientation of their medical and public health providers; economic opportunities; political philosophies; and educational opportunities.

The significance of this immense border notwithstanding, little research has been conducted to assess the health status of the populations that reside in this large geographic area. John Bruhn and Jeffrey Brandon have made a impressive contribution to our knowledge with this book on the health of the U.S.-Mexico border region.

Fernando M. Treviño, Ph.D., M.P.H.
President, World Federation of Public Health Associations

PREFACE

In October 1990 the University of Texas System organized a task force and sponsored the first annual symposium on border health. The primary purpose of the first symposium, and of those that followed, was to increase communication among health educators, professionals, and researchers working in the Rio Grande Valley from El Paso to Brownsville, Texas.

Only during the last decade has border health become a topic of significance. Numerous books and articles have been written about health conditions, services, beliefs, and practices among Mexican Americans, but only since the population along the U.S.-Mexico border increased has serious attention been given to health on the border. Many of these health problems are not new, but have become more severe, such as air and water pollution. The migration of Mexicans into the United States and the recent North American Free Trade Agreement (NAFTA) have focused more attention on the U.S.-Mexico border.

As Treviño (1982) pointed out, the United States has the sixth largest Hispanic population in the world, exceeded only by Mexico, Spain, Columbia, Argentina, and Peru, yet it was not until 1978 that the National Center for Health Statistics (NCHS) recommended, for the first time, the addition of a Hispanic identifier to birth and death certificates. While vital statistics are important in providing data on the health status of a population, data on Hispanic health in all its aspects are needed. Not until the Hispanic Health and Nutrition Examination Survey (HHANES) (1990) was launched under the auspices of the U.S. Department of Health and Human Services were any findings on the health status and health care needs of Hispanics available on a national level.

Recently funded programs and initiatives by the Pan American Health Organization, in collaboration with the Carnegie and Pew Foundations, and a large Kellogg grant awarded to the University of Texas at El Paso and Texas

Tech University Regional Health Science Center at El Paso, are examples of efforts to ascertain the health needs of border residents and explore effective ways of meeting these needs. Other projects address the needs of the Lower Rio Grande Valley in Texas and sites along the U.S.-Mexico border extending west to California.

We thought a volume focusing on border health would be a valuable text or resource for teachers and researchers, as well as for readers wanting to become better informed about the U.S.-Mexico border, its lifestyle, culture, problems, and prospects. While we do not pretend to be experts on border health, we have lived on the U.S.-Mexico border and are acquainted first hand with its health issues and problems. Our relationships with colleagues who have carried out research or provided direct health care have helped to inform us about border health. We realize that the U.S.-Mexico border constitutes a dynamic social system. The character of the border changes from day to day. As people move across boundaries, statistics change, and so do people's daily needs, including their health needs. Some information in this volume, therefore, will become dated, but we hope the general principles and approaches we suggest will remain vital for some time.

We hope this volume will not only provide information to the reader, but will arouse the curiosity of researchers and mobilize others to become involved in efforts to make the border a healthier place to live.

John G. Bruhn
Jeffrey E. Brandon

REFERENCES

Hispanic Health and Nutrition Examination Survey, 1982–84: Findings on health status and health care needs (1990). *American Journal of Public Health, 80*, Supplement, 3–72.

Treviño, F. M. (1982). Vital and health statistics for the U.S. Hispanic population, *American Journal of Public Health, 72* (9), 979–981.

ACKNOWLEDGMENTS

We are grateful to Paula Levine for her expertise in editing, her constructive comments, and for assembling the index. We also appreciate the patience and assistance of Elena Cook, Jan Russ, and Nancy Hollis, who typed many drafts of the manuscript.

INTRODUCTION

John G. Bruhn

The border between the United States and Mexico stretches from the Pacific Ocean to the Gulf of Mexico. It is the longest unfortified international boundary in the world. Four American and six Mexican states face each other along the length of the border (Carnegie Foundation, 1991).

In traveling the two thousand miles that divide the United States and Mexico it is almost impossible to find a sign that defines the border between the two countries, except at official checkpoints. The line is emotional for politicians and artificial for people who live on either side (Fromson, 1993).

With millions of legal and illegal crossings each year, it is a border that is artificially maintained. The American government spends billions of dollars a year on satellites, helicopters, and ground patrols to keep out illegal immigrants and drug smugglers, largely in vain.

Some international rituals are observed. The United States tries to straighten out the wiggles of the Rio Grande River, which forms the eastern half of the international border. The Mexicans demand compensation for every acre lost to them in the straightening process. But the day-to-day economic reality is blurring boundary lines. The border is no longer a line, it is a region (*The Economist*, 1992).

A line becomes a boundary when we imagine that it separates, but doesn't unite at the same time (Wilber, 1981). A common view of the U.S.-Mexico border is that it is a political boundary that separates two distinct countries. Yet Mexico and the United States are culturally and economically related social systems. Communities along the U.S.-Mexico border are organized around social and economic activities. Some scholars have described the border as a "culture matrix" (Gutierrez-Witt, 1990). The movement of people back and forth across the California border, for example, is historically conditioned from colonial days when people from Mexico immigrated to the U.S. for employment and people from the United States emigrated to

Mexico to maintain contact with family and friends (Alvarez, 1984). More recently the movement of people from Mexico and Latin America across the Mexican border to the United States has been viewed as a problem because of the social costs of illegal immigration. The focus on immigration has caused the public, and public policy experts, to view the border as a place of transition and border communities as temporary, rapidly changing segments of society (Alvarez, 1984). Efforts have recently been made to curtail illegal immigration into the United States by the Immigration and Naturalization Services. While the motivations for stricter border control included the greater restraint of crime and drug traffic, the timing of these enforcements, which paralleled the debates over NAFTA, was unfortunate, and generated negative feelings and attitudes on both sides of the border.

In 1900, an estimated 36,000 people lived on the U.S.-Mexico border. In 1990, the total population of the ten border states in the U.S. and Mexico was 65 million. This growth is due to several factors: (1) the population of Hispanics from Mexico and Central America is increasing in the United States; (2) drought, unemployment, and a succession of peso devaluations since the 1970s have emptied entire Mexican villages of young people, who have migrated to the border to work; (3) increasing numbers of U.S. retirees and vacationers, and the location of some U.S. industrial plants on the Mexican side of the border, have contributed to the population shift and growth; and (4) cooperation between the United States and Mexico due to the North American Free Trade Agreement is making the border an increasingly choice site for international industry. Soon the United States and Mexico will not simply meet at their common borders, they will merge, to the benefit of both (Pan American Health Organization, 1991).

Ortega (1991) regards the border not as a dividing line, but as a place where two civilizations meet. The border region constitutes a special mosaic of ethnicity, history, language, customs, climates, and landscapes. The persistence of the cultural integrity of several Indian groups indigenous to the border region shows that some cultures have been strong enough to resist some change and maintain their independence.

There are many, often competing, images of the border. To some the border is something that must be routinely crossed; to others it is a barrier to be challenged; to still others, the border is more symbol than reality. The border is also viewed in economic terms as a place of opportunity. These various views offer little help in defining the border. Chavez (1992) asks, "Where does the border begin?" He points out that defining the border as territory or political boundary emphasizes the endpoints or limits of the region. Indeed, the states which are contiguous to each other are not the only ones influenced by border activities. Chavez stresses the importance of linkages. Despite the uniqueness of the border, many activities and behaviors link both sides. Kinship, friendship, and economic ties force one to define the border by "what it is" as well as "what it isn't." The fact that the border is part of, and linked with, two larger national social systems where decisions are made and policies formulated often makes the people residing there feel isolated and somewhat incidental in shaping their own present and future.

Being on one or the other side of the border does make a difference. No common, continuous social, cultural, political, economic, or health care system exists on either side of the border. Despite overlaps in language and customs, people on opposite sides of the border respond and adapt to different cultural and social environments. Nevertheless "borderlanders" usually have a general understanding of the culture of "the other side," especially when a high level of economic interdependence exists (Pastor & Castaneda, 1989). Ways must be devised to counteract such exclusionary features inherent in boundaries as government policies. From the two governments' viewpoints, boundaries are to be monitored and regulated, with border needs and interests being of secondary importance. International boundaries have always been a source of trouble. Borders typically have served as buffer zones to diminish international disputes.

The tensions, conflicts, and misperceptions that have always characterized the U.S.-Mexican relationship are rooted in history and changes in each of the countries. These have led to policy mistakes and misconceptions. Pastor and Castaneda (1989) said, "As our children grow [up] on both sides of the border, they might relate as poorly as present and past generations have. But we hope they will understand each other better. . . . Cooperation between the United States and Mexico will always be difficult but never impossible."

Inhabitants along the U.S.-Mexico border have long fostered transborder cooperation with minimal encouragement from the two federal governments (Martinez, 1986). With a rapidly growing population, increased economic interdependence, common environmental problems, and the cross-border utilization of health services, binational initiatives are clearly needed. Air and water pollution affects people on both sides of the border. Daily, 12 million gallons of raw sewage flow into the Tijuana River, which flows into the United States from Mexico (Warner, 1991). The subsurface ground water is almost totally contaminated bacteriologically and soon may be contaminated chemically (Nickey, 1989). Serious pollution of our common airshed, and control of toxic and hazardous wastes, especially the illegal dumping of hazardous waste from one country to another, also need transborder solutions. All too often, we wait until issues become confrontational crises before we attempt to solve them. Planning for prevention and the resolution of problems usually occur independently on separate sides of the border. Planners proceed as if they are operating within self-contained systems.

Current and future problems on the U.S.-Mexico border are ecological and interrelated. They may also be political, economic, and cultural, but unless we take an ecological, holistic perspective, problems will be approached only in a piecemeal fashion. An ecological approach also recognizes the dynamism of the U.S.-Mexico border. Valenzuela (1992) has described the border as a "floating population," emphasizing the mobility and interdependence of the two countries. Efforts to plan for and prioritize resource needs and issues along the U.S.-Mexico border were begun almost a decade ago (Alba, 1984). Many of the problems anticipated then are now pressing problems. It is essential that the two countries establish priorities for access to and use of shared resources such as air and water.

The lack of universal access to good quality health care and preventive health services is one of the border's greatest problems. Along the Texas border, where more than 73 percent of the population is Hispanic, less than half of the people in some counties have private health insurance. Two-thirds of the poor are not eligible for Medicaid (Carnegie Foundation, 1991). Tuberculosis is endemic on both sides of the border, and hepatitis A, dysentery, upper respiratory infections (pneumonia and influenza), cervical cancer, diabetes mellitus, obesity, anemia, gall bladder disease, high blood pressure, teenage pregnancy, and accidents are common (Villas & Flew, 1992). Violence, drug abuse, crime, emotional and physical abuse, homelessness, and unemployment are also common in border cities where risk-taking is high and anonymity is low.

Residents cross the border for health care in both directions. Attractive to Americans are Mexico's national health care system and its devalued currency, making some services more accessible and affordable than they would be in the United States. Nonnarcotic drugs that are available only by prescription in the United States can frequently be purchased over the counter in Mexico at a much lower price. Conversely, the U.S. system with its more sophisticated technologies offers specialized services that Mexico doesn't have. The notion that a permeable border might be of benefit to each side offers a positive perspective to begin transboundary cooperation. Stoddard (1986) has proposed a "Doctrine of Mutual Necessity," which makes both parties functionally equal. Such symbiosis will be necessary if the quality of life is to be improved along the U.S.-Mexico border.

Rodriguez (1992) has said, "For Mexicans, the border is not that rigid

Puritan thing, a line; straight lines are unknown in Mexico. The border, like everything else, is subject to supply and demand. The border is a revolving door."

Wilber (1981) points out that we live in a world of conflict and opposites because we live in a world of boundaries. The solution to the war of opposites requires the surrendering of boundaries. When opposites are realized to be one, "discord melts into concord, battles become dances, and old enemies become lovers. We are then in a position to make friends with all of our universe, and not just one half of it."

As the borders of the United States and Mexico increasingly meld, the two countries will become more like relatives than distant neighbors (Riding, 1989). While economic interdependence is foremost, it is obvious that health and quality-of-life issues must be addressed soon. These issues involve values and beliefs that are markedly different in the two cultures. The greatest challenge is for the two countries to respect their differences, yet work to compromise for the long-term benefit of both. Prevention is essential to resolving common chronic problems. Preventive plans cannot be effective when only one country acts. Prevention is an ecological activity.

Weisman (1986) has aptly stated, "Except for outer space, there are no other frontiers. No place to go to escape the problems or ignore the potential. This frontera is the border between the present and the future: Along it, its people must eventually create yet a newer world."

REFERENCES

Alba, F. (1984). Mexico's northern border: A framework of reference. In C. Sepulveda and A.E. Utton (Eds.), *The U.S.-Mexico border region: Anticipating resource needs and issues to the year 2000* (pp. 21–35). El Paso, TX: Texas Western Press.

Alvarez, R. (1984). The border as a social system: The California case. *The New Scholar, 9,* 119–133.

Carnegie Foundation (1991). Promoting binational cooperation to improve health along the U.S.-Mexico border. Carnegie Corporation of New York. *Carnegie Quarterly, 36* (1, 2), 1–15.

Chavez, L.R. (1992). *Defining and demographically characterizing the southern border of the U.S.* In J.R. Weeks and R. Ham-Chande (Eds.), *Demographic dynamics of the U.S.-Mexico border* (pp. 43–60). El Paso, TX: Texas Western Press.

The Economist (1992). The Mexican-American border. December 12, pp. 21–25.

Fromson, M. (1993). *La Frontera/The Border: An enigma for two nations.* Center for International Journalism, University of Southern California, Los Angeles.

Gutierrez-Witt, L. (1990). United States-Mexico border studies and borderline. *Mexican Studies/Estudios Mexicanos, 6* (24), 121–131.

Martinez, O.J. (1986). Introduction. In O. J. Martinez (Ed.), *Across boundaries: Transborder interaction in comparative perspective* (pp. 1–7). El Paso, TX: Texas Western Press.

Nickey, L.N. (1989). Health along the United States-Mexico border. *The El Paso Physician, 12*(8), 8.

Ortega, H.H. (1991). *Present trends and future possibilities of health along the United States-Mexico border*. El Paso Field Office, Pan American Health Organization, Regional Office of the World Health Organization.

Pan American Health Organization (1991). *United States-Mexico border health statistics*. Seventh Edition, PAHO Field Office, El Paso, TX.

Pastor, R.A. & Castaneda, J.G. (1989). *Limits to friendship. The United States and Mexico* (p. 375). New York: Vintage.

Riding, A. (1989). *Distant neighbors: A portrait of the Mexicans*. New York: Vintage.

Rodriguez, R. (1992). *Days of obligation: An argument with my Mexican father* (p. 91). New York: Penguin Viking.

Stoddard, E.R. (1986). Problem-solving along the U.S.-Mexico border: A United States view. In O. J. Martinez (Ed.), *Across boundaries* (pp. 57–79). El Paso, TX: Texas Western Press.

Valenzuela, G.E. (1992). Health along the United States-Mexico border. In J.R. Weeks and R. Ham-Chande (Eds.), *Demographic dynamics of the U.S.-Mexico border* (pp. 187–200). El Paso, TX: Texas Western Press.

Villas, P. & Flew, E. (1992). Medicalization of the U.S.-Mexico border: Is it really needed? *Rio Bravo*, 2(1), 120–132.

Warner, D. C. (1991). Health issues at the U.S.-Mexico Border. *Journal of the American Medical Association*, 265(2), 242–247.

Weisman, A. (1986). *La Frontera*. New York: Harcourt Brace Jovanovich.

Wilber, K. (1981). *No boundary* (p. 29). Boston, MA: New Science Library.

BORDER HEALTH

1   BORDER CULTURE

John G. Bruhn

CHARACTERISTICS AND TRENDS

The border divides two populous countries with different historical patterns of demographic development (Martinez, 1988). In 1990, Mexico was the eleventh most populous nation in the world and the United States was the fourth most populous. Mexico has been characterized by high rates of population growth throughout the past fifty years due to declining mortality and increased fertility rates. During this same period, the United States experienced a decline in mortality and an uneven birth rate, but well below that of Mexico. Even at the height of the late 1950s baby boom in the United States, fertility levels were only half as high as in Mexico during that time (Ham-Chande & Weeks, 1992).

Until the post–World War II era, the border area was marginal to both the United States and Mexico. It was a traditional frontier between two nations in different stages of development (Herzog, 1990). American business invested heavily on both sides of the border and in northern Mexico, attracted by cheap labor in Mexico (Alba & Potter, 1986). Thus, according to Alegria (1989), it was not just adjacency, but also inequality that helped to shape the character of the border region.

The United States has not had a development strategy for the states that border Mexico and this undoubtedly accounts for the fact that the United States border counties have traditionally been economically deprived. Although poverty in Mexico increases away from the border, in the United States the reverse is true (Dillman, 1983). The ample low-wage Mexican immigrant labor force has decreased wages and increased unemployment on the U.S. side of the border (Baerresen, 1983). However, the border has become a magnet for the migration of people and industry.

It is difficult to be specific about the size and growth of the border population because it depends on how the border is defined and on the resolution of methodological problems in the censuses of both Mexico and the United States. There are important differences in the ways the two countries collect and organize data. For example, the 1990 census count for Ciudad Juárez was just under 800,000 people, while the accepted figure for this time period is 1.2 million. The City of El Paso estimates that 23,000 residents were missed in the 1990 census. Therefore, the error for the Juárez–El Paso border in the 1990 census could be as much as 423,000 (Howard, 1993). If the border is defined as all counties in the United States and municipios in Mexico that are physically adjacent to each other, the population in 1990 was found to be 7.7 million; 4.7 million on the U.S. side and 3.0 million on the Mexican side. The population on the U.S. side appears to be growing more rapidly now than on the Mexican side as a result of the high levels of migration across the border from Mexico to the United States. The number of persons entering the United States at ports of entry along the U.S.-Mexico border in fiscal year 1991 was 146 million, an increase of 49 percent since 1985. It is estimated that there are about 400 million border crossings per year from the United States to Mexico.

Population growth along the border is an urban phenomenon. One of the interesting characteristics of international borders is the development of twin cities that grow up around points of trade and commerce or natural resource bases toward which population tends to concentrate (Martinez, 1994). The relative population sizes and annual growth rates of ten urban areas on the U.S.-Mexico border are shown in Table 1.1. The largest percentage growth in the 1980–1990 decade has been in Tijuana, Nogales, and Juárez. The largest urban border cities are in California, Texas, and New Mexico. Arizona does not have a significant border population.

Despite the uniqueness of the two social environments at the border, there are many activities and behaviors which connect both sides. Kinship and friendship ties bind people together on both sides of the border. Economic ties binding the two areas are evident in the "twin plants" or maquiladoras which extend along the border region in both directions away from the border line (Chavez, 1992).

There is not one continuous system of social, cultural, political, or economic activity on both sides of the border. There is diversity on each side—for example, the Texas border is different from the California border. Likewise, Mexicans experience the same type of diversity depending upon where they live along the border on the Mexican side. The economic disparities across the U.S.-Mexico border account, in part, for immigration from Mexico to the United States. Job opportunities in the labor market have an effect on who migrates and how long they stay.

TABLE 1.1. Population Growth since 1980 in Ten Sister Counties and Municipios on the U.S. Mexico Border

	U.S.			Mexico	
County	1990 Population	% Growth since 1990	Municipio	1990 Population	% Growth since 1990
Cameron	260,120	24.0	Matamoros	303,293	27.0
Hidalgo	383,545	35.4	Reynosa	282,667	33.7
Webb	133,239	34.2	Nuevo Laredo	219,468	8.0
Maverick	36,378	15.9	Piedras Negras	98,185	22.3
Val Verde	38,721	7.8	Acuña	56,336	34.3
El Paso and Doña Ana	727,120	26.2	Juárez	798,499	40.7
Santa Cruz	29,676	45.1	Nogales	107,936	58.6
Yuma	106,895	18.0	San Luis, R.C.	110,530	19.1
Imperial	109,303	34.2	Mexicali	601,938	17.9
San Diego	2,498,016	34.2	Tijuana	747,381	62.0
10 sister communities	4,323,013	31.0	10 sister communities	3,326,233	34.3
23 border counties	5,186,090	29.8	38 municipios	3,890,485	30.3
4 border states	51,926,828	23.9	6 border states	13,246,991	23.9

Source: U.S. Bureau of the Census, Department of Commerce, 1980 and 1990 Census of Population and Housing.

Alvarez (1984) points out that because of the focus on immigration, public policy experts see the border as a place of transition that changes in direct relation to the economies of the United States and Mexico. The border is often portrayed as a marginal social region conditioned by the continual movement of the migrant. Alvarez (1984) argues that the communities on both sides of the border are organized social systems. Rather than view sister cities on the border as operating in two social spheres, they should be seen as intertwined and organized, affecting each other. Migration and mobility are intrinsic parts of the history of border cities. In the case of California, for example, exploration and a pattern of regional interaction was reinforced by missionary exploits in the interior of Baja California, by the mining circuit in southern California, and the developments of agriculture in Mexicali and of tourism in Tijuana (Alvarez, 1984). A community of kinship links and friendship networks has helped to maintain a cultural affinity to Mexico. Thus, the ebb and flow of the population along the U.S.-Mexico border has a long history which provides for a unique society which is often arbitrarily isolated by territorial lines.

FERTILITY, MIGRATION, AND MORTALITY

Demographic dynamics along the border are driven by many factors that produce demographic change, but the mix of these factors in two adjacent societies is what makes the border unique as well as what keeps it in constant flux. Ham-Chande and Weeks (1992) have offered a model to understand border demographic processes. Patterns of growth, they suggest, are largely the result of three processes, namely migration, fertility, and mortality. Migration accounts for approximately one-half of the total population growth along the border, although it may seem greater because of the transiency of the "floating population" and commuters, especially Mexican residents working on the U.S. side of the border.

Migration is the demographic phenomenon most likely to react to local change. This is complicated further by the different motivations people may have for moving to the border or across the border. Political changes, such as amendments to the immigration law, periodic enforcement of green cards by the U.S. Immigration and Naturalization Service, and economic changes may also alter the rate of migration to and across the border.

Fertility also contributes to changes in the demographics of the border. The only fertility study conducted thus far along the border shows a continuum of fertility levels with the highest in Mexico, followed by Mexican-born women residing in the United States, followed by Hispanic women born in the United States, with U.S. non-Hispanics having the lowest levels of fertility along the border (Warren, 1992).

Fertility on the border is complicated by regional diversity on both sides. Vital statistics show that the birth rate is lowest in San Diego, followed by El Paso, and highest in Laredo. Vital statistics from Mexico, however, indicate the pattern of intercity fertility differences is exactly opposite that of the U.S. side, that is, highest in Tijuana, followed by Juárez, and lowest in Nuevo Laredo.

Changes in society may also trigger changes in reproduction. For example, changes in the participation of women in the labor force and higher levels of education almost always negatively impact the birth rate. Fertility declines are also accelerated by the availability of contraceptives. Reproduction is sensitive to sociocultural influences such as across-border interactions.

Mortality patterns on the border are similar to those of fertility; that is, the border levels are higher than the national average on the Mexican side, and just below the national average on the U.S. side. State data for each side of the border indicate that infant mortality rates are about the same in California and Texas as in Tamaulipas and Chihuahua. However, other analyses of infant mortality show that infants born to Mexican immigrant women have lower death rates than those born to either U.S.-born Hispanics or Anglos. Bradshaw and Frisbie (1992) found that Mexican immigrants to the U.S. have a higher life expectancy than U.S.-born Hispanics, although the latter group has a higher life expectancy than people living on the northern border of Mexico. Part of this difference is probably due to selective immigration and part to the differences in the exposure to infectious disease and risk for certain chronic diseases. Mortality tends to decline in times of economic advancement and absence of environmental hazards. Special programs targeted toward children and prevention education directed to all ages also affect mortality trends.

Each of the three demographic processes—fertility, migration, and mortality—contributes to the demographic dynamics of the border region. While in some respects these factors help to fashion a distinctive Borderlands culture, it also true that Americans along the border have become increasingly hispanized and the Mexicans increasingly americanized.

SOCIAL CHARACTERISTICS

One in five residents of the United States lives in the border region. Hispanics represent a significant proportion (25.6 percent) of the population of this region. The majority of the Hispanic population in the border region is of Mexican origin (82 percent).

In general, the U.S. border counties have an older age structure than the Mexican municipios. In Mexico's border states a higher proportion of the population is under age 25, with the U.S. border states having a higher proportion of age 25 or more. Gender distribution is as expected, with females constituting slightly more than half of the population.

The educational indicators for the United States and Mexico are calculated in different ways, but each is appropriate to the general educational norms of each country. The U.S. indicator is based on completing high school and the Mexican indicator is based on completing primary school. On the U.S. side the lowest percentages of adult high school graduates are in Texas. In Mexico 70 percent or more of the population 15 years and older of most sister municipios have completed primary school. People in the U.S. border counties are less well educated than the U.S. average, but better educated than their counterparts in Mexico.

Indicators of poverty along the border differ for the United States and

Mexico. In the United States the definition is people living with incomes below the federally fixed poverty income level; in Mexico, the circumstance of poverty is living in a house without proper sewage service. Patterns differ among the border communities. In some cases a higher percentage of people in poverty is indicated in the U.S. county (e.g., 50.4 percent in Maverick County versus 29.4 percent in Piedras Negras). In others, the percentage is higher in Mexico (35.7 percent in Tijuana versus 11.3 percent in San Diego County), and in a few instances, the communities are similar (El Paso, 26.8 percent and Juárez, 23.9 percent) (Selwyn, 1993).

In Mexico, the percentage of people living in housing units without drainage to a sewer or septic tank ranges from 18.2 percent to 89.4 percent. In 24 of the 38 border municipios fewer than 50 percent of housing unit occupants have drainage, but all of the municipios have more than 50 percent of their residents living in housing with drainage.

In U.S. border counties, from 11.3 percent to 60 percent of the population is living below the federal poverty income level. Starr County, Texas, has the highest percentage. All but one of the U.S. border counties have a higher poverty level than the national average. The average household size in border counties and municipios is generally smaller in the U.S. than in Mexico. In U.S. border counties from 13 percent to 61.8 percent of families with children under age 18 are living in poverty. U.S. border counties have less than one-third of families with children being parented by one person.

Substantial income differentials exist for the two sides of the border. In U.S. border cities the median income is generally three to four times the level in the Mexican municipios. However, there is a wide variation among the U.S. cities. This gap in the level of earning potential on the two sides of the border obviously impacts migration.

The border represents a thriving industrial corridor intimately linking both countries through twin cities and production plants. Maquiladora plants, which literally mean "mills" in Spanish, were set up to speed up the country's industrialization process. In 1965, Mexico and the United States encouraged the establishment of export-oriented maquiladoras as a means to stimulate employment and act as a stopgap measure against massive immigration to the United States. Export-oriented maquiladoras have relied primarily on women's labor (Guendelman, 1993).

Maquiladoras have settled primarily in three cities in Mexico—Juárez, Tijuana, and Matamoros. Mexico became a desirable location after the debt crisis of 1982, which forced a large currency devaluation and subsequent unemployment. These conditions prompted many women to search for jobs in the maquiladoras. Female labor is cheaper and women are thought to have traits which make them excellent workers. Most workers are women under the age of 30. It is estimated that there are about 1,697 maquiladoras in the border states of Mexico employing approximately 475,000 young adults (Carnegie Foundation, 1991).

Typically, Mexican border cities are larger than their U.S. counterparts and tend to grow faster, making it difficult to provide city services such as drinking water, adequate sewage disposal, public transportation, housing, and solid waste disposal. There are fewer capital resources in Mexico also, which adds to the problem of keeping pace with the need. The "colonias" (unincorporated housing developments) on the U.S. side also often lack water for sewage or drinking (Selwyn, 1993). El Paso alone has at least 350 colonias with an estimated population of 28,000 to 50,000.

The economic base of the border region has been agriculture, ranching, trade, tourism, and manufacturing. Major industries along the border are agriculture aided by large irrigation projects, mining, oil, natural gas, and maquilas. For all of these industries the handling of internal plant environments and the material produced is important to the health of the workers and to the population around the industry.

BINATIONAL PROBLEMS

The Rio Grande River (U.S.)/Rio Bravo del Nor te (Mexico) forms the border of Texas and four states of Mexico, providing the means for drinking water and sewage, runoff from agricultural land, irrigating farm land, and receiving effluent from industrial plants. The border area suffers from severe pollution. Nuevo Laredo dumps 20 million gallons of raw sewage each day into the Rio Grande, a river from which communities downstream draw all of their drinking water, often in old metal containers from Mexican factories. Health hazards, such as gastroenteritis, polio, hepatitis A, cholera, dysentery, and acute and chronic poisoning are exacerbated when water is contaminated.

There are also episodes of health difficulties resulting from tire burning, auto exhaust, pesticide spraying, lead, and other hazards. Air flow and wind do not recognize human boundaries and represent binational challenges. The levels of air pollution, mainly related to motor vehicles, pose problems to public health all along the U.S.-Mexico border. The problems are particularly acute in the El Paso–Ciudad Juárez metroplex, which has the largest number of registered motor vehicles along the border. Both cities fail to meet standards for carbon monoxide. Vehicles travel on unpaved roads within and on the outskirts of the two cities, raising clouds of suspended particles. Hydrocarbons from the vehicles add to the pollution problem. They react in the atmosphere to produce oxidants. El Paso is out of compliance for acceptable ozone levels (Gray et al., 1989).

Soil pollution from the waste of various industries and agricultural fertilizers and pesticides is also a health concern. With the opening of negotiations with the maquiladora industry in Mexico, the impact that the local factories would have on environmental health was not contemplated, nor was the way hazardous wastes generated by the production processes were going to be handled. While toxic substances and residues have entered or left the U.S.-Mexico border for several decades, their movement is a relatively recent concern (Garza, 1992). In the General Ecological and Environmental Regulation Law and in Article XI of EPA Understanding and Regulation, published under the Resources, Conservation and Recovery Act (RCRA), it was established that toxic substance residues that cross the border as raw material for the production of the maquiladora industry should be returned to the original shipping point once they have been transformed. However, Garza (1992) reports evidence that suggests that compliance in Mexico by the maquiladoras for 1990 was only between 30 and 35 percent.

THE NEW MORBIDITIES

Stehney (1994) points out the health impacts of the economic and social changes on the U.S.-Mexico border which will grow as a result of NAFTA. Stehney makes an analogy between the border and American inner cities, warning that the results could be similar. He states that colonias are the equivalent of urban slums. Cross-border drug smuggling creates conditions for violence and substance abuse. Highly mobile, marginalized populations experience the erosion of traditional values and an increase in behaviors that promote pregnancy among single teens, spread of HIV infection, transborder spread of vaccine-preventable disease to unimmunized children, and partially treated drug-resistant tuberculosis among adults and children. Social transformations will create new disease morbidities, which, in turn, will increase the need to ameliorate social conditions conducive to generating disease, social problems, and unhealthy environments.

IMMIGRATION

Until disparities in wealth and income between the United States and Mexico decrease, the United States probably will continue to act as an economic magnet for Mexicans and other Latin Americans in search of employment and income opportunities. No set of data specifically identifies a person as a legal or illegal immigrant to the United States; therefore, the undocumented status of persons is an inference (Bean et al., 1986).

Two estimates have appeared in the literature based on analyses of 1980 data. One study by Bean and his colleagues (1983) utilized 1980 Mexican Census data and the other study conducted by Warren (1982) and Warren and Passel (1984) used 1980 United States data. These two independent data sets were collected at approximately the same time in Mexico and the United States. The approach taken in the research conducted by Bean and colleagues focuses on a comparison between the hypothetical sex ratio one would expect to find in Mexico in the absence of emigration to the United States and the sex ratio that was reported in the results of the 1980 Mexican Census. Bean and his colleagues estimate the size of the illegal migrant population of Mexican origin in the United States to range from about 1.5 to about 3.8 million persons. The research conducted by Warren and Passel involves the development of procedures to estimate the number of illegal migrants included in the 1980 U.S. Census. Their results indicate that 1,131,000 illegal Mexicans were included in the 1980 United States Census.

Heer (1990) states that a likely estimate of the total number of illegal Mexicans present in the United States at any one time during 1980 can be obtained by adding the 1,131,000 illegal Mexicans counted in the 1980 Census to 650,000 illegal Mexicans who were in the U.S. sometime during 1978 but were residents of Mexico. This results in a total of 1,781,000. Heer states that economic opportunity strongly affects when illegal Mexicans settle in the U.S. In his studies of the social consequences of illegal immigration in California, Heer found that while it appears that the economic effects of Mexican immigration are positive to Los Angeles County, the effects on the rest of California are mixed.

REFERENCES

Alba, F., & Potter, J. (1986). Population and development in Mexico since 1940: An interpretation. *Population and Development Review* 12(1), 47–76.

Alegria, T. (1989). *La Cuidad y la frontera en el limite de Mexico con EUA.* Tijuana: COLEF.

Alvarez, R. (1984). The border as a social system: The California case. *The New Scholar,* 9 (1–2), 119–133.

Baerresen, D.W. (1983). Economic overview. In E.R. Stoddard, R.L. Nostrand & J.P. West (Eds.), *Borderlands sourcebook* (pp. 121–128). Norman, OK: University of Oklahoma Press.

Bean, F.D., King, A.G., & Passel, J.S. (1983). The number of illegal migrants of Mexican origin in the United States: Sex-ratio-based estimates for 1980. *Demography,* 20, 99–109.

Bean, F.D., King, A.G., & Passel, J.S. (1986). Estimates of the size of the illegal migrant population of Mexican origin in the United States: An assessment, review and proposal. In H.L. Browning & R.O. de la Garza (Eds.), *Mexican immigrants and Mexican Americans* (pp. 13–36). Austin, TX: Center for Mexican American Studies Publications.

Bradshaw, B.S. & Frisbie, W.P. (1992). Mortality of Mexican immigrants: Comparisons with Mexico. In J.R. Weeks & R. Ham-Chande (Eds.), *Demographic dynamics of the U.S.-Mexico border* (pp. 125–150). El Paso, TX: Texas Western Press.

Carnegie Foundation (1991). Promoting binational cooperation to improve health along the U.S.-Mexico border, Carnegie Corporation of New York. *Carnegie Quarterly 36*(1, 2), 1-15.

Chavez, L.R. (1992). Defining and demographically characterizing the southern border of the U.S. In J.R. Weeks & R. Ham-Chande (Eds.), *Demographic dynamics of the U.S.-Mexico border* (pp. 43–60). El Paso, TX: Texas Western Press.

Dillman, C.D. (1983). Border urbanization. In E. Stoddard, R. Nostrand, & J. West (Eds.), *Borderlands sourcebook*. Norman: University of Oklahoma Press.

Garza, V. (1992). Transborder movement of toxic substances and its risks for public health. *Border Health Journal* 8(4), 1–6.

Gray, R., Reynoso, J., Conrado, D.Q., & Applegate, H.G. (1989). *Vehicular traffic and air pollution in El Paso-Cd. Juarez*. El Paso, TX: Texas Western Press.

Guendelman, S. (1993). Working women and the maquila industry. Symposium "Foundation for the future: The health of the family in the United States-Mexico border." February 17–19, El Paso, TX: Pan American Health Organization.

Ham-Chande, R. & Weeks, J.R. (1992). A demographic perspective of the U.S.-Mexico border. In J.R. Weeks & R. Ham-Chande (Eds.), *Demographic dynamics of the U.S.-Mexico border* (pp. 1–27). El Paso, TX: Texas Western Press.

Heer, D.M. (1990). *Undocumented Mexicans in the United States*. New York: Cambridge University Press.

Herzog, L.A. (1990). *Where North meets South: Cities, space and politics on the United States-Mexican border*. Austin, TX: University of Texas Press.

Howard, C.A. (1993). Demography of the U.S.-Mexico border region. In H.C. Daudistel & C.A. Howard (Eds.), *Sociological explorations: Focus on the Southwest* (pp. 161–170). St. Paul, MN: West Publishing Co.

Martinez, O.J. (1988). *Troublesome border*. Tucson, AZ: University of Arizona Press.

Martinez, O.J. (1994). *Border people: Life and society in the U.S.-Mexico borderlands*. Tucson, AZ: University of Arizona Press.

Selwyn, B.J. (1993). Epidemiological issues in family health along the U.S.-Mexico border. Symposium "Foundation for the future: The health of the family on the United States-Mexico border." February 17–19, El Paso, TX: Pan American Health Organization.

Stehney, M. (1994). Ghettoization of the border: The potential health impact of free trade. *Border Health Journal, 10,* 15–19.

Warren, C.W. (1992). Determinants of Anglo and Mexican American fertility on the U.S.-Mexico border. In J.R. Weeks & R. Ham-Chande (Eds.), *Demographic dynamics of the U.S.-Mexico border* (pp. 105–124). El Paso, TX: Texas Western Press.

Warren, R. (1982). Estimation of the size of the illegal alien population in the United States. Paper presented at the annual meetings of the Population Association of America, San Diego, CA.

Warren, R. & Passel, J. (1984). A count of the uncountable: Estimates of undocumented aliens counted in the 1980 Census. Revised version of paper presented at the 1983 annual meetings of the Population Association of America, Pittsburgh, PA, April.

2 HEALTH

ITS MEANING AND EXPRESSION

John G. Bruhn

INTRODUCTION

Fabrega (1974, 1979) theorizes that health and illness are physiologically and chemically grounded, but socially and culturally conditioned. Epidemiologic studies have shown that several ethnic groups, such as African Americans, Mexican Americans, and Asian Americans, have rates of heart disease, cancer, diabetes, mental illness, drug abuse, and other health problems well above the national norm. In seeking an explanation for these elevated risk levels, some analysts have pointed to the diet, living conditions, health care behavior, and lifestyles of these groups as the sources of many of their health problems. Taken together, the patterns of behavior of these peoples and their beliefs about the causes and cures of illnesses, which deviate from the norms of the larger Anglo society, have come to be labeled "health care subcultures" (Weaver, 1979).

There is no doubt that health care subcultures are associated with certain mortality and morbidity profiles. However, a useful model to help us to understand why some people get sick and others remain well must be additive and interactive: it should combine consideration for the culture, the beliefs, values, attitudes, and behaviors of the individual as well as the ways in which key factors interact to affect health and illness. Health is a dynamic, changing process. Similarly, individuals and the physical and social environments in which they live continually undergo change. As Fabrega (1974) pointed out, health and disease have different expressions and individualistic consequences—health and disease are not independent variables. The language and grammar of health and disease must be interpreted within behavioral and cultural frameworks.

The U.S.-Mexico border does not divide discrete cultures from one another. It is an interactive border. Cities often have more in common with their immediate neighbors across the border than with other cities on their own side of the border. The culture of health and illness of the people who live along the border is a collage of beliefs, attitudes, and behaviors that are modified as the residents change.

We do not fully understand the health beliefs, attitudes, and behaviors of border residents because they are not uniform. There have been relatively few studies of border health behavior, and some border locations have been studied more than others. It is not our intention to generalize to all border residents what has been learned from these studies. Our purpose is to promote a better understanding of the forces that affect the value placed on health, and the priority given it, on both sides of the border, so that progress can be made in solving common health problems.

THE CONCEPT OF HEALTH AND ITS MEANING

The definition of health often is taken for granted in studies that attempt to understand why some people use certain health services and others do not. We often focus on what people do, or do not do, when they get sick to understand their ideas about health. As a result, the information we obtain reflects only a limited aspect of what they consider health and how they value it in comparison to other aspects of their lives. Zola (1966) notes an interplay between culture and health. What people think, believe, and do regarding their health "fit" the values of the society in which they live. A society's values, in turn, usually specify preferred actions and solutions to problems. Differences in people's beliefs and the actions they take when they are sick, therefore, reflect their enduring cultural values.

A. Harmony and Balance

Mexican-Americans do not divide the natural and the supernatural into separate components. A harmonious relationship between the natural and the supernatural is considered essential to human health and welfare, while disharmony precipitates illness and misfortune (Madsen, 1964a).

Views vary on the extent of supernatural causation. The lower class sees the natural and the supernatural blended into one functional entity. Therefore, the members of this class rely heavily on supernatural techniques to deal with illness and other problems. Conservative members of the middle class have a more secular orientation toward the problems of daily life, but still perceive a supernatural power pervading the universe. The conservative elite preserves a religious philosophy, but scorns the superstitions of the lower class. The anglicized upper class tends to adopt popular scientific concepts of natural order and causation. Through education and other contacts with the Anglo world, the younger generation of all classes has become increasingly skeptical of the supernatural beliefs derived from Mexican folk medicine (Madsen, 1964a).

Faith in folk medicine is strongest among members of the lower class who see supernatural forces in every phase of life, from conception to death. Pregnancy is considered to be a dangerous period for the unborn child. It is believed that the emotional and physical state of the pregnant woman may affect the health and development of the fetus. Natural forces, such as a lunar eclipse or a full moon, are also thought to be dangerous.

An expectant mother must remain in harmony with the universe throughout pregnancy. Health and well-being after birth continue to depend on the maintenance of a God-given balance in life. Any disruption of the balanced relationship between parts of the body, between the individual and society, or between human beings and supernatural beings can produce illness and distress (Madsen, 1964a).

B. *Perceived Health*

Roberts and Lee (1980a) found self-rated health to be the most powerful predictor of subsequent illness among adults. Perceived health is a function of culture, yet health care providers on the U.S. side of the border do not understand the concept of health among the Mexicans whom they treat. Folk medicine beliefs, determined among 100 Mexicans seeking treatment at an urban clinic in California, were compared to the awareness and understanding of these beliefs by the medical residents treating them. Fifty percent or more of the physicians claimed never to have encountered the beliefs expressed by their patients. There was no evidence that increased years of residency, speaking Spanish, or being of Mexican ancestry increased knowledge. Residents did best at identifying the expectations of patients when they came for specific reasons, such as injections or a blood test (Mull & Mull, 1981).

Lantican and Lara (1992), in a study of Mexican-Americans in El Paso, found a mixture of folk and western influences in both the perception and treatment of illness conditions. The perception of the seriousness of an illness was related to its perceived cause. This finding emphasizes how important it is that the health care provider probe and understand the patient's perception of the cause of illness. Mexican-American patients rarely reveal to physicians their folk medicine beliefs and practices for fear of criticism or ridicule. Belief in folk illnesses and the use of folk healing methods continues to be widespread among urbanized Mexican-Americans. Participation in the system of folk beliefs and curative practices does not preclude the reliance upon physicians and the use of scientific medicine not defined by folk concepts. Thus, many Mexican-Americans participate in two insular systems of health beliefs and care. Medical care that ignores this is inadequate (Ripley, 1986; Martinez & Martin, 1966; Creson, McKinley & Evans, 1969; Clark, 1970).

At one extreme is a lack of knowledge and understanding of culturally based beliefs about health on the part of health care professionals; at the other extreme is the desire of young Anglo physicians to convert the beliefs of their Mexican patients to the health beliefs of Anglo culture. Rubel (1966) noted the latter behavior in his extensive study in the lower Rio Grande Valley. As Graham (1976) points out, there is no void of theories and cures to be filled by Anglos. Mexicans have a folk medicine system that can be traced to seventeenth-century Spain. Furthermore, health beliefs and practices are not a random collection, but constitute a body of knowledge that includes ideas about the nature of man and his relationships with the natural, supernatural, and human environments. Folk beliefs flourish because they are an integral part of the whole culture.

Schulman and Smith (1963) studied the concept of health held by Spanish-speaking mountain villagers of New Mexico and Colorado who have retained a folk medical system which, at times, is at odds with that of Anglo culture. Schulman and Smith found three criteria for health across all ages and for both sexes: (1) a high level of physical activity; (2) a well-fleshed body; and (3) the absence of pain. "Adequate functioning" is an integral part of the image of health among the villagers. This implies that adults will carry out expected daily tasks successfully. One is considered "healthy" until normal daily activity is no longer possible. Therefore, some symptoms may be tolerated or accepted without a person being labeled "sick." In Mexican-American culture, illness and health are considered a matter of chance; therefore, a person who does become sick is rarely held responsible for being ill (Clark, 1970; Schreiber, Homiak & Harwood 1981). Spector (1979) points out that some Chicanos describe health as a reward for good behavior. People are expected to maintain their own equilibrium in the world by acting in a proper way, eating proper foods, and working the proper amount of time. The prevention of illness is accomplished by praying, wearing religious medals, and keeping religious relics in the home. Eating herbs and spices also enhances prevention.

In contrast to Anglos, who believe in individual responsibility for one's health, Mexican Americans involve others in matters concerning individual well-being. Group consultation with kin regarding major decisions such as surgery, hospitalization, or referral to treatment in another city is common. Almost invariably, the wife or mother makes the initial assessment of a symptom. An increasingly important aspect of assessment and treatment relates to the concurrent use of folk and scientific practitioners. By simultaneous reliance on both types of care, Mexican American patients increase their chances of a successful outcome. Kay (1977) studied what health and illness meant to 60 Mexican American women between the ages of 22 and 78 who lived in a barrio in a large southwestern city in the U.S. The Mexican American woman believes that much illness is due to the way in which one lives. She has specific ideas about what kinds of activity, rest, recreation, and nourishment lead to good or poor health. As the regulator of the diet and preparer of food, the Mexican American woman is almost solely responsible for the nutrition of family members. When she thinks someone is sick, she tries to discern the cause and prescribe treatment. Kay found that women pray for cures, but deny that God sends illness.

Studies have shown positive relationships between parental perceptions of children's health status and their children's actual health status. Eisen, Ware, Donald, and Brook (1979) found that parental ratings of children's health status were significantly associated with their own self-perceived health status. It has been suggested that this association may be the result of common genetic or environmental factors, or of the effects of the child's health on the family. Mexican American mothers were more likely to rate their children's health as poor if their children were over 12 or not fully acculturated—that is, spoke Spanish in the home. Mothers of children under the age of 12 were influenced in rating their children's health status if a chronic medical condition existed in their home. It is quite clear that the perceptions of health held by Mexican American mothers may influence their behavior toward their children and that the children's self-perceived health status is influenced by their mothers' perceptions of their health. All of these factors could impact upon a child's functioning. Mexican Americans clearly are not homogeneous in their health beliefs and behavior (Mendoza, Ventura, Saldivar, Baisden & Martorell, 1992).

Most studies of the utilization of health services by Mexican Americans have focused on adults. Gilman and Bruhn (1981) recorded the utilization of school health services and community primary care sites by Mexican American and Anglo children in grades K–5 over one year. No significant differences were found between the two groups with respect to visits, nonvisits, or frequency of visits. Two unobtrusive measures were used to ascertain the degree of acculturation of the Mexican American children and their parents: the return of Spanish language questionnaires and the enrollment of the child in bilingual classes. No significant differences were found in the proportion of visitors/non-visitors in each group or the total number of visits for health services made by these children. Mexican American and Anglo children did not differ in the types of health problems presented, but fewer Mexican American than Anglo children made visits for emotional, behavioral, or learning problems. The results indicate that when health services are available and accessible, and when the barriers of language and income are minimized, Mexican American and Anglo children do not differ in their use of health services in the community.

Children who do not feel well tell their mothers they are sick. The mother questions the child, feels the child's forehead, looks at the place where it hurts, and decides what illness or disease the child has. She asks expert help when the illness is beyond her knowledge. Once an illness has been named, the barrio woman thinks in terms of three kinds of medicine: (1) home remedies; (2) doctors' prescriptions; and (3) proprietary drugs. The barrio woman is best informed about home remedies, such as herbs.

The Mexican American women studied by Kay (1977) believed that vulnerability to illness is influenced by age, or stage in the life cycle. The stages are as follows: *criatura* (fetus or newborn), *bebe* (child under age 3), *nino* (small child, 3–15), *muchacho* (children 15 and over), *joven* (youth aged 18–21), and *senor* or *senora* (adult over age 21). Menstruation, pregnancy, childbirth, and postpartum care all have cultural prescriptions related to keeping healthy.

C. Categories of Illness

Ideas about illness and its cause are varied. Some concepts clearly are derived from Mexican folk beliefs; others are "scientific" syndromes recognized in the United States and Mexico. It is not always easy to place an illness in a single category, but six general groups of illnesses are assembled for purposes of organization (Lyndon B. Johnson School of Public Affairs, 1979). Diseases of hot and cold imbalance are derived from the Hippocratic theory of pathology, which postulates that the human body in a state of health maintains a balance between four humors. Some of the humors are thought to be "cold." A disproportion of hot and cold foods are thought to result in illness. While not many people know all of the foods that are classified as hot and cold, dietary regulation is thought to be essential to good health.

In the tradition of preindustrial Mediterranean culture, hot implies consumption and cold implies giving. These qualities reflect the orientation of two social strata—the strong and the weak—and their mutual relationship. The effort to balance hot and cold is a symbolic attempt to secure an equitable social order, or reciprocity (Ingham, 1970). According to Ingham, "getting ahead" is a common orientation in a consumer economy, whereas conspicuous giving is valued more in a primitive society. Peasant societies encompass features of both civilized and primitive orders, and these features evoke conflicting motives of greed and generosity. Through the mediation of hot and cold, the Mexican expresses an adjustment to extremes.

A second category of illness results from the real or imagined dislocation of internal organs, such as lumps or irregularities in limbs or organs. Disease also can result from a third category, magic. *Mal ojo* or the evil eye is perhaps the best known condition in this category. It is believed that if someone, especially a woman, admires someone else's child, and looks at that child without touching it, the child may fall ill of *ojo*. Other conditions can result from witchcraft. A fourth category of illness is of emotional origin. Mexican Americans do not distinguish between emotional and physical illness; rather, they distinguish illness by cause (Graham, 1976). Intense or prolonged emotional states, such as fright and anger, can cause some illnesses (Clark, 1970). Fright or *susto* is a common folk disease. Rubel and his colleagues (1984), after an intensive study of *susto*, concluded that the boundaries between the emotional and physical parameters of *susto* are complex and interrelated, but that *susto* is real, producing a deterioration in health and possibly death. A fifth category of illness includes other folk-defined illnesses, such as palpitation (*latido*) and surfeit (*empacho*). Palpitation is thought to be caused by going without food for a long time. *Empacho* is the presence of a large ball in the stomach that produces swelling of the abdomen. The final category of illness, considered "scientific," includes asthma, pneumonia, cancer, and so on. Mexican Americans may believe the causes of these illnesses to be quite different than do Anglo physicians. Therefore, folk treatments may be used in lieu of, or in concurrence with, scientific prescriptions. Faith is an especially important element whatever the cure.

Empacho, susto, mal ojo, and *caida de la mollera* (a fragile skull formation among infants) have remained firmly embedded in the sociocultural framework despite alternate systems of belief and competing healing ways. It has been argued that *empacho, susto,* and *mal ojo* function to sustain dominant values of Mexican American culture, especially those that maintain the solidarity of the family unit and those that prescribe the appropriate role behavior for males and females and for old and young individuals (Rubel, 1960). Rubel was unable to demonstrate an association between *caida de la mollera* and values. He attributes this to the fact that this illness occurs only in children under three and generally in those under six months of age, children who have not yet been socialized to appropriate role expectations. Not one of these four illnesses is amenable to the understanding or treatment of the trained physician, Mexico American or Anglo. They affect only people of Mexican background (Rubel, 1960) and create anxiety in all sectors of the Mexican American population. People who have adopted Anglo sociocultural behavior tend to disparage these concepts of illness as ingenuous beliefs, but others vouch for their authenticity. The four illnesses are important not just as pathological conditions, but as distinct symbols of a traditional way of life.

Folk diseases in South Texas provide a mechanism for avoiding or relieving situations that involve conflicts with Mexican American values. Value conflicts are increasing with the increasing acculturation of Mexicans. Individuals who have internalized values from both subcultures usually are aware of cognitive dissonance (Madsen, 1964b). Their self images lose focus, and decision making can produce anxiety. Some seek geographical escape from the border, moving to other states or to large cities. Those who retreat usually are affected by a series of folk illnesses.

Many *curanderismo* are knowledgeable about the nature of value conflicts. Folk treatment involves a return to the ideal values and social relationships of a conservative way of life. Thus, it is not surprising that Mexican patients who have considerable difficulties in reconciling culture conflicts often use two different systems of health care. Nor is it surprising that folk medicine often is successful when scientific medicine fails.

Chesney and his colleagues (1980), in their study of 40 Mexican American families living in close proximity to a large university health care facility in Texas, found that the use of conventional medical services and folk medicine are related. Most families used conventional medical treatment for problems they defined as serious illness. Their response to specific physical symptoms, however, varied. Symptoms associated with folk illnesses were treated with home remedies. More dramatic symptoms, such as chest pain or blood in stools, received medical attention. They sought help for serious symptoms of depression from religion or from family, whereas help for minor symptoms of anxiety was sought from medical personnel.

The researchers point out that folk medicine appears to be well integrated into Mexican American families and communities that appear to be assimilated into Anglo culture. A myriad of patterns of utilization were found, depending upon the alternatives available to the family.

Chesney and his colleagues (1982) studied the health care utilization patterns of 152 families in a small, rural town on the U.S.-Mexico border. They tried, in particular, to understand the relative contribution of acculturation, social class, and social isolation to utilization patterns. Acculturation was found to have a direct effect on whether or not health services were used, while social class and social isolation interacted to produce a weak effect, independent of acculturation. They suggest that all three factors should be taken into consideration when trying to understand the use of health services by Mexican Americans.

D. Interpersonal Relations and Mental Health

Anglos tend to view external reality as something they can influence. Mexican Americans, however, have a passive attitude toward nature and feel subjugated by it. Mexican Americans tend to assume that interpersonal reality can be modified, and that interpersonal reactions are evaluated on the basis of the immediate pleasure and satisfaction they bring. They consider the interpersonal exchange to be valuable and enjoyable. Anglos often have elaborate and rigid ideas about interpersonal relationships. Therefore, Anglo mental health professionals ask their clients to "face reality." Mexican Americans see reality as fluid, changing, and interactive, not something to be avoided or eliminated. Mental health professionals also focus on forces *within* an individual, such as self identity, whereas Mexican Americans focus on *interactions* between persons and the feelings emanating from these interactions, such as "together feelings" (Diaz-Guerrero, 1976).

R. Diaz-Guerrero (1976) notes that many neurosis-provoking conflicts in Mexicans are "inner" conflicts provoked more by clashes of values than by clashes between individuals and reality. Aspects of the Mexican family, such as cohesiveness and closeness, seem to help prevent juvenile delinquency. Therefore, the "togetherness" of interpersonal reality is important and highly valued in Mexican culture. This, undoubtedly, is a positive force in maintaining good mental health.

As the individual owes allegiance to the family, so the family owes protection to its members. Because of the strict definition of familial relations, however, certain types of problems usually are solved without family help. For example, sexual difficulties are rarely taken up with parents. Conflicts between conservative Latin culture and values acquired at school rarely are discussed at home (Madsen, 1964a). The child in an integrated school develops agility in shifting values in everyday behavior.

Children and young adults seek advice in many areas outside the home, for example, close friends (*palomilla*). Because personal shortcomings or failures are not admitted easily, personal gains or advancements may be concealed. This prevents envy in others (*mal ojo*).

The magnitude of Mexicans' mental health problems has been inferred from their socioeconomic and migratory experiences. Many conclusions of past epidemiological research have been equivocal and have been hindered by methodological and sampling problems (Rogler, Malgady & Rodriguez, 1989). Hispanics present a profile that is associated with increased risk of mental disorder, but the literature is inconclusive.

Migration from one culture to another inserts a person into a different socioeconomic system. The stresses of not knowing the language of the new culture understandably may create economic hardships and result in depression and anxiety related to subsistence. Migration also disrupts the immigrant's supportive bonds, accentuating feelings of loneliness and despair (Ruiz, 1982).

Stress and coping skills in different individuals exposed to the same stimuli vary. Generalizations about Mexican migrants are not warranted. The emotions investigated most often in Mexican Americans are depression and distress. While depression is as prevalent among Mexican Americans as among Anglos, in Mexican Americans economic factors often are a precursor. Substance abuse appears to be a significant source of death and disability among some Hispanic populations, such as Puerto Ricans in New York City. Alcohol and substance abuse may be palliative coping responses to stress. Large differences exist across ethnic groups in the type of drug, quantity, and degree of intoxication considered to be within a culture's limits of social acceptability and normalcy (Cervantes & Castro, 1985). The behavioral dynamics of personal drug use among Mexican Americans need further research.

Shrout and his colleagues (1992) found Mexican American immigrants to have fewer mental health problems than island Puerto Ricans, U.S.-born Mexican Americans, and non-Hispanic whites. Discrimination and deprivation, symptom counts, or diagnoses did not explain these differences. They noted that selection factors associated with immigration may be a factor; perhaps only healthier persons migrate. On the other hand, Acosta (1979) states that the most difficult barriers between Mexican Americans and therapists are social class and cultural dissimilarities. Thus, Mexican Americans who need mental health services, especially migrants, are unlikely to seek the services of Anglo mental health professionals.

Lopez (1981) conducted an extensive survey of the literature on utilization of mental health services by Mexican-Americans from the 1950s to the 1970s. He found equivocal support for underutilization during each decade. As a result of his survey, Lopez concluded that underutilization of mental health services by Mexican Americans was not well documented.

The findings, however, indicate that Mexican Americans are using mental health services in parity with their representation as a total group in the southwestern United States. Lopez points out serious methodological problems in past studies. These include: (1) non-representative samples, (2) non-useful classification of diagnostic categories, (3) lack of consideration of the variation between mental health facilities, (4) different methods of identifying Mexican Americans, (5) lack of consistency in defining catchment areas, (6) reliance on census data, and (7) collection of data on only one aspect of the service delivery system, that is, admissions. Lopez recommends methods for improving future research and needed directions.

E. Interventions to Modify Health Behavior

Weaver (1973) pointed out the need for more information about the health behavior of a new generation of Mexican Americans, Mexicans who reside on the U.S.-Mexico border and live and work in two cultures. Their values, including health values, are becoming a blend of the values of the two cultures. Their health status is heterogeneous. As a result, health professionals on both sides of the border face the enormous challenge of detecting and controlling diseases which transcend culture. As this new generation uses the health services of two cultures, their health concepts and beliefs will be modified. They will also be at risk for the illnesses of two cultures.

Obesity, which is common among Mexican Americans, is a risk factor for cardiovascular disease. Cousins and her colleagues (1992) found it possible to develop a weight loss program that is consistent with the foods and values prevalent in Mexican American culture. Working with existing systems, such as churches, community organizations, clinics, and the natural networks of friends and relatives was found to be more effective than a community-wide education program. Balcazar and Cobas (1993) point out that Mexican American attitudes toward being overweight need not be modified. Indeed, these attitudes are similar to those of non-Hispanics. Therefore, weight reduction programs aimed at Mexican Americans might not differ in content from those for Anglos, but they must take into consideration different cultural values, attitudes, and beliefs. An intervention or treatment which is relevant to Mexican Americans, both linguistically and culturally, and the involvement of powerful significant others, has been shown to increase compliance (Tamez & Vacalis, 1989).

Nader and his research group (1992) demonstrated the value of family involvement in health behavior interventions to reduce cardiovascular risk behavior in volunteer healthy Mexican American and Anglo families. Part of their rationale for studying family-based interventions was that increasing family support of health-promoting behavior should enhance the maintenance of gains. Over a three-year period, the researchers noted great gains in blood pressure reduction in both Mexican Americans and Anglos. Nader (1992) notes, "This study demonstrated that with interventions that are culturally adapted and group facilitators who are sensitive to cultural needs and practices, health behavior change methods can be effective, even with a Mexican American population that is disadvantaged in terms of income and education" (pp. 71–72).

F. Curanderismo

Curanderismo is an essential part of the Mexican American belief system. Curanderismo defines health and illness, and diagnoses and treats illnesses, within a framework that focuses on the relationship between the spiritual, physical, and mental status of the client. Curanderismo is a holistic approach to health care. The power to heal is seen as a gift from God, and all treatments appeal to God or to one of the saints (Madsen, 1964a). Diagnosis by the curandero, or folk healer, is a dynamic formulation of all of the relevant information and observations derived from the client, his/her family, and the supernatural (Romero, 1983). While folk healers, or curanderos, may specialize in particular treatments, their approach to the definition of health and illness remains holistic. Traditional use of curanderos varies throughout the Southwest. An estimated 20 to 80 percent of Mexican Americans use the services of a curandero (Romero, 1983).

Romero (1983) outlines arguments for utilizing curanderos' services in mental health clinics. The incorporation of curanderismo services into clinics could increase the number of mental health service consumers in Mexican American communities. Mental health professionals have observed cures by curanderos of cases that might not have responded to therapy or medication. Inclusion of a curanderismo in the clinic might decrease the mental health profession's failure rate.

Curanderos and psychiatrists share similar professional characteristics. In general, they use the same treatment model: both view society as healthy and the client as being in need of adjustment. Several studies have reported positive results on the utilization of curanderos in mental health programs.

Romero (1983) describes two major strategies for incorporating curanderismo services: (1) contracting with the curanderos in a neighborhood, and (2) hiring a curandero as a staff member in a mental health clinic. The second strategy was adopted at a mental health clinic in Colorado. Incorporation of curanderismo into the mental health system denied the use of a holistic approach because medical practitioners had already divided the territory into specialties. Hence, the mental health staff became engaged in classifying "curanderismo-related things." A dichotomy was proposed between all the "things" cured by drugs and psychotherapy and all that were not. Clients first had to be evaluated by a therapist to determine where in the traditional mental health model the client fell. The mental health staff would decide what the problem was and provide the necessary treatment. The curandero lost autonomy in this institutionalization plan; the mental health staff maintained control throughout the process. Cases not successfully treated by modern medicine were labeled "curanderismo-related."

This example illustrates the intolerance of the Anglo system of health care toward the health beliefs of other cultures, and the enormous pressure clients from other cultures feel when seeking help from the Anglo system.

Curanderismo is changing because Mexican Americans are changing. Distrust and avoidance of the Anglo health care system has declined, especially as Mexican Americans undergo cultural, educational, and occupational changes. The isolation of Mexican Americans, as far as health care is concerned, is changing (Trotter & Chavira, 1981). Increased educational levels; better jobs, especially with companies that provide health benefits; health clinics; and initiatives by health departments regarding immunizations and well-baby care have all affected the Mexican American's concept of health.

One reason for the continued existence of curanderismo is the curandero's use of natural support systems, such as the family. For most Mexican Americans, the social structure of health and illness is determined by the family system. Curanderos provide counseling for their clients. These healers use their knowledge of the client's background and personality to provide advice that fits the client's needs within the context of his/her culture. It has been observed that the curandero is more of a psychiatrist than a physician (Kiev, 1968). Trotter and Chavira (1981) call the curandero the caretaker of mental hygiene in the barrio.

The curandero is expected to continue to play an important role in the health status of Mexican Americans, especially in the lower Rio Grande Valley of Texas. Curanderismo can be viewed as a model of a health care system that incorporates the social and behavioral sciences in its therapeutic regimen. It combines self-reliance with cultural relevance and family systems and gives Mexican Americans who choose it a sense of stability and continuity in the face of change. One of the most important tools of the health care provider is the ability to communicate with patients with a common language and cultural expectations. The ability of curanderos to use culturally and socially appropriate modes of therapy helps Mexican Americans experiencing change or crises in their lives maintain some link between the past and present (Trotter & Chavira, 1981).

Keefe (1981) conducted two large-scale surveys and in-depth interviews with 24 Mexican Americans in three Southern California towns. She found folk medicine to be a persistent, but ancillary, health care system. Most

Mexican Americans know something about folk medicine, but few maintain a strong belief in it, and only a small number of Mexican Americans consult folk healers. Scientific medicine is their primary health and mental health system. Folk medicine endures as an alternative, primarily in the treatment of minor health problems that require little extrafamilial attention, or severe health problems that persist despite professional scientific care. There is evidence that folk medical terms and treatments have changed and become integrated with scientific medicine in the minds of many Mexican Americans. Keefe (1981) posits that we need to study actual health care behavior rather than focus on Mexican Americans' use of traditional or scientific medicine.

THE HEALTH SUB-CULTURE OF THE MIGRANT

Health is not only a matter of beliefs and attitudes but is tied to the realities of the environment. Health is directly related to the social and physical environment of the Mexican migrant (Shenkin, 1974). There are five proximate causes for illness among migrants: Migrants obtain little medical care, and medical care for injury or illness generally is sought at hospital emergency rooms; migrants are subjected to detrimental environmental influences, such as poor and crowded housing, poor sanitation, and poor water, and to detrimental occupational influences: the high accident rates of farm labor, exposure to pesticides, and the taxing nature of their work lead to exhaustion and lowered resistance; migrants are malnourished; discrimination contributes to an unhealthy lifestyle; and mobility is a source of stress and continual adaptation and precludes continuity of health care and a stable lifestyle.

The health beliefs and lifestyle of Mexican migrants have a direct relationship to their use of health services. Mexican immigrants in San Diego County were found to exhibit a pattern of health service utilization that is the reverse of the pattern typical of the general U.S. population. Respondents who were in the country legally generally made much greater use of hospital outpatient clinics than did their undocumented counterparts. Recently arrived undocumented migrants relied to a great extent upon emergency room service. Many migrants have had to be hospitalized because they postponed seeking health care. Use of emergency rooms also reflects a lack of knowledge of sources of available care. This is especially true of migrants from rural areas of Mexico (Chavez, Cornelius & Jones, 1985).

Preventive health care is relatively uncommon among Mexican migrants. Preventive care is least common among recent undocumented migrants and more common among long-term legal immigrants.

In general, the health service utilization rates of Mexican migrants fall below those of the general U.S. population, especially in areas of preventive dental and perinatal care (Chavez, Cornelius & Jones, 1985). Clearly, the high cost of health care is a barrier for many migrants. Their reasons for failing to seek health care, however, are complex and varied. The Mexican migrant population exhibits considerable diversity in its use of health services.

Walker (1979) determined the kinds and costs of medical care used by Mexican migrants in Laredo who were enrolled in a prepaid insurance study in which financial barriers were eliminated or reduced. He found that even when economic barriers to care were reduced or removed, migrants used fewer medical services. There is evidence that Mexicans residing on the U.S.-Mexico border, when given a choice, use health services in Mexico; confine their utilization of services on the U.S. side to reproductive health services; and use services on the Mexican side according to the priority they place on health. They do not seek health services until they think that they are needed (Guendelman, 1991; Guendelman & Jasis, 1990; Warner, 1992; Andersen, Lewis, Grachello, Aday & Chui, 1981). There also is evidence that when identified barriers to utilization are controlled, Mexicans achieve their expected utilization. Major utilization differences between Mexican American and Anglo American clients appear primarily to be socioeconomic (Trevino, Bruhn & Bunce, 1979; Estrada, Trevino & Ray, 1990). Roeder (1982) points out that it is easy to blame the failure of Mexican Americans to use health services to the same degree as Anglos on socioeconomic, institutional, or cultural barriers. Seeking "the" reason for underutilization, rather than attempting to improve the system of health care so that it will serve diverse clients better, has its dangers.

Several studies have shown that delays in seeking health care cannot be blamed on the availability and use of curanderos (Higginbotham, Trevino & Ray, 1990). The utilization of health services has been found to relate to social class and age differences (Welch, Comer & Steinman, 1973). However, Roberts and Lee (1980b) found ethnic status to exert an independent effect on health and illness behavior—that is, differences in health care use remain after controlling for a number of social, economic, and demographic factors. Acculturation and "closeness to the family unit" may have a more profound effect on utilization. Mexican Americans who are less acculturated are less frequent users of health services than the more acculturated. However, this appears to pertain more to the importance of a person's social integration into the Mexican culture than to a commitment to folk beliefs (Wells, Golding, Hough, Burnam & Karno, 1989; Nall and Speilberg, 1967). Indeed, there is evidence that acculturation was one of the most important determinants of sexual socialization and the spread of AIDS among Mexicans in California (Magana & Carrier, 1991).

Dutton (1978) convincingly argues that neither socioeconomic factors nor cultural attributes sufficiently explain the lower use of health services by the disadvantaged. Her research suggests that such differentials can also be attributed to inadequacies in the health care systems used by the disadvantaged. She found that differences in care were reduced more by controlling for the effects of variables that represented the usual system of care than by financial or demographic factors or health-related attitudes. These results substantiate the argument that omitting health-care system characteristics impedes our understanding of health care behavior.

Slesinger and Richards (1981) examined the medical behavior of a group of Hispanic migrant workers who traveled from the border region of Texas to Wisconsin. Through their interviews, the researchers found that migrants use aspects of both folk and clinical medical traditions, often choosing between various therapies on the basis of the availability and geographic location of specific providers and services as well as their cultural conceptions of illness, healers, and therapies. Although a small number of migrants were discovered to prefer either folk or scientific therapies, the great majority believed in both traditions and selectively utilized them both. There generally appeared to be few problems of incompatibility between the two systems.

Grebler, Moore, and Guzman (1970) pointed out that it is tempting to construct a social continuum ranging from folk to acculturated in understanding the health beliefs and behavior of Mexican Americans. Neither end of this continuum can be defined clearly. There is probably not just one continuum, but many. Changes in social environments are so complex, and extend in so many directions, there is little reason to assume a linear continuum in beliefs from those who are more Mexican to those more Anglo. This explains why the findings on the health status or utilization patterns of border residents are contradictory.

New Health Issues on the Border

Fernandez (1989) describes a new civilization along the U.S.-Mexico border in which the "Mexican factor" is keyed to the future of the U.S. economy. Probable implications for the Mexican health sector of NAFTA are large-scale privatization and deregulation (Laurell & Ortega, 1992). In this context, the Mexican health sector, which traditionally has been dominated by public institutions, is undergoing a deep restructuring. NAFTA is likely to force a change in Mexican health legislation, which includes health services in the public social security system and recognizes the right to health and to accelerated selective privatization. The U.S. insurance industry and hospital corporations are interested in promoting these changes in order to gain access to the Mexican market. This would lead to the deterioration of public institutions, increasing inequalities in health, and a strengthening of the private sector (Laurell & Ortega, 1992).

Most visits to the U.S. health system are to private facilities (Warner, 1991). Recent surveys of U.S. physicians on the Arizona and Texas borders have shown that Mexican nationals use primary medicine and specialist providers on the U.S. side of the border (Zinnecker, 1990; Warner & Reed, 1993). The patterns of binational health service utilization are certain to change as the Mexican and U.S. health care systems change.

Although twin plants along the U.S.-Mexico border have been operating since 1965, it is only recently that worker health has become a focus of inquiry. The maquila industry is noted for its turnover rates and the mobility of its workers. An increase in the number of American companies opening plants on the Mexican side of the border will bring about an increase in daily contact between workers from a developed country and workers from a developing country. Reviews of medical consultation reports in three twin plants indicate a high incidence of gastrointestinal problems, respiratory disorders, and headaches (Sizemore, 1992). Hovell and his associates (1988) did not find maquiladora workers less healthy than workers from the same colonias who did not work in maquiladoras. These researchers state that it is possible that maquiladora workers are generally healthier than others because pre-employment physical exams are given in some plants. Guendelman & Silberg (1993) point out that despite long working hours, low pay, and less latitude in decision making, maquiladora workers are no worse off than electronics workers. They conclude that the previously reported adverse effects of maquiladoras are exaggerated. Subjective factors, such as negative attitudes toward economic adversity and work dissatisfaction, were stronger predictors of health than were objective indicators (Guendelman & Silberg, 1993).

A UNIFIED VIEW OF HEALTH

Markides and Coreil (1986) have indicated that a low acculturation lifestyle may protect Hispanics against various diseases, although what these factors and mechanisms are is not yet clear. These authors mention an "epidemiological paradox" because of the lower morbidity rates for several chronic diseases than would be expected for Hispanics, given the prevalence of conventional risk factors in the Hispanic population. Castro and Baezconde-Garbanati (1988) have speculated about the reasons for the epidemiological paradox with respect to coronary heart disease. How much does acculturation and lifestyle contribute to the lower-than-expected rates of heart disease among Hispanics? How much do personality and behavior patterns contribute? Or, does the methodology need to improved?

Farge (1977), in his study of generational differences in the health care beliefs and behaviors of Mexican Americans in Houston, reported findings which conflicted with previous studies. Speculations attempting to explain these differences included the fact that many early studies of Mexican American health beliefs and behaviors were conducted in rural settings, and were based on observations which precluded replication.

Researchers carefully examine the possible reasons why results do not fit expected patterns. The reasons why the studies of people's health beliefs and behavior result in inconsistencies and discrepancies are, perhaps, too obvious. Change is an aspect of life. The subjects being studied and the researcher both change while research is in progress. Hence, research findings reflect what was observed or measured at one particular point in time. This is why longitudinal and followup studies are crucial; they map change at several points in time. A second reason for differing results is the fact that researchers usually study only one or more aspects of a phenomenon. Hence, the influence or impact of larger, often subtle, effects is missed or ignored. Cultural norms and expectations constantly are at play. Subjects carry these norms and expectations with them; they may not be known, expressed, or measured, but they affect how people think, what they believe, and how they behave. Health needs, and individuals' perceptions of them, have many dimensions (Bruhn & Trevino, 1979). Individuals' perceptions determine whether or not care will be sought, from whom, and its degree of success. Therefore, it is essential that attempts to understand Mexican Americans' health behavior include an understanding of their concept of health.

Figure 2.1 illustrates several key variables involved in an individual's formation of a concept of health and subsequent health-seeking behavior. It also shows the importance of social, psychological, and cultural factors in influencing an individual's concept of health. The figure shows that at least five key variables—age, sex, generation, socioeconomic status, and degree of acculturation—help to shape the value an individual places on health and his/her health beliefs. Health value and health beliefs, in turn, are essential components of an individual's concept of health. How an individual conceptualizes health will influence the options perceived for care and, in turn, his/her health behavior.

Antonovsky (1987) has pointed out that health and illness have a complementary relationship; to understand either one there must be a "sense of coherence," or what is referred to here as a "unitary" concept of health and disease—one that places health and disease in a cultural context, which is continually subject to change. This is precisely the context in which "border health" must be viewed. The U.S.-Mexico border is a blend of cultures

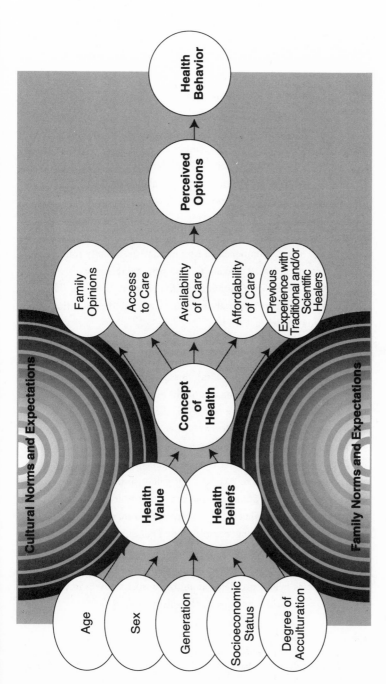

Figure 2.1. Key variables affecting an individual's concept of health and health-seeking behavior.

continuously influenced by economic, political, social, physical, environmental, and other factors, all of which interact to affect the behavior of residents on both sides of the border at specific points in time.

Quesada and Heller (1977) note many kinds of barriers that can affect the use of health care services: sociocultural, communication, alternative sources of care, political, and health manpower barriers. The use of health services in Texas, especially in the border community, also relates to the availability of Mexican American health professionals. Mexican Americans are located in 81 of the 254 counties in Texas. They are concentrated in 28 counties, where they constitute 50 percent or more of the population. The ratio of primary care physicians to the population in 24 of these 28 counties is lower than the Texas state ratio of physicians to the general population—4 have no physicians at all. One-third of these 28 counties have no practicing dentists. Twenty-one counties have fewer pharmacists than the state average, and 5 counties have no pharmacists. Twenty-four of these counties have no nurses. There are no occupational therapists in 21 of the 28 counties. A similar distribution exists for physical therapists. Thus, the availability of health professionals is a critical factor in the utilization of services (Quesada & Heller, 1977).

Political decisions by organized groups of health professionals influence the economics of the health care market. Decisions by state and local health departments, medical, dental, nursing, pharmaceutical, and other health professional groups all impact on the availability of health care in the border communities. If we are to provide effective health services for the people living along the U.S.-Mexico border, we must strive to understand the different attitudes, values, and perceptions of these people in regard to health and illness. If prevention is to be a part of these services, we must make a vigorous attempt to reconcile our values so that health services in Mexico and the United States and the issues that bear on health and welfare can achieve a somewhat equal priority. The future approaches for dealing with the rapidly changing, complex health concerns on both sides of the border must be ecological. Single-issue approaches cannot be successful because all issues are interdependent. The concept of health will become a more political issue as health problems along the border worsen; however, the solutions to those problems must not be solely political.

REFERENCES

Acosta, F.X. (1979). Barriers between mental health services and Mexican Americans: An examination of a paradox. *American Journal of Community Psychology*, 7, 503–520.

Andersen, R., Lewis, S.Z., Giachello, A.L., Aday, L., & Chiu, G. (1981). Access to medical care among the Hispanic population of the Southwestern United States. *Journal of Health and Social Behavior, 22,* 78–89.

Antonovsky, A. (1987). *Unraveling the mystery of health.* San Francisco, CA: Jossey-Bass.

Balcazar, H. & Cobas, J.A. (1993). Overweight among Mexican Americans and its relationship to life style behavioral risk factors. *Journal of Community Health, 18,* 55–67.

Bruhn, J.G. & Trevino, F.M. (1979). A method for determining patients' perceptions of their health needs. *Journal of Family Practice, 8,* 809–818.

Castro, F.G. & Baezconde-Garbanati, L. (1988). *Cardiovascular disease in Hispanics: A bio-behavioral perspective.* Washington, DC: The National Coalition of Hispanic Health and Human Services Organizations.

Cervantes, R.C. & Castro, F.G. (1985). Stress, coping, and Mexican American mental health: A systematic review. *Hispanic Journal of Behavioral Sciences, 7,* 1–73.

Chavez, L.R., Cornelius, W.A., & Jones O.W. (1985). Mexican immigrants and the utilization of U.S. health services: The case of San Diego. *Social Science and Medicine, 21,* 93–102.

Chesney, A.P., Chavira, J.A., Hall, R.P., & Gary, H.E. (1982). Barriers to medical care of Mexican-Americans: The role of social class, acculturation, and social isolation. *Medical Care, 20,* 883–892.

Chesney, A.P., Thompson, B.L., Guevara, A., Vela, A., & Schottstaedt, M.F. (1980). Mexican-American folk medicine: Implications for the family physician. *The Journal of Family Practice, 11,* 567–574.

Clark, M. (1970). *Health in the Mexican-American culture.* Berkeley, CA: University of California Press.

Cousins, J.H., Rubovits, D.S., Dunn, J.K., Reeves, R.S., Ramirez A.G., & Foreyt, J.P. (1992). Family versus individually oriented intervention for weight loss in Mexican American women. *Public Health Reports, 107,* 549–555.

Creson, D.L., McKinley, C., & Evans, R. (1969). Folk medicine in Mexican-American sub-culture. *Diseases of the Nervous System, 30,* 264–266.

Diaz-Guerrero, R. (1976). *Psychology of the Mexican.* Austin, TX: University of Texas Press.

Dutton, D.B. (1978). Explaining the low use of health services by the poor: Costs, attitudes, or delivery systems? *American Sociological Review, 43,* 348–365.

Eisen, M., Ware, J.E. Jr., Donald, C.A., & Brook, R.H. (1979). Measuring components of children's health status. *Medical Care, 17,* 902–921.

Estrada, A.L., Trevino, F.M., & Ray, L.A. (1990). IV. Health care utilization barriers among Mexican Americans: Evidence from HHANES 1982–84. *American Journal of Public Health, 80,* 27–31.

Fabrega, H. Jr. (1974). *Disease and social behavior: An interdisciplinary perspective.* Cambridge, MA: M.I.T. Press.

Fabrega, H. Jr. (1979). Disease and illness from a bicultural standpoint. In P.I. Ahmed & G.V. Coelho (Eds.), *Toward a new definition of health: Psychosocial dimensions* (pp. 23–51). New York: Plenum.

Farge, E.J. (1977). A review of findings from "Three Generations" of Chicano health care behavior. *Social Science Quarterly, 58,* 407–411.

Fernandez, R.A. (1989). *The Mexican-American border region.* Notre Dame, IN: University of Notre Dame Press.

Gilman, S.C. & Bruhn, J.G. (1981). A comparison of utilization of community primary health care and school health services by urban Mexican-American and Anglo elementary school children. *Medical Care, 19,* 223–232.

Graham, J.S. (1976). The role of the curandero in the Mexican American folk medicine system in West Texas. In W.D. Hand (Ed.), *American folk medicine: A symposium* (pp. 175–189). Berkeley, CA: University of California Press.

Grebler, L., Moore, J.W., & Guzman, R.C. (1970). *The Mexican- American people: The nation's second largest minority.* New York: The Free Press.

Guendelman, S. (1991). Health care users residing on the Mexican border. *Medical Care, 29,* 419–429.

Guendelman, S. & Jasis, M. (1990). Measuring Tijuana residents' choice of Mexican or U.S. health care services. *Public Health Reports, 6,* 575–583.

Guendelman, S. & Silberg, M.J. (1993). The health consequences of maquiladora work: Women on the U.S.-Mexico border. *American Journal of Public Health, 83,* 37–44.

Higginbotham, J.C., Trevino, F.M., & Ray, L.A. (1990). V. Utilization of curanderos by Mexican-Americans: Prevalence and predictors. Findings from HHANES 1982–84. *American Journal of Public Health, 80,* 32–35.

Hovell, M.F., Sipan, C., Hofstetter, C.R., DuBois, B.C., Krefft, A., Conway, J., Jasis, M., & Isaacs, H.L. (1988). Occupational health risks for Mexican women: The case of the maquiladora along the Mexican-United States border. *International Journal of Health Services, 18,* 617–627.

Ingham, J.M. (1970). On Mexican folk medicine. *American Anthropologist, 72,* 76–87.

Kay, M.A. (1977). Health and illness in a Mexican American barrio. In E.H. Spicer, E. Bauwens, M.A. Kay, M.E. Shutler, & L.F. Snow (Eds.), *Ethnic medicine in the Southwest* (pp. 99–166). Tucson. AZ: University of Arizona Press.

Keefe, S.E. (1981). Folk medicine among urban Mexican Americans: Cultural persistence, change, and displacement. *Hispanic Journal of Behavioral Sciences, 3,* 41–58.

Kiev, A. (1968). *Curanderismo: Mexican American folk psychiatry.* New York: Free Press.

Lantican, L. & Lara, J.B. (1992). Perceptions of illness conditions and their treatment among Mexican-Americans in a border community. Paper presented at Second Border Symposium, March 11–13, El Paso, Texas.

Laurell, A.C. & Ortega, M.E. (1992). The Free Trade Agreement and the Mexican health sector. *International Journal of Health Services, 22,* 331–337.

Lopez, S. (1981). Mexican-American usage of mental health facilities: Underutilization considered. In A. Baron, Jr. (Ed.), *Explorations in Chicano psychology* (pp. 139–164). New York: Praeger.

Lyndon B. Johnson School of Public Affairs (1979). *The health of Mexican-Americans in South Texas.* Policy Research Project Report No. 32. Austin, TX: The University of Texas at Austin.

Madsen, W. (1964a). *Mexican-Americans of South Texas.* New York: Holt, Rinehart and Winston.

Madsen, W. (1964b). Value conflicts and folk psychotherapy in South Texas. In A. Kiev (Ed.), *Magic, faith, and healing* (pp. 420–440). New York: Free Press.

Magana, J.R. & Carrier, J.M. (1991). Mexican and Mexican American male sexual behavior and spread of AIDS in California. *The Journal of Sex Research, 28,* 425–441.

Markides, K.S. & Coreil, J. (1986). The health of Hispanics in the Southwestern United States: An epidemiological paradox. *Public Health Reports, 101,* 253–265.

Martinez, C. & Martin, H.W. (1966). Folk diseases among urban Mexican-Americans. *Journal of the American Medical Association, 196,* 147–164.

Mendoza, F.S., Ventura, S.J., Saldivar, L., Baisden, K., & Martorell, R. (1992). The health status of U.S. Hispanic children. In A. Furino (Ed.), *Health policy and the Hispanic* (pp. 97–115). Boulder, CO: Westview Press.

Mull, J.D. & Mull, D.S. (1981). Residents' awareness of folk medicine beliefs of their Mexican patients. *Journal of Medical Education, 56,* 520–522.

Nader, P.R., Sallis, J.F., Abramson, I.S., Broyles, S.L., Patterson, T.L., Senn, K., Rupp, J.W., & Nelson, J.A. (1992). Family-based cardiovascular risk reduction education among Mexican- and Anglo-Americans. *Family and Community Health, 15,* 57–74.

Nall, F.C. & Speilberg, J. (1967). Social and cultural factors in the responses of Mexican-Americans to medical treatment. *Journal of Health and Social Behavior, 8,* 299–308.

Quesada, G.M. & Heller, P.L. (1977). Sociocultural barriers to medical care among Mexican-Americans in Texas: A summary report of research conducted by the Southwest medical sociology ad hoc committee. *Medical Care, 15,* 93–101.

Ripley, G.D. (1986). Mexican-American folk remedies: Their place in health care. *Texas Medicine, 82,* 41–44.

Roberts, R.E. & Lee, E.S. (1980a). The health of Mexican Americans: Evidence from the human population laboratory studies. *American Journal of Public Health, 70,* 375–384.

Roberts, R.E. & Lee, E.S. (1980b). Medical care use by Mexican-Americans. *Medical Care, 18,* 266–281.

Roeder, B.A. (1982). Health care beliefs and practices among Mexican Americans: A review of the literature. *Aztlan, 13,* 223–256.

Rogler, L.H., Malgady, R.G., & Rodriguez, O. (1989). *Hispanics and mental health: A framework for research.* Malabar, FL: Robert E. Krieger Publishing Co.

Romero, M. (1983). Institutionalization of folk medicine: The mental health profession and curanderismo. In J.H. Morgan (Ed.), *Third world medicine and social change* (pp. 189–202). New York: University Press of America.

Rubel, A.J. (1960). Concepts of disease in Mexican-American culture. *American Anthropologist, 62,* 795–814.

Rubel, A.J. (1966). *Across the tracks: Mexican-Americans in a Texas city.* The Hogg Foundation for Mental Health. Austin, TX: University of Texas Press.

Rubel, A.J., O'Neill, C.W., & Collado-Ardon, R. (1984). *Susto, a folk illness.* Berkeley, CA: University of California Press.

Ruiz, P. (1982). The Hispanic patient: Sociocultural perspectives. In R.M. Becerra, M. Karno & Escobar, J.I. (Eds.), *Mental health and Hispanic Americans: Clinical perspectives* (pp. 17–27). New York: Grune & Stratton.

Schreiber, J.M., Homiak, J.P., & Harwood, A. (Eds.) (1981). *Ethnicity and medical care.* Cambridge, MA: Harvard University Press.

Schulman, S. & Smith, A.M. (1963). The concept of "health" among Spanish-speaking villagers of New Mexico and Colorado. *Journal of Health and Human Behavior, 4,* 226–234,

Shenkin, B.N. (1974). *Health care for migrant workers: Policies and politics.* Cambridge, MA: Ballinger Publishing Co.

Shrout, P.E., Canino, G.J., Bird, H.R., Rubio-Stipec, M., Bravo, M., & Burnam, M.A. (1992). Mental health status among Puerto Ricans, Mexican Americans, and non-Hispanic whites. *American Journal of Community Psychology, 20,* 729–752.

Sizemore, M.H. (1992). Health problems of Mexican and American workers at three maquilas in Ciudad Juárez, Mexico. *International Quarterly of Community Health Education, 12,* 137–149.

Slesinger, D.P. & Richards, M. (1981). Folk and clinical medical utilization patterns among Mejicano migrant farmworkers. *Hispanic Journal of Behavioral Sciences, 3,* 59–73.

Spector, R.E. (1979). *Cultural diversity in health and illness.* New York: Appleton-Century-Crofts.

Tamez, E.G. & Vacalis, T.D. (1989). Health beliefs, the significant other and compliance with therapeutic regimens among adult Mexican Americans with diabetes. *Health Education, 20,* 24–31.

Trevino, F.M., Bruhn, J.G., & Bunce, H. (1979). Utilization of community mental health services in a Texas-Mexico border city. *Social Science and Medicine, 13A,* 331–334.

Trotter, R.T. & Chavira, J.A. (1981). *Curanderismo: Mexican American folk healing.* Athens, GA: University of Georgia Press.

Walker, G.M. (1979). Utilization of health care: The Laredo migrant experience. *American Journal of Public Health, 69,* 667–672.

Warner, D.C. (1991). Health issues at the U.S.-Mexican border. *Journal of the American Medical Association, 265,* 242–247.

Warner, D.C. (1992). Health care on the U.S.-Mexico border. In A. Furino (Ed.), *Health policy and the Hispanic* (pp. 182–195). San Francisco, CA: Westview Press.

Warner, D.C. & Reed, K. (1993). Health care across the border: The experience of U.S. citizens in Mexico. *U.S.-Mexico Policy Report No. 4.* Lyndon B. Johnson School of Public Affairs, The University of Texas at Austin.

Weaver, J.L. (1973). Mexican American health care behavior: A critical review of the literature. *Social Science Quarterly, 54,* 85–102.

Weaver, J.L. (1979). Toward a definition of health risks for ethnic minorities: The case of hypertension and heart disease. In P.I. Ahmed & G.V. Coelho (Eds.), *Toward a new definition of health: Psychosocial dimensions* (pp. 255–268). New York: Plenum Press.

Welch, S., Comer, J., & Steinman, M. (1973). Some social and attitudinal correlates of health care among Mexican Americans. *Journal of Health and Social Behavior, 14,* 205–213.

Wells, K.B., Golding, J.M., Hough, R.L., Burnam, M.A., & Karno, M. (1989). Acculturation and the probability of use of health services by Mexican Americans. *Health Services Research, 24,* 237–257.

Zinnecker, A.K. (1990). *The use of U.S. health services by Mexican nationals along the Texas-Mexico border.* Austin, TX: Lyndon B. Johnson School of Public Affairs, University of Texas.

Zola, I.K. (1966). Culture and symptoms—An analysis of patients' presenting complaints. *American Sociological Review, 31,* 615–630.

3 BORDER HEALTH ISSUES

Jeffrey E. Brandon, Frank Crespin, Celinda Levy,
and Daniel M. Reyna

INTRODUCTION

An ecological approach to health issues along the U.S.-Mexico border recognizes that to be most effective, disease prevention efforts must be developed and implemented binationally. This approach will be recommended for the variety of issues considered in this chapter. The diversity in ethnic groups and illness patterns found along the 2,000-mile border creates unique challenges when describing major border health issues. This chapter will discuss the differences in the distribution of health concerns among the population living in the U.S.-Mexico border region. Mortality and morbidity figures, child health issues, specific communicable and noncommunicable diseases, mental health and drug abuse problems, and environmental issues will be addressed.

BORDER HEALTH DEMOGRAPHICS

"A common culture 'artificially' separated by a geo-political boundary. Problems worse than I thought," was the description by a recent Washington, D.C.–based visitor to the border (National Health Policy Forum, 1994, p. 1). This visitor was describing his most immediate post-visit impression of the shared border between Mexico and the United States that includes the six Mexican states of Baja California, Sonora, Chihuahua, Coahuila, Nuevo Léon, and Tamaulipas, and the four U.S. states of California, Arizona, New Mexico, and Texas.

In 1900, only about 36,000 persons lived along the entire border. The total 1990 border population is estimated at 9,089,508. Although the border stretches a great distance, the majority of its population is centered in a limited area. According to the United States–Mexico Border Health Association (USMBHA), the border is lined on the Mexican side with 39 principal municipalities with a population of 3,889,578 and on the U.S.

side with 24 counties with a population of 5,199,930, based upon 1990 census data from both countries (USMBHA, 1994). Over 56 percent of the border population in the United States and over 45.3 percent of the population in Mexico reside in the 12 bordering counties and municipalities (USMBHA, 1994). It is estimated that these 12 primary binational pairs of sister cities represent 7,803,306 inhabitants, or 86 percent of the total border population, with 4.4 million of the population from these 12 binational pairs coming from the U.S. (USMBHA, 1994). Of these population centers on the U.S.-Mexico border, San Diego County is the most populated, followed by El Paso County, Texas, and Doña Ana County, New Mexico (USMBHA, 1994).

There is no argument that the growth of the border states and communities has increased at a very high rate during the last two decades. The growth can be attributed to numerous political, social, and economic phenomena, including the uncontrolled migration to the border created by the maquiladora industry (Pan American Health Organization, 1989a). The problems brought about by this growth are mirrored in each of the primary sister cities that dot the border: the pollution of surface and groundwater, air pollution, the lack of proper disposal and recycling of solid and hazardous waste, lack of affordable housing, lack of access to health care, and the spread of communicable disease (Sevrens, 1992).

One of the unique aspects of the border region on the U.S. side is the difference in the ethnic makeup of the border populations compared to the racial and ethnic makeup of the country as a whole. While only nine percent of the U.S. population as a whole were Hispanic in 1990, more than one-quarter of the population of the U.S. border states is Hispanic, with the border counties exceeding thirty-six percent (Ortega, 1995). Though California and Texas have the largest Hispanic populations, the state of New Mexico has the largest proportion of Hispanics (more than 38 percent) (Ortega, 1995). The range among the border counties differs from that of San Diego County with the lowest proportion of Hispanic population (20.4 percent), to Webb County, Texas, exceeding 93 percent (USMBHA, 1994). For Mexico, there is no ethnic distinction per se between the border region and the nation as a whole, which explains the omission of any discussion in the *Profiles* data set (USMBHA, 1994).

The Hispanic population has increased substantially along the U.S.-Mexico border during the 1980s. While the increase in population in Mexico from 1980–1990 was 21.5 percent, the growth for the border region was 33.9 percent, and while the growth for the U.S. border counties was 31 percent, the national population grew by only 10 percent (USMBHA, 1994).

The impact of this population growth has influenced the border's economy, trade, industrial and economic development, and most directly the significant population movement between the two countries.

With regard to age and sex distributions there are some notable differences between the two countries and their border counties, influenced in particular by the social and economic attributes of their regions. The U.S. border population as a whole is younger than the average for the U.S., with the mean age in 1988 being 25.5 years compared with 32.2 years for the U.S. as a whole (Marin & Marin, 1991). While Mexico in 1990 measured over 38 percent of its population under age 15, the U.S. percentage was just under 22 percent (USMBHA, 1994). Somewhat surprising, the percent under age 15 is less in the Mexican municipalities (33.9 percent) than the nation as a whole, while the percentage for the U.S. counties (24.1 percent) exceeds the U.S. national rate (USMBHA, 1994).

The fluidity of the U.S.-Mexico border was notably visible to a group of federal congressional and regulatory health staff and foundation program officers on a visit to the Texas-New Mexico border region in April, 1994, sponsored by the National Health Policy Forum (NHPF), as indicated by the impressions noted in the Forum's report (NHPF, 1994):

> Although several had grown up along the U.S.-Mexico border or conducted previous work there, most site visit participants had not seen the El Paso-Doña Ana County-Juárez area. As participants looked across the winding, narrow, sewage-filled Rio Grande separating El Paso and Juárez, they commented on its physical insignificance. . . . The contrast between the often humble dwellings on the Mexican side and the usually larger, more solidly constructed buildings on the U.S. side, was a reminder that the Mexican economy is the biggest reason Mexican nationals cross the border, legally or illegally, to the United States. There were more than 35 million legal crossings over the three bridges from Juárez to El Paso in 1992. It is hard to say how many illegal crossings occurred, but the holes in the fences to El Paso and the paths over the mountains into Doña Ana County bear witness to the numbers (p. 1–2).

Just as many health professionals in the border region of Juárez, El Paso and Las Cruces recognize that "we must view the three sister communities as a single epidemiological unit when developing health services strategies" (Crespin & Kalishman, 1991, p. 5), it is now equally recognized throughout the length of the border that the border's population movements have created a distinguishable zone which is displaying unique epidemiological disease patterns, with specific health characteristics unique to the border region. This awareness is being validated repeatedly in spite of the differences of each country's political and legal systems, and cultural, language and economic development levels.

Considering the figures for life expectancy, it would seem that past the early years, residents of the border, at least for three of the four U.S. border states (the exception being Texas), can expect to live a long life (USMBHA, 1994). The quality of that life will nonetheless be affected to a great extent by the disease morbidity of the communities in which people live. The spread and control of infectious disease is further complicated due to the high level of interdependence and constant movement of people back and forth across the border (Martinez, 1994). Laurence N. Nickey, M.D., director of the El Paso City–County Health and Environmental District, spoke directly to the issue of the mutual dependency of the sister-city communities of El Paso and Juárez in stating that:

> even though there are two distinct sovereign nations, two states and two distinct cities involved, for purposes of public health, there is a population base of almost 2,000,000 sharing the same air, the same water, the same pollution, and the same diseases almost on an immediate basis. What affects the public's health on one side affects the other side and does so almost instantly. (Nickey, 1991, p. 2)

Distribution of Disease among Border Populations

While Hispanic mortality rates are similar to those of non-Hispanic whites, there are various differences in the top causes of death between the groups. Among Hispanics as a whole, when compared to non-Hispanic whites, Hispanics are more likely to have increased risks for diabetes, hypertension, tuberculosis, alcoholism, cirrhosis, specific cancers, violent deaths, and HIV infection (Council on Scientific Affairs, American Medical Association, 1991). Poverty and the lack of health insurance are the greatest obstacles to health care among Hispanics as a group. Further complicating factors include the fact that Hispanics are more likely to be unemployed or underemployed and thus lack adequate health insurance, and to have less education than non-Hispanic whites. Warner (1991) suggested that other factors contributing to higher rates for certain health problems along the U.S.-Mexican border include water and air pollution, the lack of availability of potable water, and the lack of indoor plumbing and electricity in many areas.

Women of reproductive age make up 25 percent of the population on the Mexican side of the border, and 24 percent of the population on the U.S. side. Birth rates among Hispanic border women are higher than average, ranging from 89.1 to 107.3 per 1000 females aged 15–44 years in the U.S. in 1988, and 127 per 1000 in Mexico in 1986 (PAHO, 1993).

The border experiences a lower rate of first trimester prenatal care than the rest of the United States (JUNTOS UNIDOS, 1994). Approximately 73.6 percent of the women on the U.S. side of the border received early maternity care, while only 20.7 percent received such care on the Mexican side.

Ninety-five percent of births in the U.S. are attended by a physician as compared to 92 percent in the border counties. Although only a small percentage of births are attended by a nurse midwife in the United States, it is more common in certain border counties such as Doña Ana, New Mexico (12.3 percent), San Diego, California (6.9 percent), and Cameron, Texas (7.0 percent) (USMBHA, 1994).

The differences between the two countries and their respective border regions is evident in the rates of infant mortality. While all the Mexican municipalities combined had an infant mortality rate of 25.2 deaths per 1,000 births, the U.S. counties combined had a rate of only 7.0 (USMBHA, 1994). Both data collection systems, however, suffer from suspected underreporting of infant mortality, more so in Mexico than in the United States.

The differences are significant between the two countries with regard to the leading causes of infant deaths. The main causes of infant mortality in the Mexican border communities are lack of prenatal care, low birth weight, intestinal infectious disease, and nutritional deficiencies. Diseases of the perinatal period are the leading cause of infant death in both border regions, followed by congenital anomalies (USMBHA, 1994). Beyond the first two primary causes the areas differ. In Mexico, the remaining causes are pneumonia and influenza, intestinal infectious diseases, and accidents. For the United States, these causes are Sudden Infant Death Syndrome (SIDS), accidents, and pneumonia and influenza (USMBHA, 1994).

For certain vaccine-preventable diseases such as measles, mumps, and rubella, the rates are much higher in Mexico nationally and in the border region than in the United States. One reason is that mumps and rubella vaccination is part of the standard U.S. vaccination program, which is not the case for Mexico (USMBHA, 1994).

Mexican Americans have one of the highest birth-weight-specific fetal and neonatal mortality rates for low birth weights of any ethnic group in the U.S. This may be attributed to their status as a medically underserved population and to the low rates of medical intervention during the perinatal period. Despite this, infant mortality rates for Mexican Americans are comparable to whites and half those of Blacks (Scribner & Dwyer, 1989).

This contradiction can be understood by the fact that Mexican Americans are at the lowest risk of low-birth-weight births of any racial or ethnic group or minority. Even U.S. mothers who were born in Mexico of lower socioeconomic status have been found to have lower rates of low-birth-weight infants than the overall population. This suggests that there is a strong protective factor associated with Mexican culture that safeguards against the risk of low birth weight (Scribner & Dwyer, 1989).

Scribner and Dwyer (1989) studied the self-reports from 1,645 Mexican American mothers who participated in the Hispanic Health and Nutrition Examination Survey (HHANES) conducted by the National Center for Health Statistics during 1982–1984. They found that the aspects of Mexican cultural orientation that were associated with a favorable prenatal experience are seen primarily in highly Mexican-oriented Hispanics. These protective factors were lost when the mothers became more acculturated.

In a report prepared for the Bureau of Primary Care, Guendelman and English (1992) looked at the effects of U.S. residency on birth outcomes of mothers of Mexico. They found that after only five years of residence in the U.S. there was a deterioration in pregnancy outcomes. Even though long-term immigrants were better educated, had higher family incomes, and had greater access to health care, they were 87 percent more likely to have a preterm delivery than newcomers. Fewer pregnancies were planned among long-term immigrants. These mothers were more likely to work during pregnancy and the prevalence of smoking, drinking, and drug use among them was higher than among new immigrants.

De la Torre and Rush (1987) found that these same indications of acculturation (smoking, drinking, working) reduced the likelihood that Mexican migrant mothers would breast-feed. Gorman, Byrd, and VanDerslice (1995) point out that breast-feeding practices are especially important on the U.S.-Mexico border because breast-feeding provides an uncontaminated source of nutrition for the infant. The quality of water is poor in communities on the border and the sewage systems are lacking. Breast-fed infants have a lower incidence of diarrheal disease and a lower mortality rate. Another important benefit of breast-feeding is that it requires no financial output, and the lactation amenorrhea which results from exclusively breast-feeding infants may contribute to a reduction in unwanted pregnancies and an increase in birth intervals.

These same researchers surveyed 268 Hispanic women from three colonias (rural, undeveloped plots of land, often without water supply or sewage) near El Paso, Texas, and conducted focus groups with women and men. They found a lower incidence of breast-feeding initiation (54.3 percent) than Romero-Gwynn and Carias (1989) found in Southern California (63.8 percent). In addition to the low proportion of women initiating breast-feeding, only 16 percent of the women breast-fed for six months or longer.

As with efforts to address other health concerns in the border region, maternal child health programs must be binational and geared toward the specific needs of families in border communities. Differing levels of acculturation among families must also be taken into account. Maternal child health recommendations (Committee on Health and Social Implications of Increased Trade along the Border Region, 1994) to the 1994 Border Governors' conference included: (1) supporting and strengthening public health programs for prenatal care (especially the first three months of life), (2) coordinating records between the U.S. and Mexico and conducting further epidemiological studies of the causes of maternal mortality in Mexico, (3) continuing efforts to prevent infectious and nutritional causes of infant death, (4) beginning a border-area birth defects registry, (5) continuing immunization campaigns, and (6) continuing epidemiological and social analysis of accidental and violent deaths of children and adolescents, child abuse, and abandonment.

NONCOMMUNICABLE DISEASES

Accurate data on Hispanic death rates have not been available since death certificates did not include Hispanic identifiers prior to 1988 (Council on Scientific Affairs, American Medical Association, 1991). Information specifically on rates among Mexican Americans living along the border with Mexico is also rare. The AMA Council on Scientific Affairs (1991) noted higher death rates among Mexican Americans as a whole for alcoholism and cirrhosis, violent deaths, and accidents. Warner (1991) noted that mortality rates in the Texas border counties were lower than those for the rest of Texas and the U.S. overall, and added that "the rates for Hispanics are lower in the Texas border counties than for whites alone in the United States for each of these age groups" (p. 243).

Information on the border Mexican American population suggests that some noncommunicable health problems are genetically linked, such as diabetes. Other problems are due to barriers in obtaining health care. Problems of access to health care result in significant cross-border utilization of services. These access problems occur on both sides of the border (U.S. General Accounting Office, 1988).

For all ages, the leading cause of death for both countries nationally and for the border region is heart disease (USMBHA, 1994). Notably, cerebrovascular disease is more important as a cause of death in the U.S. than in Mexico and diabetes is a higher cause of death in Mexico than in the U.S., even in the border regions (USMBHA, 1994).

According to Marin, Burhansstipanov, Connel, Gulen, Helitzer-Allen, Lorig, Morisky, Tenney, and Thomas (1995), differences in understanding and use of preventive and disease control measures are also evident among Mexican Americans living along the U.S.-Mexico border. They compared the proportion of the general population aware of hypertension as having reached 90 percent, with higher levels for both treatment and control of hypertension. In comparison, according to the National Health and Nutrition Examination Survey (HANES), only one-third of Mexican Americans with hypertension were being treated, with only 14 percent achieving control. (The need for group-specific health promotion/education programs will be addressed in Chapter 7).

Mexican Americans in the border region may be more prone to obesity, gallbladder disease, and diabetes (Diehl & Stern, 1989). For example, they reported that Type II diabetes is 2–2.5 times more prevalent among Mexican Americans than the rest of the U.S. population. They suggest that the increased risk for obesity, gallbladder disease, and diabetes may be due to a high level of admixture of Native American genes in the Mexican American population, influenced by environmental or dietary factors.

Prevalence data for obesity, hypertension, and diabetes were also observed to be higher than the national average for Mexico among a group of civil servants in the city of Monterrey, Nuevo Léon, Mexico (Villareal, 1990).

Again, diabetes mellitus is an example of one of those noncommunicable illnesses more common along the U.S.-Mexico border Mexican American population. Mortality data generally showed a larger than expected number of deaths from diabetes (USMBHA, 1994). Because of its insidious course, deaths from the disease tend to be underreported. Complications of diabetes include retinopathy, kidney failure, heart disease, and stroke, and according to the Council on Scientific Affairs of the American Medical Council (1991), these conditions tend to be much worse among Mexican Americans.

Hispanics more commonly have certain genetically linked health problems, including diabetes. Nutritional problems are also prevalent, especially obesity. Because of the large concentration of Hispanics in the border area these problems are seen more frequently there (Warner, 1991).

Increased rates of communicable diseases along the border have been noted (Furino & Munoz, 1991). There are some notable differences between the countries and border regions as to morbidity and mortality data on communicable diseases, complicated by cross-border mobility, which significantly contributes to the threat of such diseases being shared between the United States and Mexico (Warner, 1991). For infectious and parasitic diseases, the death rates in Mexico are higher than in the United States. Tuberculosis is a much more significant cause of death in Mexico at both the national level and in the border regions. Measles is more a factor in Mexico, especially for children under the age of five. On the other hand, the death rate due to HIV infection is more a factor in the United States than in Mexico (USMBHA, 1994). Gastrointestinal illness, tuberculosis, and syphilis are communicable illnesses with a high incidence in border states. Diarrheal illness remains a major cause of childhood morbidity and mortality in Mexico (Pan American Health Organization, 1990).

Health officials are concerned about the resurgence of vaccine-preventable communicable diseases. With Mexico and the United States having different systems of immunization delivery and vaccination schedules, there is increased risk of vaccine-preventable illness. In the United States, the Centers for Disease Control and Prevention (CDCP) have shown that there is a high proportion of infants less than two years old who are inadequately immunized (CDCP, 1992). These inadequately immunized children may be at particular risk along the border.

The potential for the occurrence of communicable disease on the border is high due to several factors. Not only do the United States and Mexico have different immunization practices, which can increase the possibility of importation of communicable diseases, but differences in surveillance and reporting practices between the two countries also make binational comparisons difficult. For example, the U.S. reports of diarrheal diseases are based on etiology (e.g., shigella), while in Mexico notification is based on pathology (e.g., gastroenteritis) (Pan American Health Organization, 1993).

Poor sanitary conditions on both sides of the border contribute to the threat of communicable disease. For example, approximately 22 million gallons of raw sewage from Ciudad Juárez flow daily into the Rio Grande. Ciudad Juárez is a city of approximately 1.5 million residents with no sewage treatment capability (Reavis, 1989).

It is important to note that the true incidence of many communicable diseases is likely to be higher because underreporting of illness may occur. Individuals who are at greatest risk for developing communicable diseases are also less likely to seek attention due to lack of accessible medical care. Many individuals are more likely to cross the border for care, also resulting in underreporting of communicable diseases.

For tuberculosis and typhoid fever the rates on both sides of the border are overall significantly higher than at the national level (USMBHA, 1994). The CDCP has reported higher rates of tuberculosis in foreign-born persons as compared to persons born in the U.S. (CDCP, 1991). Persons originating from six countries, including Mexico, account for over 60 percent of the tuberculosis cases in the U.S. Fifty-two percent of Hispanic tuberculosis patients in the U.S. were foreign-born. The impact of tuberculosis in some areas of the U.S. border is even now at a crisis stage. For example, in El Paso County in 1991, there were more cases of tuberculosis than in 23 individual states (Nickey, 1993). The CDCP has recommended that state and local health departments ensure appropriate tuberculosis screening, prevention, and treatment of foreign-born immigrants (CDCP, 1990).

Some of the so-called "emerging" infectious diseases, such as dengue and cholera, are of great concern in the region. Dengue is a mosquito-transmitted illness that has surfaced along the border. The incidence of dengue has been increasing in Latin America since 1982. In 1994, there were numerous outbreaks of dengue in many countries throughout Latin America, including Mexico. The CDCP (1995) reported 46 persons in the U.S. with laboratory-confirmed dengue, with 10 of the cases most likely resulting from travel to Mexico and Central America. The majority of the cases (21) were probably acquired in the Caribbean islands (CDCP, 1994).

Cholera, after almost a century's absence in the western hemisphere, resurfaced in Peru. The infection rapidly spread throughout Latin America and into Mexico. In the United States, nearly all cases of cholera have been imported from Latin America. In 1992 more cases of cholera were reported in the U.S. than any other year since 1962, when cholera surveillance began (CDCP, 1994). Although the rate of amebiasis morbidity in the U.S. border is about the same as the national level and the Mexico border rate is lower than the Mexican national rate, the difference in the border region is still significant, with the Mexican border rate at 798.8 cases per 100,000 and the U.S. border rate at 1.4 (USMBHA, 1994). The border region also does not fare very well with regard to hepatitis A. For both countries, morbidity rates are much higher in the border regions, with the U.S. border rate (37.1 per 100,000) three times higher than the national level and the Mexican border rate (50.1) 2.5 times the national rate (USMBHA, 1994).

A discussion of communicable disease problems in the border area would not be complete without mentioning HIV infection (see Chapter 5).

For Acquired Immunodeficiency Disease Syndrome (AIDS), the morbidity rate is more than five times higher in the United States than in Mexico nationally, while the rate for the U.S. border is slightly higher than the national level, with the opposite true for the Mexican border (USMBHA, 1994). With a growing population in the border area, we can expect an increase in the absolute number of cases of AIDS. It is not clear what may happen to the rate of AIDS transmission on the border. Even without an increase in the rates, any increase in the total number of cases can have significant human and financial consequences. In Mexico a significant proportion of cases originate in the border states (Warner, 1991).

UTILIZATION OF MEDICAL SERVICES ALONG THE U.S.-MEXICO BORDER

Use of medical services along the U.S. border with Mexico has been highly publicized in recent years. Just as U.S. citizens are consumers of health services in Mexico, often due to the potential significant cost savings, Mexican nationals also have their different reasons for pursuing care in the United States.

The Use of Mexican Medical Services by U.S. Residents

The lack of medical services along the U.S.-Mexico border has created a phenomenon that may occur nowhere else in the world. This phenomenon is the crossing of an international border by citizens of one country into another country to obtain affordable medical services. Every day large numbers of U.S. citizens cross into Mexico to obtain medical care or to purchase affordable prescription medications.

According to a survey conducted by the Washington, D.C.–based Families USA Foundation (1992), U.S. citizens have been priced out of medical care in their own country and are forced to seek services in Mexico. Families USA surveyed consumers who reported that they would much rather obtain their services in the United States, but were unable to afford the high cost of those services.

The survey found that the cost of a doctor's office visit in the United States was, on the average, three times the cost of a visit to a Mexican physician. The cost differential of prescription medications was even more striking. The extent to which U.S. residents travel to Mexico to purchase medications is not known. However, U.S. health care workers believe the problem is extensive. In 1992 the El Paso Times conducted a survey of pharmacies in El Paso, Texas, and Ciudad Juárez, Chihuahua. The purpose of the survey was to determine the price of commonly used prescription drugs. Table 3.1 shows the cost comparisons of these medications (Negron, 1994).

TABLE 3.1. Cost Comparisons of Medicines at Pharmacies in the City of El Paso and Ciudad Juárez, 1994

Name of Medication (Use)	Walgreens Pharmacy, El Paso	Furrs Pharmacy El Paso	Farmacia Benavides Cd. Juárez	Farmacia Alameda, Cd. Juárez
Ranitidine 150 mg./60 tablets (anti-peptic ulcer medication)	$82.29	$104.24	$30.00	NA
Lovastatin 20 mg./30 tablets (cholesterol-lowering agent)	$51.39	$56.15	NA	$57.00
Diltiazem 60 mg./30 tablets (antihypertensive)	$20.39	$18.46	$7.50	NA
Fluoxetine 20 mg./14 tablets (antidepressant)	$29.99	$28.10	$33.60	NA
Cefaclor 250 mg./15 capsules (antibiotic)	$34.29	$40.79	$24.44*	$23.30**
Cimetidine 300 mg./100 tablets (anti-peptic ulcer medication)	$72.49	$90.96	NA	$27.00

Source: *El Paso Times,* Friday, July 15, 1994, 1A.
*250 mg./30 tablets
**500 mg./15 capsules

Tabet and Wiese (1990) surveyed clients of a community health center in southern New Mexico. The researchers found that 87 percent of those surveyed had purchased medications in Mexico at some point during the previous 60 days, with the predominant reason given being lower cost. Although the medical services for clients of the community health centers are probably more accessible, the cost of medications may still be problematic. Many individuals purchase medications in Mexico in order to self-treat illness. Others are under the care of U.S. doctors but are shopping Mexican pharmacies for lower prices (Bolio, 1993).

Self-diagnosis and self-medication pose significant risks to individuals. Many of the medications purchased without a prescription in Mexico have dangerous side-effects and require strict monitoring (Tabet & Wiese, 1990).

The cross-border utilization of health services by U.S. residents has definite economic benefit for Mexican health care providers. The Families USA Foundation survey found that, on the average, U.S. residents made up one-fourth of Mexican physicians' clientele (Families USA Foundation, 1992). Ninety-nine percent of the physicians surveyed provided services to U.S. residents.

Even in Mexican communities slightly more distant from the border, health services researchers have found that U.S. citizens were frequent utilizers of medical and dental services. In Hermosillo, Sonora, 34.5 percent of physicians and 40 percent of dentists provide care for U.S. residents. U.S. citizens paid cash for medical services 88 percent of the time and for dental services 69 percent of the time (Chacon-Sosa & Otalora-Soler, 1988).

The pattern of use of services indicates that U.S. residents most often seek care for acute, episodic illnesses. The routine use of Mexican health care providers for preventive services and disease screenings is unlikely. There may be a small proportion of U.S. residents who regularly see Mexican physicians for the management of chronic medical problems, such as diabetes and hypertension.

Use of U.S. Medical Services by Mexican Residents

Very few issues stir as much controversy as that of Mexican nationals coming to the United States to avail themselves of health care and other social programs. The controversy over California's Proposition 187 is a testament to this. The stereotype of the border-crossing Mexican national is that of a pregnant woman who arrives at a U.S. hospital in labor in order to have a baby. By virtue of being born in the United States, the child will be entitled to all of the attendant benefits (Jarique, 1993).

In November 1994, Californians voted in support of Proposition 187, which denied medical care to illegal immigrants and required that health care providers report illegal immigrants to the government. Supporters of Proposition 187 claimed that the provision of medical care to illegal immigrants was bankrupting the state's government. Opponents of the measure argued that denying medical care to the undocumented endangers the public health and undermines health professionals' ethics (Ziv & Lo, 1995).

Studies indicate that the stereotyped view of large numbers of Mexican immigrants crossing the border for medical care in the United States may not reflect an accurate picture. Guendelman and Jasis (1990) conducted a study of Tijuana residents to determine the extent to which they utilized U.S. health services. The researchers found that only 2.5 percent of those who had used medical services in the previous six-month period utilized services in the United States. Of the users of U.S. services, the largest proportion were older individuals, lawful permanent residents, citizens of the U.S. living in Mexico, and middle- to high-income Mexican nationals.

LaBrec (1990) conducted a study of the utilization of medical services at the Yuma Regional Medical Center (YRMC) by Mexican nationals. The researcher conducted a retrospective review of YRMC records during a two-year period from 1988–1990 to determine a pattern of use of hospital services by Mexican nationals. Although the study did not address the proportion of total services provided by YRMC to Mexican nationals, the study did show the types of services provided. The pattern of services provided in the medical facility suggests that Mexican nationals often used the emergency room for primary care and trauma services. Pregnancy-related diagnoses predominated inpatient services provided. (For a more extensive discussion of the impact of cross-border utilization of services on hospitals, see the discussion by Fairbanks in Chapter 4.)

The availability of medical services on both sides of the border influences the extent to which Mexican nationals use medical services in the United States. For example, if the availability of medical services is limited on the Mexican side of the border, Mexican nationals may be more likely to obtain services in the United States. The extent to which Mexican nationals are working and living in the U.S. may also reflect the likelihood that they would use medical services in the United States.

The use of medical services by Mexican nationals is not confined to U.S. hospitals. Nichols, LaBrec, Homedes, Geller, and Estrada (1991) surveyed physicians, dentists, nurse practitioners, physician assistants, and pharmacists practicing in Tucson, Arizona, and in several border counties to determine the utilization of health services by Mexican nationals. Of the 412 Arizona health care providers surveyed, 70 percent reported having seen one Mexican national per week in 1988. Of the health care providers responding, 52 percent believed that Mexican nationals caused problems with the health care system, while 48 percent believed they did not. Those providers who believed there were problems cited uncompensated care, overutilization of services, obstetrical care, and quality of care as the leading problems.

Uncompensated care is a serious issue concerning health care providers along the border. Overutilization of health services by the undocumented may be more a problem of perception than of fact. Hubbell, Waiztkin, Mishra, Dombrink, and Chavez (1991) studied access to medical services by Latinos in Orange County, California, and found that Latinos were less likely to utilize medical services than Anglos. The parameters included regular sources of medical care, access to health insurance, barriers to obtaining care, and physician visits within the previous year. When compared to Anglos, Latinos were less likely to have: (1) health insurance, (2) a regular source of medical care, (3) easy access to medical services, and (4) a record of a visit to a physician within the previous year. There was no significant difference in the utilization rates between undocumented Latinos and Latino citizens. The reasons found to be responsible for less frequent use of medical services were socioeconomic factors, including lack of medical insurance.

The provision of obstetrical care to Mexican nationals is a controversial issue. There are very real incentives for Mexican women to have children in the U.S. The advantages include better educational opportunities for their children, access to public health insurance (e.g. Medicaid), access to supplemental food and nutritional programs (WIC), lower likelihood of being deported, and more access to public housing and other social programs (Jaurique, 1993).

There are many factors that influence quality of care provided to Mexican nationals in the U.S. These factors include barriers to patient communication (language barriers), obstacles to continuity of care, and lack of background medical information on the patient (Nichols et al., 1991).

MENTAL HEALTH ISSUES

U.S.-Mexico border communities share unique characteristics which place their residents at increased risk for experiencing high levels of stress, mental health problems, alcohol, tobacco and other drug abuse (ATODA), and violence. Chief among these characteristics are infrastructure problems associated with the dramatic increase in population growth being experienced on the border, poverty and poor living standards, immigration and acculturation.

As previously cited, population growth along the U.S.-Mexico border has been high. The Pan American Health Organization (1995) estimates that there will be 10 million people on the border by the end of this century. Concomitant improvements in public health and safety infrastructure are not being provided to keep up with such population growth. Serious environmental problems exist in these communities, including housing shortages, poor air quality, water pollution, water shortages, toxic chemical contamination, soil contamination, and a lack of waste water treatment facilities. The quality of available housing is also a problem. According to a U.S. General Accounting Office study (1988), over 200,000 residents of New Mexico and Texas live in colonias (rural unincorporated subdivisions with substandard or no water and sewerage facilities). It has been estimated that more than 350,000 people in Ciudad Juárez live in colonias (Pan American Health Organization, 1995).

The areas of extreme poverty on both sides of the border and high unemployment on the U.S. side contribute to chronic stress, mental health issues, and the problems of substance abuse and violence. The minimum wage in Mexico is established on a regional basis and varies in the north but averages about $4.00 per day. The minimum wage in the U.S. is $4.25 per hour (Pan American Health Organization, 1995). Access to health care is reduced in the face of poverty, and other factors pose significant barriers to access to health care, such as limited availability of providers, language and cultural differences, lack of understanding of the system, and prohibitive U.S. laws.

Other characteristics of border communities also influence these mental health issues. Border communities experience a constant influx of cultural influences and a high level of economic and cultural transition. In 1991, the EPA estimated that annual border crossings approached more than 200 million and in 1993, the Immigration and Naturalization Service (INS) estimated that there will be 400 million crossings of the U.S.-Mexico border per year (Pan American Health Organziation, 1995). The continual influx of new residents, combined with the transient nature of the community, create a constant pressure for cultural diffusion.

A primary cause of stress for some Hispanic migrants from Mexico is related to the legality of their status as residents or the residency status of family members and friends. Fear of deportation is constant. Establishing new social contacts is often viewed as dangerous, as people fear that others may report them to immigration officials. Increased loneliness and isolation result from this stress and fear (Cervantes & Castro, 1985; Melville, 1978).

The mean age of residents is younger than in non-border communities, which means that stabilizing societal effects from older family members are less present. Anecdotal evidence suggests that U.S. and Mexican border communities are more comparable to each other than to the countries in which they exist (Kennedy, 1991). The pattern of drug and alcohol use is increasing with the same rapidity and magnitude as the number of people who cross the border each day.

The sum of all of these community risk factors is a level of daily stress and change that has a negative impact on health. Family ties that offer support to buffer this stress are broken. People exist in greater isolation. Transportation and child care necessary for mothers to obtain prenatal care is not available. Excess stress often leads to increased drug and alcohol use as a coping mechanism. Rates of intentional and unintentional injuries (suicide, homicide, drowning, motor vehicle accidents, fire, falls, and firearms) increase with drug and alcohol use (LaCerva, 1993). This cluster of stressful life conditions has been shown to correlate with impaired mental health (Swanson, Linskey, Quintero-Salinas, Pumariega & Holzer, 1992).

The Committee on Health and Social Impacts of Increased Trade along the Border Region (1994) reported to the Border Governors' Conference on the morbidity and mortality of intentional and unintentional injuries in the border region. In 1988–1990, three of the four U.S. border states had higher rates of deaths related to motor vehicle traffic accidents than the U.S. rates. New Mexico's rate of motor vehicle deaths per 100,000 was the highest at 32.4; next were Arizona at 24.5 and Texas at 20.4, compared with the overall U.S. rate of 19. The 1990 rate of motor vehicle deaths per 100,000 in the Mexican state of Sonora was 47.5 (Committee on Health and Social Impacts of Increased Trade Along the Border Region, 1994). According to statistics collected by PAHO (1990), accidents and homicides were the major causes of mortality in the 15–44 age group in the state of New Mexico and in the northern border region of Mexico, and child abuse is a concern on both sides of the border.

Swanson, Linskey, Quintero-Salinas, Pumariega, and Holzer (1992) found that adolescents on the border in the Rio Grande region of Texas used drugs to relieve their feelings of psychological distress. This study compared self-report of illicit drug use, depressive symptoms, and suicidality among 4,157 secondary students in six border cities in the neighboring states of Texas and Tamaulipas. A total of 1,775 students participated from Mexico and 2,382 participated from the U.S. On the Texas side, nearly half of the students in grade seven and higher reported high levels of current depressive symptoms. Twenty-one percent reported the use of illicit drugs in the prior month and 23 percent reported thinking about suicide in the previous week. Although suicidality and drug use were less prevalent on the Mexican side of the border, 40 percent of the adolescents there reported high levels of current depression. Levels of psychological distress and drug abuse contributed significantly to suicidality in this population.

Migration and Acculturation

The positive and negative aspects of migration and acculturation are key aspects to understanding all three of these mental health issues, especially for recent immigrants. Effects of acculturation among Mexican Americans, as well as methods to measure acculturation levels, have been studied for the past 15 years and are now being addressed in terms of border health.

Acculturation is the process whereby immigrants change their behavior and attitudes toward those of the host society (Rogler, Cortes & Malgady, 1991). Changes in acculturation involve changes in a person's relationship to the external world and require significant internal psychological changes (Rogler, Cortes & Malgady, 1991). Not all of these psychological changes are positive.

Immigrants low in acculturation have been recently uprooted and have not yet reconstructed social bonds. Their world remains unfamiliar and uncontrollable, with language barriers and isolation. This lowers self-esteem and impinges on mental health (Padilla, Cervantes, Maldonado & Garcia, 1988). On the other hand, higher levels of acculturation contribute to increased alienation from traditionally supportive primary groups. Less acculturated Mexican Americans experience less alienation and have been found to retain more traditional cultural beliefs and practices (Kranau, Green & Valencia-Weber, 1982).

Increased acculturation involves internalization of the host society's cultural norms. This is not necessarily positive in terms of mental health. Some of these norms internalized by immigrants involve negative and damaging stereotypes and prejudices towards Hispanic people. The incorporation of such norms into a person's self image can be disruptive and harmful to self-esteem and psychological health (Rogler, Cortes & Malgady, 1991).

As explained above, the mental health status of people who reside in border communities is greatly affected by the variables that contribute to stress, mental health problems, drug abuse, and violence. In addition to these stress factors, the process of acculturation is key to understanding mental health issues on the border.

There is evidence that the dynamics of assimilation of Hispanics into Anglo culture are unlike the dynamics for European immigrant groups. The research suggests that Latinos retain a strong identification with their ethnicity and language and that their self-image involves being both Latino and part of American culture. Thus, it is important to avoid generalizing research studying acculturation of European immigrants to effects of acculturation among Hispanic immigrants.

Furthermore, there are differences among Hispanics in terms of country of origin. Significant research has been conducted on immigrants from Mexico, which is relevant to the mental health status along the U.S.-Mexico border. It has also been hypothesized that the acculturation process and socioeconomic stressors experienced by migrant farm workers produce a greater risk of mental health distress (Lovato, Litrownik, Elder, Nunez-Liriano, Suarez & Talavera, 1994). Since a large percentage of residents on the border are migrant workers, these data are important for understanding mental health on the border. Also, the literature suggests that individuals who emigrate after the age of 14 experience higher levels of stress than those who emigrate at younger ages. The cultural context in which childhood and early adolescence socialization takes place is an important determinant of successful integration/adaptation (Vega, Kolodny, Valle & Hough, 1986). Also, mental health research, including research on the role of acculturation, has specifically addressed issues associated with Latina migration.

Female Hispanic immigrants suffer higher rates of depression and generalized distress than non-immigrants. Pre-migratory stressors such as economic, political, and family trauma can cause women to remain marginalized after migration (Vargas-Willis & Cervantes, 1987).

Role theory has been used to understand how immigration affects women's mental health. Empirical studies conducted in Mexico suggest that women in Mexico are assigned very traditional roles (Salgado de Snyder, 1987). Mexican women tend to assign to themselves, and to each other, rigid and traditional sex roles that require them to be passive and men to be active. Research indicates that Mexican women who immigrate to the U.S. do not experience these rigid, traditional roles. Women who migrate are more authoritarian, less submissive, and exhibit a stronger need for achievement than women who do not migrate. Women who migrate without their families are less traditional than women who do not migrate or who migrate with their families (Lovato et al., 1994).

In her article on women's roles and health, Wilson (1995) described the numerous roles and role changes which women experience during the process of immigration. Immigration can serve to increase or decrease the number of roles that a women has, and can change the nature of the roles. This change is stressful and affects mental health. The parental roles include childbearing as well as socialization of children. A woman immigrating from Mexico faces a number of difficulties accessing health care for her children and herself. She must first realize that there is a need for prenatal or pediatric care, and then she must have the funds, time, transportation, and child care necessary to access these services. Accessing care entails overcoming language barriers and culturally unfamiliar or unacceptable practices. The parental role is also altered by the common experience of guilt that women feel about having taken their children away from familiar surroundings, especially when the neighborhoods to which they move are not safe. Alternatively, if the mother has left children behind and sends money to support them, she is likely to experience ambivalence about the separation. Another mental health-related concern, prevalent on both sides of the border, is drug abuse.

Drug Abuse

According to Nancy Kennedy, the project officer of the Epidemiology Studies and Surveillance Branch of the Division of Epidemiology and Prevention Research of the National Institute on Drug Abuse (NIDA), the epidemiology of substance abuse is in its infancy. Epidemiology began to be applied to substance abuse in the 1970s and 1980s when the use of illicit drugs (especially heroin) increased. There are unique measurement problems which make data collection of substance abuse use patterns very different than data collection on rates of infectious and chronic illnesses. Measurement of substance abuse depends on objective reports of users or treatment facilities. Obtaining reports from users is difficult, as use of drugs is not socially acceptable or legal (Kennedy, 1991). Furthermore, the disease of addiction itself is most often marked by denial. The psychoactive properties of the drugs themselves and the behaviors in which addicts must engage in order to survive make users and addicts unreliable sources of information.

In 1989, NIDA and the Office for Substance Abuse Prevention funded a joint investigation by the PAHO El Paso Field Office and the USMBHA. The purpose of the investigation was to review available data on substance abuse and treatment in the border region and to make recommendations. The completed report (Pan American Health Organization, 1989b) provides a historical perspective on substance abuse in the United States, Mexico, and on the border, and provides information on the substance abuse treatment and prevention services available in the border region. The report concluded that little quantitative data regarding drug abuse on the border were available, and questioned the validity of the available studies. Again, the report strongly recommended that binational efforts be made to address this issue.

An example of the limitation of available studies and why the validity of such studies is questioned involves a 1989 study referenced in this Pan American Health Organization report (Montoya, 1989). This study used 1985 population estimates to provide an empirical translation of NIDA estimates of substance abuse for young (ages 12–17 years) Hispanic males to the associated populations in the southwestern counties along the U.S.-Mexico border. These estimates were drawn from the 1985 National Household Survey on Drug Abuse (NHSDA), and the specific observed estimate used was "used in the past month." While the use of alcohol (27 percent) and cigarettes (14.5 percent) were the most frequently cited drugs, marijuana, either used separately (5.6 percent) or along with other drugs (11.9 percent), and cocaine (2.8 percent) were also fairly common. The author, however, questioned the validity of applying national estimates to local areas, and suggested that these numbers represent the minimal experience at the local level.

Although there is a lack of epidemiological data regarding the prevalence of substance abuse on the border, there is definite agreement among border health professionals and residents that substance abuse is a priority health concern. Project Consenso (USMBHA, 1991), supported by the U.S. Public Health Service and the Mexican Ministry of Health, and carried out by the Pan American Health Organization El Paso Field Office, was initiated in 1991 to identify border health concerns best addressed through binational cooperation. Results from a mailout Delphi survey (n=667 responses) identified substance abuse as one of the six most important health priorities. Substance abuse was identified also as a priority concern by health professionals in the four regional meetings held as part of Project Consenso.

This binational work recommended by the 1989 PAHO report has been undertaken. In 1992, the four U.S. border governors pledged greater cooperation among their state agencies emphasizing prevention of alcohol, tobacco, and other drug abuse (ATODA). The recommended prevention strategies were to: (1) increase the use of mass media and other information resources, (2) enhance educational efforts to create an attitude and culture that rejects drugs and that allows the family and community to play a fundamental role, and (3) encourage cooperation between the countries for the provision of appropriate technical assistance to communities for the education and training of human resources in this area. In 1994, the 10 U.S. and Mexico border governors signed a Joint Communiqué, which added an emphasis on demand reduction strategies (Committee on the Health and Social Implications of Increased Trade along the Border Region, 1994). Another example of binational efforts has been the formation of a binational policy group to work on substance abuse–related issues. The Center for Substance Abuse Prevention (CSAP) commissioned the Arizona-Mexico Border Health Foundation (AMBHF) and the USMBHA to bring substance abuse prevention experts together to identify: (1) prevention efforts, (2) current prevention, treatment, and research gaps, and (3) future policy options for CSAP consideration. The U.S.-Mexico Border Policy Group, consisting of over 30 border experts from Mexico and the United States, was formed and its report was finalized in 1995 (Pan American Health Organization, 1995).

In this report, the availability of drugs on the border was noted as a community risk factor for increased substance abuse. The border is an international drug transportation route. The northern border states of Mexico have registered the highest number of drug seizures (marijuana and cocaine) in comparison to other parts of the country. In 1993, Mexican border agents seized 233 tons of marijuana, representing a 38 percent increase from the previous year. Drug seizures are also increasing on the U.S. side. Other factors influencing the availability of drugs are that the border is crossed by youth to buy alcohol, and that people of all ages cross the border to buy pharmaceutical products (Pan American Health Organization, 1995). Policy recommendations resulting from this report were that CSAP should: 1) make ATODA prevention and treatment for the border region a priority, 2) strengthen disease prevention networks that operate along the border, 3) support the establishment of a "U.S.-Mexico Border Substance Abuse Educational Training Center," and 4) promote an ongoing program for prevention and epidemiological research that responds to the border's culturally diverse and transitioning population.

This report agrees with the earlier Pan American Health Organization (1989b) report in suggesting that prevalence studies have not produced valid data. In support of this, the Pan American Health Organization (1995) report cited a study by Harrison and Kennedy that reviewed data collected from the 1988 and 1990 NHSDAs. They combined the data from both surveys in order to increase the sample size to 591. Their results, presented in Table 3.2, are surprising as they suggest little difference between prevalence rates for people who live on the U.S. side of the border compared with people who live in non-border areas of the U.S.

TABLE 3.2. Percentage of Drug Users among Border vs. Non-Border Residents

	Lifetime use	Use in the past year	Use in the past month
U.S. border residents	43.0%	18.6%	6.9%
U.S. non-border residents	38.0%	14.4%	7.0%

Source: Pan American Health Organization, 1995

The difficulty with these data is that the sample size is small. High risk populations have to be oversampled in order to obtain sufficient data. Many people living on the border are hard to reach due to lack of telephones, crowded living conditions, and fear of responding because of immigration status. Thus, the concern persists that the methodology frequently used does not yield a valid representation of the prevalence of drug use along the border.

The Pan American Health Organization (1995) report also cited a study which used an alternative methodology in a 1991 investigation in Mexico City. In this study, Maria Elena Medina-Mora, head of the Division of Epidemiology and Social Science at the Mexican Institute of Psychiatry, used an ethnographic case-finding approach in conjunction with the survey methodology used in the Mexican Household Survey. Results of the study when these two methodologies were used simultaneously were different than when the survey methodology was used without the ethnographic approach. With this innovative approach, a clearer picture of drug use emerged that more realistically represented the depth of the problems. "The results showed findings that differed significantly in demographic characteristics of drug users, in the drugs consumed, and in the patterns of use. The differences were staggering" (Pan American Health Organization, 1995, p. 37).

The Swanson and colleagues (1992) study previously cited showed a higher prevalence of drug abuse and also found that country of birth plays an important role in drug use patterns. Their study, which was conducted binationally, included use of a self-administered, anonymous questionnaire that was given directly to adolescents attending public secondary schools in three southern Texas cities (Brownsville, Edinburg, and Rio Grande City) and three adjacent Mexican cities (Matamoros, Reynosa, and Camargo). The prevalence rates of drug use reported in this study were higher than those reported in the NIDA and HNSDA studies. This study found that 21 percent of Texas youth reported using illicit drugs in the past month. Of the Mexican youth, only 4.95 percent reported using illicit drugs. In terms of country of origin, this study found that youth who lived in the U.S. with both parents born in the U.S. had significantly higher rates of drug use than those who had one or both parents born in Mexico. The Mexican youth whose parents were both born in Mexico were significantly less likely to use drugs than peers with at least one parent born in the U.S. (Swanson et al., 1992). This study underscores the importance of a methodology geared to the binational nature of the border. It also points to the role that acculturation plays in drug use. Further support for the hypothesis that increased acculturation levels among Hispanic youth are associated with increased drug use comes from Gfroerer and De La Rosa (1993). Utilizing data from the 1988 NHSDA, they found that children whose fathers' primary language was English and whose education levels were higher had increased levels of drug use.

A study of cigarette and alcohol use among migrant Hispanic adolescents (Lovato et al., 1994) also examined the factor of acculturation. This study used a sample of 214 Hispanic migrant adolescents who were enrolled in the National Migrant Education Program in San Diego County. They found that females who scored higher on measures of acculturation reported higher use of alcohol in their lifetime. Males and females who scored higher on measures of acculturation were more likely to report binge drinking in the past 30 days. Such results support the need for prevention efforts at an early age.

An example of a successful binational, community-based prevention program that addresses the use of ATODA by school age youth is the VENCINOS network, a CSAP community partnership (JUNTOS UNIDOS, 1994). This project is an expansion of the Community Partnership JUNTOS

UNIDOS, which began in 1991 and which serves Santa Cruz County, Arizona, and adjacent Nogales, Sonora, Mexico. VENCINOS includes the border communities of Yuma County and Cochise County in Arizona and the adjacent sister cities in Sonora, Mexico.

The VENCINOS project serves 170,000 people on the 150 miles of the Arizona-Sonora border. The target population is primarily Hispanic (47 percent) with some communities being 98 percent Hispanic. A large segment of the population, only recently arrived from Mexico, are migrant farm workers and seasonal workers. The area is characterized by high unemployment, low per capita income, and a population in which 34 percent are under the age of 19. The goals of VENCINOS include: (1) to reduce underage initiation and use of alcohol, tobacco, and other drugs, (2) to decrease the frequency of substance use–related incidents, (3) to establish community systems that support an integrated, community-based approach to substance abuse prevention, (4) to alter community norms and perceptions regarding the utilization of alcohol, tobacco, and other drugs, 5) to establish sustained, collaborative relationships with counterparts in Sonoran sister cities, and 6) to impact local, state, national, and binational policy and resources in favor of ATODA prevention programming at the Arizona-Sonora border. While evaluation results from this project are still unavailable, addressing ATODA concerns binationally through such prevention efforts is consistent with current practice and should hold promise. (See Chapter 7 for more examples of such health promotion/education efforts.)

ENVIRONMENTAL HEALTH CONCERNS

No discussion of border health issues would be complete without a consideration of environmental pollution. Water and air pollution are the major factors affecting the environmental health of the U.S.-Mexico border region (Council on Scientific Affairs, 1990). While inadequate water supplies and water pollution are concerns throughout the region, air pollution is more severe in major urban areas. Increased agricultural export development (Cech & Essman, 1992), population growth, and the expanded development of factories along the northern border of Mexico (maquilas) (Shields, 1991) have contributed to these environmental problems.

The need for cooperative U.S.-Mexican efforts to address and improve environmental conditions along the border remains a concern of residents of the region. The challenge has been the lack of official recognition by both governments and their mutual participation in identifying and developing resources to meet those needs. This section will review the border's environmental problems as recognized by border residents, experts, and government agencies, and those actions recently implemented. See Chapter 6 for more detailed information on environmental health issues.

The first effort outside of the creation of the International Boundary and Water Commission (IBWC) was the signing of the 1983 U.S.-Mexico Border Environmental Agreement, better known as the La Paz Agreement. This agreement was reaffirmed in a November 1990 Joint Presidential Communiqué that directed the development of the Integrated Border Environmental Plan (IBEP) (Office of International Activities, U.S. Environmental Protection Agency, 1992). Most recently, the effort has been moved forward by the signing of the North American Free Trade Agreement (NAFTA) in the fall of 1992, and more specifically by the signing of the Environmental Side-Agreement that created the Commission for Environmental Cooperation, the North American Development Bank (NAD Bank), and the Border Environment Cooperation Commission (BECC).

"Disease knows no border. It does not need a visa. It travels at will. And it kills at will" (Nixon, 1991, p. 6). These and other statements made by Dr. Sam Nixon at the 1991 Border Health Conference held in McAllen, Texas, continue to echo throughout the border region as if spoken just yesterday. He challenged the conference participants by exhorting that:

> This is the challenge we must meet. How and if we meet this challenge will determine the fate of our border. That fate swings like a pendulum between two very different worlds, two very different futures. One is a future of economic growth at the risk of further environmental and health devastation along both sides of the border. The other is a future that improves the health of the border area's infrastructure while it comes alive with increased trade. Without a sound infrastructure, which the border area does not have at this time, the strain of increased trade could cause the area to collapse. From Texas to California, the border area cannot support the weight of unbridled change. The border area lacks the health care services needed; the sewage treatment facilities needed; the public water systems needed; and the environmental enforcement necessary to control industrial waste dumping and air emissions. (Nixon, 1991, p. 6)

The needs of the environment and its impact on health were also a significant concern of participants in Project Consenso. Environmental health was determined to be one of the six priorities for the border. Project Consenso's recommendations related to environmental health specifically addressed: (1) the assurance of proper disposal of hazardous waste generated by the maquila industry, (2) the establishment of a binational entity such as the now-approved U.S.-Mexico Border Health Commission, (3) the need to increase potable water and the establishment of additional sewage disposal facilities along the border, (4) the prevention of food contamination by pesticides, (5) the reduction of environmentally related disease conditions, (6) the identification and reduction of pollution sources affecting water quality in the Rio Grande River, and (7) the necessity to quantify the level of contaminants in the environment and initiate abatement efforts as necessary (USMBHA, 1991).

There is no question that the quality of the environment plays a major role along the U.S.-Mexico border in contributing to health problems (NHPF, 1994). This environmental impact was clearly enumerated in the initial Environmental Plan for the U.S.-Mexico Border Area which became known as the Integrated Border Environmental Plan (IBEP). The IBEP was developed in response to the charge from both Mexican President Salinas de Gortari and U.S. President George Bush, which called for U.S. and Mexican environmental authorities to cooperate in preparing a comprehensive plan to protect the environment along the border (Office of International Activities, U.S. Environmental Protection Agency, 1992). The plan summarized the problems of congestion, uncontrolled urban development, and the lack of basic public health and sanitation facilities among the growing sister cities communities. Although specific to each side of the border, the problems are clearly more severe on the Mexican side where:

> tens of thousands of families attracted to the border area by job opportunities in the maquiladoras are straining existing road, drinking water, and wastewater treatment systems. In some places with high population densities, centralized wastewater collection and treatment systems have never been built. The lack of land available for housing, together with unplanned land use, have resulted in the growth of settlements which lack basic services such as public transportation and solid waste disposal. In addition, the hazardous wastes generated by the maquiladoras have caused widespread concern on both sides of the border, because little is known about the kinds, quantities, or disposal of such wastes. (Office of International Activities, U.S. Environmental Protection Agency, 1992, p. 11)

The primary focus on the U.S. side has been and will continue to be the remediation of the poor environmental conditions created by the proliferation of unincorporated communities called colonias. These colonias, which are the homes of over 200,000 people in Texas and New Mexico alone, are characterized by substandard housing, inadequate roads and drainage, and barely adequate water and sewer systems, if such systems exist at all. For example, less than one percent of Texas colonias, and about 7 percent of New Mexico colonias, are covered by wastewater treatment systems. (Office of International Activities, U.S. Environmental Protection Agency, 1992, p. 11)

Although the problems of the border may have been generally identified by the IBEP, reaction to the completed plan was not favorable, as indicated by the findings and recommendations of the Public Advisory Committee to the IBEP. The Committee found that the plan was not in fact an integrated plan, that the long-term water supply demands were ignored, and that "at the current time, crisis management and political agendas, rather than long-term interests, drive funding and priorities for environmental programs along the border" (Udall Center, 1993, p. 3).

The Committee further identified five priority recommendations after review of the completed plan. The recommendations emphasized more efficient, and non-duplicative, binational coordination of data gathering; the requirement for suitable and appropriate institutional responsibility, which included support for a binational commission; the need for more rational funding allocations; the urgent need for funding resources commensurate with the problems; and greater responsiveness to border residents and their problems, such as emphasis on environmental health. It further described environmental health as "perhaps the most pivotal principle underlying the topics of critical attention" (Udall Center, 1993, p. 10).

Soon after NAFTA, and most assuredly reinforced by the experience of the IBEP, a final agreement was reached with the Mexican government on new binational mechanisms to facilitate border environmental cleanup and to provide additional support for community adjustment and investment related to NAFTA. Two new organizations (BECC and the NAD Bank) were created as components of the North American Agreement on Environmental Cooperation (U.S. Department of the Treasury, 1994).

The BECC, with headquarters in Ciudad Juárez, Chihuahua, Mexico, was charged with assisting border states and local communities in coordinating, designing, and implementing environmental infrastructure projects with cross-border impact (U.S. Department of the Treasury, 1994). The BECC's specific functions include:

1) To work with state and local governmental entities, to organize,

develop and arrange public and private financing to develop environmental infrastructure projects in the region 100 km (62 miles) on either side of the U.S.-Mexico border, and to coordinate and oversee such projects,

2) to assess the technical and financial feasibility and evaluate social and economic benefits of environmental infrastructure projects,

3) to provide technical assistance, giving preference to projects involving potable water supply, wastewater treatment, municipal waste management and other related projects. (BECC, 1995, p. 1)

The NAD Bank, with headquarters in San Antonio, Texas, is charged with providing over $2 billion in financing for both border environmental projects and, more broadly with the United States, ten percent of the U.S. and Mexican shares of the NAD Bank for NAFTA-related community adjustment and investment.

The newest addition to the border planning and coordinating community has been the Good Neighbor Environmental Board. The Board was created by the Enterprise for the Americas Initiative Act of 1992 to advise the President and the Congress concerning environmental and infrastructure needs within the states contiguous to Mexico (Good Neighbor Environmental Board, 1995). The Board includes members from U.S. government agencies, from the state governments of Arizona, California, New Mexico, and Texas, and from private organizations and nongovernmental entities with expertise on environmental and infrastructure problems along the southwest border (Good Neighbor Environmental Board, 1995).

The Board paid considerable attention to the results of the Integrated Border Environmental Plan (IBEP) and to its successor, the plan to be referred to as "Border 21." The Board emphasized that "Border 21" should: (1) be more comprehensive than previous efforts, (2) establish short-term goals and objectives, (3) employ a binational, regionally-based approach for addressing transboundary issues, (4) include meaningful public participation, (5) address environmentally related public health issues, and (6) incorporate domestic components as determined by the two governments (Good Neighbor Environmental Board, 1995, pp. 5–6).

Specific to the environment, the Board made a number of recommendations, including the following:

1) that federal agencies, BECC, NAD Bank, and other public and private funders incorporate sustainable development in planning or funding border environmental programs and projects;

2) that federal agencies support and encourage local binational efforts toward cross-border environmental planning;

3) that a binational air quality management basin (AQMB) be formed in timely fashion for the El Paso-Juárez airshed;

4) that the responsible federal agencies continue to improve the efficiency and reliability of the notification and monitoring process for hazardous materials transported across the border;

5) that federal funding be continued at existing levels for infrastructure, health facilities, and training in U.S. colonias for at least the next ten years; and,

6) that in view of the importance of limited water resources and the impact of contaminated water on border residents' health, that federal agencies develop and implement an integrated, borderwide and bilateral strategy for the use, reuse, and treatment of limited water resources. (Good Neighbor Environmental Board, 1995, pp. 16–18)

As is widely recognized, the border does not lack for the effort to understand its problems, for specific recommendations to address those problems, for federal legislation, or for community and organizational mechanisms to implement the necessary functions. What the border does lack are the necessary resources from both federal governments to bring about those results. Improvement of environmental conditions can only be achieved by long-term, comprehensive, and binational integrated planning with appropriate community and state input. According to Nixon (1991):

> The border is extremely vulnerable right now. It is oscillating between those two futures I described earlier. It is up to us to ensure the pendulum swings in a positive direction—toward stabilization. That's what we hope to accomplish through our efforts. . . . The health and environmental conditions along both sides of the border will not improve without our push. As the population grows, as it does every day, and as demographics change, the situation will worsen. . . . We face a tremendous challenge. A challenge that will keep us busy for a long time to come. But also a challenge we pledge . . . to meet and overcome. (p. 12)

SUMMARY

Flack (1985) has referred to the U.S.-Mexico border as "a region which could easily be out of control" (p. 17). Problems associated with population growth in border cities, illegal immigration, illicit drug use, increased violence, and economic development, accompanied by failure to address environmental health concerns, are among the many issues to address. Falck attributes such increased risks to the rise of maquiladora industries along the border, with the associated northern migration in Mexico, with the increased prevalence of tuberculosis and other infectious diseases; with the increased risks of HIV/ AIDS as the result of increased drug use and prostitution; with environmental pollution; and inadequate availability of and access to health care. Falck contends that we are living in a time when daring and radical solutions, including binational cooperation, must be tested. The observations made by the U.S.-Mexico Border Health Task Group reinforced loudly and clearly the strategies needed to combat the public health problems of the border in stating that:

> the problems of the border are far from insoluble, but because they exist on both sides, and because border communities must be treated as single epidemiological units, health-status issues must be approached from a binational perspective with an understanding that public health agencies and workers in both countries, from the federal to the local levels, must work in partnership to solve them. (U.S. Public Health Service, 1991, p. 3)

This chapter has provided an overview to some of the major health issues confronting citizens living along the U.S.-Mexico border. While much uncertainty remains regarding the impact of continued economic and population growth, there remains the question of how much longer a strained and inadequate health care system can continue to adapt to meet such challenges. The one resounding recommendation for increasing the effectiveness of the current public health infrastructure is to make further use of the ecological approach in addressing problems on the binational level. There is widespread recognition that solutions to many of the health issues unique to the border region must incorporate this binational perspective. One of the six policy recommendations made by the XII Border Governors' Conference (Committee on Health and Social Implications of Increased Trade along the Border Region, 1994) called for the establishment of a U.S.-Mexico Border Health Commission, and for the ten border state governors to work with their national governments to "encourage the development of complementary and interactive sub-commissions on each side of the border" (p. 6).

This "participatory approach" was recommended to minimize border health problems and build strong, binational community projects. Over the past six years, there has been growing professional and governmental support from both countries for such a commission. The XII Border Governors' Conference suggested that:

> The overall purpose of the U.S.-Mexico Border Health Commission is to reinforce organizational structures needed to improve medical and public health practices in a unique environment that requires a cooperative multi-state and binational approach. This Commission is particularly necessary in a region that has two distinct operational and legal systems, yet share geographic and epidemiologic environments. The establishment of a Border Health Commission follows the recognition that *border population centers should be considered as a single epidemiologic area.* The U.S.-Mexico Border Health Commission will be established on the border to: (1) facilitate the implementation of public health and prevention programs within existing structures, (2) facilitate and coordinate the development of public and private partnerships to deal with general health problems at the border (e.g., disease prevention, emergency care, perinatal care, selected health services, and developing an appropriate system of medical care insurance), (3) establish criteria for community health guidelines as they relate to urban planning standards, and (4) design/develop a continuing public health assessment system and hearing process for implementation in the border region. (Committee on Health and Social Implications of Increased Trade along the Border Region, 1994, p. 10–11)

The governors intended for the Commission to be responsive to local needs and to work closely with local and state governments to encourage collaborative strategies for resolving border health problems. While the Border Health Commission Act was authorized by the U.S. Congress in 1993, no funds have been appropriated for implementation. The endorsement of such a binational commission has yet to be even considered by the Secretariat of Health in Mexico. Therefore, binational ratification of the Commission may still be a long way off. In the meantime, most binational activities will continue to occur at the local level, such as the sister communities projects supported by the U.S.-Mexico Border Health Association.

REFERENCES

Bolio, D. (1993, June 29). To avoid the cost of U.S. prescription drugs, more Americans shop south of the border. *Wall Street Journal*, B1.

Border Environment Cooperation Commission (BECC). (1995). *Guidelines for project submission and criteria for project certification.* Ciudad Juárez, Chihuahua: Border Environment Cooperation Commission.

Cech, I. & Essman, A. (1992). Water sanitation practices on the Texas-Mexico border: Implications for physicians on both sides. *Southern Medical Journal, 85*(11), 1053–1064.

Centers for Disease Control (1990). Tuberculosis among foreign-born persons entering the United States: Recommendations of the Advisory Committee for the Elimination of Tuberculosis. *Morbidity and Mortality Weekly, 39*(RR18), 1–13, 18–21.

Centers for Disease Control (1991). Tuberculosis transmission along the U.S.-Mexican Border-1990. *Morbidity and Mortality Weekly Report, 40*(22), 373–375.

Centers for Disease Control and Prevention (1992). A retrospective assessment of vaccination coverage among school-aged children. *Morbidity and Mortality Weekly, 41*(6), 103–107.

Centers for Disease Control and Prevention (1994). *Addressing emerging infectious disease threats: A prevention strategy for the United States 1994.* Atlanta, GA: Department of Health and Human Services, U.S. Public Health Service.

Centers for Disease Control and Prevention. (1995). Imported dengue—United States, 1993–1994. *Morbidity and Mortality Weekly Report, 44*(18), 353–356.

Cervantes, R.C. & Castro, F.G. (1985). Stress, coping, and Mexican-American mental health: A systematic review. *Hispanic Journal of Behavioral Sciences, 7*(1), 1–73.

Chacon Sosa, F. & Otalora-Soler, M. (1988). Utilization of health services in Hermosillo, Sonora by United States residents. *Border Health, 4,* 27–35.

Committee on Health and Social Implications of Increased Trade along the Border Region (1994). *Preliminary recommendations for the 1994 border governors' conference.* Tijuana, Baja California.

Council on Scientific Affairs, American Medical Association (1990). A permanent U.S.-Mexico Border Environmental Health Commission. *Journal of the American Medical Association, 263*(24), 3319–3321.

Council on Scientific Affairs, American Medical Association (1991). Hispanic health in the United States. *Journal of the American Medical Association, 265*(2), 248–252.

Crespin, F.H. & Kalishman, N. (1991). New Mexico's health status: A natural experiment in border industrialization. Border Health Conference. McAllen, TX.

De la Torre, A. & Rush, L. (1987). The determinants of breastfeeding for Mexican migrant women. *International Migration Review, 21,* 728–739.

Diehl, A.K. & Stern, M.P. (1989). Special health problems of Mexican-Americans: Obesity, gallbladder disease, diabetes mellitus, and cardiovascular disease. *Advances in Internal Medicine, 34,* 73–96.

Economics and Statistics Administration (1993). *Hispanic Americans today.* (Bureau of the Census Document No. P23– 183). Washington, D.C.: U.S. Government Printing Office.

Families USA Foundation (1992). *Crossing to Mexico: Priced out of American health care.* Washington, D.C.: Families USA Foundation.

Flack, V. T. (1985). Bringing about change along the United States-Mexico border. *Border Health, 1*(Special Issue), 17– 23.

Furino, A. & Munoz, E. (1991). Health status among Hispanics: Major themes and new priorities. *Journal of the American Medical Association, 265*(2), 255–257.

Gfroerer, J. & De La Rosa, M. (1993). Protective and risk factors associated with drug use among Hispanic youth. *Journal of Addictive Diseases, 12*(2), 87–107.

Good Neighbor Environmental Board (1995). *First annual report.* A Presidential and Congressional Advisory Committee on U.S.-Mexico Border Environmental and Infrastructure Issues.

Gorman, T., Byrd, T.L., & VanDerslice, J. (1995). Breast-feeding practices, attitudes, and beliefs among Hispanic women and men in a border community. *Community Health Journal, 18*(2), 17–27.

Guendelman, S. & English, P.B. (1992). *The effects of U.S. residency on birth outcomes among Mexican-born women in California* (Bureau of Primary Care, Maternal and Child Health Branch Contract No. 90–11768). Sacramento: California Department of Health Services.

Guendelman, S. & Jasis, M. (1990). Measuring Tijuana residents' choice of Mexican or U.S. health care services. *Public Health Reports, 105*(6), 575–583.

Hubbell, F.A., Waitzkin, H., Mishra, S.I., Dombrink, J., & Chavez, L.R. (1991). Access to medical care for documented and undocumented Latinos in a southern California county. *Western Journal of Medicine, 154*(4), 414–417.

Jaurique, M. (1993, June 21). Crossing the border to have a baby. *El Paso Times*, 1A.

JUNTOS UNIDOS (1994). *VENCINOS: Arizona, Sonora Substance Abuse Prevention Coalition*. Nogales, AZ: Arizona-Mexico Border Health Foundation.

Kennedy, N.J. (1991). Epidemiology of substance abuse: The U.S.- Mexico border area. *Border Health, 7*(3), 1–7.

Kranau, E.J., Green, V., & Valencia-Weber, G. (1982). Acculturation and the Hispanic woman: Attitudes toward women, sex role attribution, behavior, and demographics. *Hispanic Journal of Behavioral Sciences, 4*(1), 21–40.

LaBrec, P.A. (1990). *Utilization of Yuma Regional Medical Center by Mexican nationals. Southwest Border Rural Research Center, Monograph No. 16*. Tucson, AZ: University of Arizona.

LaCerva, V. (1993). *Let peace begin with us: The problem of violence in New Mexico, Vol. 2*. Medical Director's Office, Maternal and Child Health. Santa Fe, NM: New Mexico Department of Health.

Lovato, C.Y., Litrownik, A.J., Elder, J., Nunez-Liriano, A., Suarez, D., & Talavera, G.A. (1994). Cigarette and alcohol use among migrant Hispanic adolescents. *Community Health, 16*(4), 18–31.

Marin, G., Burhansstipanov, L., Connell, C.M., Gielen, A.C., Helitzer-Allen, D., Lorig, K., Morisky, D.E., Tenney, M., & Thomas, S. (1995). A research agenda for health education among underserved populations. *Health Education Quarterly, 22*(3), 346–363.

Marin, G. & Marin, B.V.O. (1991). *Research with Hispanic populations*. Newbury Park, CA: Sage.

Martinez, O.J. (1994). *Border people: Life and society in the U.S.-Mexico borderlands*. Tucson: University of Arizona Press, 40–44.

Melville, M.B. (1978). Mexican women adapt to migration. *International Migration Review, 12*(2), 225–235.

Montoya, M. (1989). Prevalence of 1985 substance abuse in the U.S.-Mexico border: Hispanic males ages 12–17 years. *Border Health, 5*(4), 11–17.

National Health Policy Forum (1994). *Diversity in health systems reform: The implications of U.S.-Mexico border issues*. Site Visit Report. Washington, D.C.: The George Washington University.

Negron, S. (1994, July). Farmacias boasting bargains: Customers drawn from across U.S. *El Paso Times*, 1A.

Nichols, A.W., LaBrec, P.A., Homedes, N., Geller, S.E., & Estrada, A.L. (1991). *Utilization of health services along the U.S.-Mexico border*. Southwest Border Rural Health Research Center, Monograph No. 23. Tucson, AZ: University of Arizona.

Nickey, L.N. (1991, September). *The United States-Mexico border health & environmental problems*. Oral testimony for public hearing at the University of Texas at El Paso National Health Policy Forum (1994). Diversity in health systems reform: The implications of U.S.-Mexico border issues. Site Visit Report. Washington, D.C.: The George Washington University.

Nickey, L.N. (1993, July). *U.S.-Mexico border health and environmental* issues. Paper presented to the United States Congressional Border Caucus, Washington, D.C.

Nixon, S.A. (1991, October). *Address by Sam A. Nixon, M.D., President Texas Medical Association*. Paper presented at TMA's Third Annual Border Health Conference, McAllen, TX.

Office of International Activities, U.S. Environmental Protection Agency (1992). *Summary, environmental plan for the Mexican-U.S. border area, first stage (1992–1994)*. Washington, D.C.: U.S. Environmental Protection Agency.

Ortega, H. (1991). Promoting binational cooperation to improve health along the U.S.-Mexico border. *Carnegie Quarterly, 36*(1–4), 1–8.

Ortega, H. (1995). *United States-Mexico border: Vital statistics review*. El Paso, TX: The Interamerican Institute for Border Health and Environment, p. 10.

Padilla, A.M., Cervantes, R.C., Maldonado, M., & Garcia, R.E. (1988). Coping responses to psychosocial stressors among Mexican and Central American immigrants. *Journal of Community Psychology, 16*, 418–427.

Pan American Health Organization (1989a). *Population distribution*. El Paso, TX: El Paso Field Office, PAHO.

Pan American Health Organization (1989b). *Report on substance abuse along the U.S.-Mexico border*. El Paso, TX: El Paso Field Office, PAHO.

Pan American Health Organization (1990). *U.S.-Mexico border health statistics*. El Paso, TX: El Paso Field Office, PAHO.

Pan American Health Organization (1993). Maternal mortality in the Americas. *Epidemiological Bulletin, 14*(1), 1–9.

Pan American Health Organization (1995). *Substance abuse in the U.S.-Mexico border region*. El Paso, TX: El Paso Field Office, PAHO.

Reavis, R. (1989). *Border Health Conference proceedings*. El Paso, TX: Pan American Health Organization, El Paso Field Office, 23–24.

Rogler, L.H., Cortes, D.E., & Malgady, R.G. (1991). Acculturation and mental health status among Hispanics: Convergence and new directions for research. *American Psychologist, 46*, 585–597.

Romero-Gwynn, E. & Carias, L. (1989). Breast-feeding intentions and practice among Hispanic mothers in southern California. *Pediatrics, 84*(4), 626–632.

Salgado de Snyder, V.N. (1987). Factors associated with acculturative stress and depressive symptomatology among married Mexican immigrant women. *Psychology of Women Quarterly, 11*, 45–48.

Scribner, R. & Dwyer, J.H. (1989). Acculturation and low birth weight among Latinos in the Hispanic HANES. *American Journal of Public Health, 79*(9), 1263–1267.

Sevrens, G. (1992). *Environmental, health, and housing needs and nonprofit groups in the U.S.-Mexico border area*. Arlington, VA: World Environment Center.

Shields, J. (1991). Ambient air arsenic levels along the Texas- Mexico border. *Journal of the Air Waste Management Association, 41*(6), 827–831.

Swanson, J.W., Linskey, A.O., Quintero-Salinas, R., Pumariega, A.J., & Holzer, C.A. (1992). Binational school survey of depressive symptoms, drug use, and suicidal ideation. *Journal of the American Academy of Child Adolescent Psychiatry, 31*(4), 669–678.

Tabet, S.R. & Wiese, W.H. (1990). Medications obtained in Mexico by patients in southern New Mexico. *Southern Medical Journal, 83*, 271–273.

Udall Center for Studies in Public Policy (1993). *State of the U.S.-Mexico Border Environment*. Report of the U.S. Environmental Protection Agency U.S.-Mexico Border Environmental Plan, Public Advisory Committee. Tucson, AZ: University of Arizona.

United States Department of the Treasury (1994). *Fact sheet on the U.S.-Mexican Agreement on the Border Environment Cooperation Commission (BECC) and the North American Development Bank (NAD Bank)*. Washington, D.C.: U.S. Department of the Treasury.

United States General Accounting Office (1988). *Health Care: Availability in the Texas-*

Mexico border area. (GAO Document # HRD-89–12). Washington, D.C.: Governmental Accounting Office.

United States-Mexico Border Health Association (1991). *Project Consenso final report.* El Paso, TX: Pan American Health Organization, El Paso Field Office.

United States-Mexico Border Health Association. (1994). *Sister communities health profiles: United States-Mexico border, 1989–1991.* El Paso, TX: Pan American Health Organization, El Paso Field Office.

United States Public Health Service (1991). *U.S.-Mexico Border Health Task Group report.* Rockville, MD: U.S. Department of Health and Human Services, U.S. Public Health Service.

United States Public Health Service (1994). *Health United States 1993.* Hyattsville, MD: Department of Health and Human Services, U.S. Public Health Service.

Vargas-Willis, G. & Cervantes, R.C. (1987). Consideration of psychosocial stress in the treatment of the Latina immigrant. *Hispanic Journal of Behavioral Sciences, 9*(3), 315–329.

Vega, W.A., Kolodny, B., Valle, R., & Hough, R. (1986). Depressive symptoms and their correlates among immigrant Mexican women in the United States. *Social Sciences in Medicine, 22*(6), 645–652.

Villareal, R.V. (1990). Prevalence of obesity, high blood pressure and diabetes in an urban population sample at I.S.S.S.T.E. in Nuevo Léon, Mexico. *Border Health, 6*(1), 2–10.

Warner, D.C. (1991). Health issues at the U.S.-Mexican border. *Journal of the American Medical Association, 265*, 242–247.

Wilson, D. (1995). Women's roles and women's health: The effect of immigration on Latina women. *The Jacobs Institute of Women's Health, 5*(1), 8–14.

Ziv, T.A. & Lo, B. (1995). Denial of care to illegal immigrants: Proposition 187 in California. *New England Journal of Medicine, 332*(16), 1095–1098.

4 HEALTH CARE ACCESS AND UTILIZATION ON THE U.S.-MEXICO BORDER

Jo Fairbanks

Just what constitutes "health" has long been debated. The health of a population depends on a variety of factors, many of which are not well understood. It is clear, however, that there is a direct relationship between health and socioeconomic status (Blane, 1995). Data have shown a relationship between low socioeconomic status and a range of poor health indicators including high blood pressure, obesity, low birth weight, premature birth, and acute and chronic disease rates, among others. Consistently, persons who live in poverty, with all the stresses that accompany that lifestyle, experience much higher levels of morbidity and mortality than those who are more affluent (Syme & Berkman, 1994). Poverty is a shared condition of most of the people who live along both sides of the border. While access to medical providers can improve the health of individuals, it cannot eliminate the root causes of illness. Many people living along the U.S.-Mexico border are living in deplorable conditions which contribute to their susceptibility to illness. Poverty undermines health, and the resources of both countries will be required to provide the public health measures necessary for a healthier border population.

There are many barriers, in addition to poverty, that contribute to ill health and reduce access to health care for citizens of both the U.S. and Mexico, and they, too, are formidable. With the exception of a few binational sister cities, such as San Diego-Tijuana and El Paso-Juárez, most of the border area is rural geographically and residents in rural border areas face the same problems as rural residents everywhere. In general, the health of rural residents is poorer than their urban counterparts. Consistently the National Health Interview Survey, conducted annually by the U.S. Department of Health and Human Services, indicates that a higher percentage of rural residents perceive themselves to be in fair or poor health than do those of the metro population (Straub & Walzer, 1992).

Rural residents in general are older, economically poorer, and have lower levels of education than their urban counterparts. These socioeconomic factors are themselves tied to poorer health status (McCoy & Brown, 1978). Eggebeen and Lighter (1993) reported that rural residents, regardless of age, consistently rate their physical health more poorly than residents of metro areas. Even though rural residents seem to be in poorer health, they have fewer physician contacts per year, which is most likely due to socioeconomic factors and the maldistribution of health care providers in rural areas (Straub & Walzer, 1992).

For rural residents who live in sparsely populated areas along the U.S.-Mexico border, the nearest medical services could be many dozens of miles away. The barriers to accessing a health care system are considerable. In addition to geographic or distance barriers, other barriers to access and utilization fall into the general areas of health care delivery system, facility, and provider shortfalls. Cultural barriers are imbedded within each of these areas as well.

HEALTH CARE DELIVERY SYSTEM SHORTFALLS

The rapidly growing population on both sides of the U.S.-Mexico border contains a disproportionate share of uninsured individuals. The health care systems of the United States and Mexico are fragmented in their services, and each has its own advantages and disadvantages.

Although Mexico has a national health system, with a constitutional "right to health care," access to care is segmented, with different groups in the population receiving care from different health care systems. The Mexican government is the major provider of services and financing for health care. The social security system (Instituto Mexicana de Seguridad y Servicios Sociales Para los Trabajadores del Estado) provides health care to workers, including those in government, employees of large factories and corporations, the armed services, and members of unions and rural cooperatives. Social Security in Mexico has developed an extensive network of providers and facilities, and it is responsible for the largest segment of health care. The Health and Welfare Ministry (Servicios Coordinado de Salud Publica en los Estados) provides care essentially to the unemployed, and the rural and urban poor (Warner, 1991a). Other private providers and facilities are available on a fee-for-service basis to those who can afford it.

In Mexico, 55 percent of the population subscribe to a social security institution, 35 percent receive care from agencies serving the uninsured, and four percent use private health care services. The Mexican system for the provision of health care differs widely among these entities and, while coverage is broad, quality of care varies (Frenk, Gomez-Dantes, Cruz, Chacon, Hernandez & Freeman, 1994). Rural residents of Mexico, like their U.S. counterparts, often have no local access to providers or facilities.

While both countries have gaps in coverage, the least equitable in coverage is the U.S. system, with its high levels of medically indigent. The 1987 Medical Expenditures Survey indicates that 35 to 40 million U.S. citizens are uninsured (Short, Monheit & Beauregard, 1989). The U.S. system is highly technical and specialized and is experiencing a crisis in escalating costs. Mexico is, by comparison, economically depressed, which results in diminished funding for health care. Mexico currently spends less than one percent of U.S. expenditures for health care, but the U.S. system has become largely unaffordable, especially for the uninsured. All of this results in a fragmented system of care on both sides of the border.

Health Care Provider and Facility Shortages

On the U.S. side of the border there is an extreme shortage of providers, and, among those who do practice there, it is very difficult to find providers who offer care to the medically indigent. Many U.S. counties along the border are federally designated Health Professional Shortage Areas (HPSAs). HPSA designation by the U.S. Department of Health and Human Services Department makes areas eligible for placement of National Health Service Corps (NHSC) personnel (see educational strategies, later in this chapter). Primary care providers, such as family practice physicians, family nurse practitioners, physicians' assistants, and dentists in the NHSC program exchange service in underserved areas for student loan repayment. The criteria for designation include an area population-to-primary care provider ratio of at least 3,500 to 1 or a ratio of 3,000 to 1 combined with unusually high demand for services (Primary Care Bureau, 1995). Most U.S. counties along the U.S.-Mexico border are designated HPSAs. In Texas, for example, all or part of 14 of the 15 border counties are HPSAs (Texas Governor's Office, 1993). In New Mexico, all areas contiguous to the border are severe shortage areas with population-to-provider ratios more than twice as high as needed for designation (Primary Care Bureau, 1995). This lack of providers is extreme in rural areas as well as in the very poor sections of the inner cities.

The lack of a supporting health care infrastructure on the U.S. side also discourages providers. In fact, the existing system is eroding. Rural pharmacists cannot compete with large discount drug stores or mail order companies. According to Berchem and Dankmyer (1994), more than 1,000 independent pharmacies have gone out of business in the U.S. in the last two years.

While most border states have Federal Qualified Health Centers (FQHCs) providing care in border countries, these facilities are often over-whelmed by the large patient population. It has been extremely difficult to recruit and retain providers to practice in these clinics because of the poor economic base that results in lower provider salaries.

Low levels of reimbursement from Medicare and Medicaid for drugs and primary care make it very difficult for physician providers or pharma-cists in underserved areas to earn what they could if they were practicing in a more affluent population base. Rural communities and clinics are increas-ingly exploring the use of less costly non-physician providers such as physician's assistants (PAs), nurse practitioners (NPs), and certified nurse midwives (CNMs) to fill their need for primary care services. Many states have liberalized the practice acts for these providers to make it easier for them to treat patients more autonomously. NPs and PAs in several states can prac-tice without direct physician supervision and can prescribe medication in-dependently. The U.S. Office of Technology Assessment (1986) has shown that NPs, PAs, and CNMs can manage 60 to 80 percent of patients' primary care needs independently. As cost controls on health care become more strin-gent, the use of non-physician providers will likely increase, especially in underserved areas.

DEMAND FOR MEDICAL SERVICES

Utilization of the existing U.S. Federally Qualified Community/Migrant Health Centers (FQHCs) along the border is very high, primarily because these clinics accept Medicaid patients and provide care through a sliding-scale fee schedule. There are long waiting periods for appointments in many of these clinics. For example, La Clinica de Familia, a Community/Migrant Health Center with five satellite offices located in southern New Mexico, treats approximately 20,000 patients with more than 35,000 medical/den-tal encounters and 50,000 educational/social service visits each year. La Clinica, which is funded by both federal and state dollars, has special medi-cal and service related programs unique to the needs of the border popula-tion. Waiting times for appointments can be three months or more. Demand is very high for primary care, a situation that is exacerbated by this rapidly growing, mobile population. La Clinica, like all FQHCs, provides services to everyone on a sliding fee schedule regardless of citizenship. Patients come from both sides of the border to seek care.

In fact, there is a considerable amount of crossutilization of health care services by people on both sides of the border. Research indicates that U.S. and Mexican citizens "cross over" to use health care providers on both sides. Guendelman (1991a) found that in her sample of Mexicans residing in Tijuana, 2.5 percent crossed the border for health care in the U.S. during a six-month period. Those seeking treatment in the U.S. were more likely to come from middle- and upper-income sectors and were those who had previously lived in the U.S. Ten percent of women in the survey who had been pregnant in the last five years indicated they had used California services for delivery.

Recent surveys in Arizona and Texas indicate that U.S. physicians see Mexican patients. Nichols et al. (1991) reported the mean number of Mexican patients seen by Tucson, Arizona, physicians was nine per week. Hilts (1992) reported that a Families USA study found that U.S. citizens were accounting for 25 percent of patients for Mexican physicians practicing along the border. U.S. citizens go to Mexico for primary care, dental care, reduced cost of drugs, and cancer therapies. Warner (1991a) reported that more than one-fourth of low-income respondents living in the lower Rio Grande Valley went to Mexico to purchase drugs and 40 percent of dentists in Hermosillo, Mexico, served U.S. patients.

For the medically indigent, the shortage of primary care providers and facilities in the United States leads to the use of hospital emergency rooms for treatment. Patients without access to primary care often do not get medical assistance until illnesses have worsened. U.S. federal law requires hospitals to provide emergency care to all who need it regardless of immigration or insurance status. This places a heavy burden on border state hospitals, which are not fully reimbursed by the U.S. government for that care. The difference in what the hospitals charge and what is reimbursed can be less than half of actual costs. Most undocumented immigrants are treated in public hospitals; thus the major cost of that treatment is shouldered by state and county governments. The number of Mexicans crossing over can be high. For example, Holy Cross Hospital in Nogales, Arizona, a border community, provided one-third of their emergency room services in 1990 to Mexican nationals who could not pay for treatment. One-fifth of the births at Holy Cross are to Mexican nationals. While many patients pay for treatment, because Holy Cross is a Catholic hospital it accepts its charity care as bad debt, something all hospitals cannot do (Lutz, 1990).

A current proposal in the U.S. House of Representatives to fully reimburse states for the care of non-citizens (Perry, 1995) had not been enacted at the time of this writing. Currently, rural hospitals serving the border population are struggling to survive on Medicaid and Medicare reimbursement rates because they do not have the paying patient base upon which to shift the costs for this uncompensated care.

Even when hospitals and clinics are within reach, there is often mistrust and fear of the system. Cultural differences exist about the causative factors of illness and, thus, the appropriate treatment. Language barriers compound other cultural differences. For example, Diehl and Stern (1989) reported ethnic differences in attitudes about such behaviors as dieting, food choices, and the use of alcohol and tobacco. Expanded, affordable and culturally appropriate primary care is badly needed along the border, and when hospital care becomes necessary, an equitable system of hospital reimbursement should be implemented by both countries.

FACTORS AFFECTING HEALTH CARE UTILIZATION

As the border population grows, rapid and extensive changes are occurring to an area that was once remote and practically deserted. These changes are being fueled by the North American Free Trade Agreement (NAFTA). The migration of farm workers is yet another factor affecting health care utlization along the border.

NAFTA

In 1965, the Mexican government opened a limited area along the border to foreign investment. This project, the Border Industrialization Program, began what has now become known as the maquiladora plants. These opportunities for foreign investment have been broadened through the more recent North American Free Trade Agreement (NAFTA) with the United States, Mexico, and Canada. NAFTA is having a major impact on the border. Since 1965 there had been a slow, steady growth in border industrialization, but the approval and implementation of NAFTA in 1994 has dramatically increased this rate of growth. Today, more than 2,000 factories called maquiladoras have been established in border cities in Mexico. The maquila industry allows foreign companies to establish plants to assemble imported components and raw materials into products for export out of Mexico. Eighty percent of the maquila industries and assembly plants are U.S.-owned, and employ more than 500,000 Mexican workers (La Botz, 1994).

The elimination of tariffs on trade brought about by NAFTA made it possible for U.S. and Canadian companies to use inexpensive Mexican labor to assemble products which are then returned to the country of origin for sale or future export. The word "maquila" refers to the unit of grain a miller retains for grinding a farmer's grain. While the finished products don't remain in Mexico, Mexico's "maquila" is the employment opportunity for hundreds of thousands of workers (Guendelman, 1991b).

Wages for Mexican workers may be as low as $3.75 to $4.50 per day.

In Mexico's extremely depressed economy, which has undergone repeated devaluations of the peso, the opportunity for jobs has lured large numbers of people to the border cities of Tijuana, Nogales, Matamoros, and Juárez. Because of that depressed economy, however, the cities have been unable to provide the infrastructure of services needed to support growth rates currently over 5 percent per year. As a result, workers who do get jobs live in substandard housing in areas (colonias) where there is often no access to potable running water, sewers, electricity, or adequate roads. Workers who do not get jobs further exacerbate the cities' problems (La Botz, 1994).

Two-thirds of the maquila workers are women and much has been written about their exploitation. "There are a whole series of problems which are linked to the maquiladora," reports Theresa Almada, a social worker in Juárez. "There are problems with the urban infrastructure such as the lack of water, sewers and electric lights." Other problems include low wages, industrial pollution, and pervasive sexual harassment of women workers. "The issue of the maquiladora isn't just the factory which comes here, but rather that in cities along the border, the size of the maquiladora industry is so great in relation to the city, that the maquiladora limits and determines the entire social reality of the city" (La Botz, 1994, p. 404).

Reports have been made about the use of hazardous chemicals and pollutants in poorly ventilated buildings, excessive noise levels, and unsafe equipment in the maquiladoras. However, few research studies have looked at the worker satisfaction in the plants or the effect the plants' condition has on these workers (Guendelman, 1991b).

Many believe that the maquiladoras are not perceived by employees as bad places to work and, in fact, offer better wages than service jobs, greater access to health care, vacations, training opportunities, and subsidized food in company cafeterias. Guendelman (1991b) reported that women working in the maquiladoras felt they had little control over their working lives, but also felt they had substantially better benefits than those in the service sector (Guendelman, 1991b).

The stress of the burgeoning population seeking jobs along the border is not isolated to the Mexican side. In fact, cities and states on both sides of the border are economically hard-pressed to provide a health care and services infrastructure to this rapidly growing group of people. Workers who cannot find jobs in the maquiladoras often enter the U.S. both legally and illegally to do farm or service work in order to survive. Hundreds of illegal housing subdivisions called "colonias" have proliferated on the U.S. side in every state along the border, as Mexican workers cross over hopeful of obtaining work. The subdivisions are extremely substandard, with limited or no water or sewage available to the landowners. Many of these workers are so desperate to own their own land, which is practically impossible for them to do in Mexico, that they buy land in the illegal subdivisions even when told there are no wells or sewers. Often, however, the potential buyers are not informed about water quality and quantity, liquid and solid waste disposal, roads, and terrain management. Owners are not aware of the add-on costs of bringing electricity to the property ("Five Colonias Illegal," 1994). Many residents use outhouses in low-lying areas that frequently flood. Ground water, often the only source of water, can be badly contaminated with floating human waste. The subdivisions endanger the health and safety of residents and often violate state law, but it has been difficult to prosecute the developers. Taxpayers in U.S. border counties, already burdened by poverty, are frequently unable to rectify these very unhealthy living conditions.

Because so many residents are living in extreme poverty, the border population is experiencing severe threats to human health. As was noted in Chapter 3, acute infectious diseases that rarely occur in other parts of the U.S. are endemic on the border. Communicable diseases such as tuberculosis and hepatitis are more common there. Drug resistant tuberculosis rates are high along the border, as high as 43 percent of the total cases in Juárez. This is due to the misuse of the medicine prescribed to treat the disease. Patients typically take drugs until they feel better and then stop instead of continuing the medicine for six to nine months. This allows the bacteria that are strongest to flourish. The widespread availability of antibiotics without a prescription in Mexico also adds to the problem (Beil & Rivas, 1994).

Mexican Americans have a prevalence rate of Type II diabetes that is two to three times that of the general population. They are afflicted with high rates of diabetic retinopathy and end-stage renal disease (Furino & Munoz, 1991). Common diseases among children include hepatitis A, various forms of dysentery, and intestinal parasites linked to poor sanitation, as well as upper respiratory infections that cause death and disability. Diabetes, overweight, anemia, and high blood pressure are common disorders in Mexican and Mexican American women (Ortega, 1991).

Migrant Workers

A migrant farm worker is defined by the U.S. Public Health Service as "an individual whose principal employment is in agriculture on a seasonal basis, who has been so employed for the last twenty-four months, and who establishes for the purposes of such employment a temporary abode" (Texas Governor's Office, 1993, p. 5). Currently, over 4.2 million migrant and seasonal farm workers make up more than 75 percent of the U.S. agricultural work force. Alan Dever (1991) reported that the health status of these workers is poorer than that of the general population and that they have different health problems. Dever has found the following:

> Migrant farm workers have different and more complex health problems from those of the general population. Migrant farm workers suffer more frequently from infectious diseases than the general population. Farm workers have more clinic visits for diabetes, medical supervision of infants and children, otitis media, pregnancy, hypertension, and contact dermatitis and eczema. Clinic visits for general medical exams account for only 1.4 percent of all visits to migrant health clinics, 39 percent below the U.S. average.
>
> Demographic analysis of the study area counties indicates that the farm worker population has more young people and fewer older people than the general U.S. population. (Dever, 1991, p. 2)

Concerning health status, Dever also reported:

> Clinic visits for ages 1–4 are mostly for infectious and nutritional health problems. Health problems for ages 5–9 are also primarily infectious, but dental problems also appear for the first time in this group. Dental disease is the number one health problem for patients aged 10–14. Pregnancy is the most frequent presenting health condition for females aged 15–19; dental disease is number one for males. Females age 20–29 visit clinics primarily for pregnancy, diabetes, common cold, and reproductive problems. Males visit primarily for contact dermatitis and eczema, strep throat and scarlet fever, and dental problems. In the 30–44 age group, two of the top three problems for both males and females are diabetes and hypertension. Nearly half of all clinic visits for men and women in the 45–64 age group are for diabetes, hypertension, or arthropathies. Among the elderly, over 60 percent of clinic visits by males and 80 percent by females are for diabetes and hypertension. (Dever, 1991, page 2)

Most migrant farm workers are citizens or have legal status in the U.S. Legal residency has increased since the amnesty program of 1986 (Stehney, Guzman, Barnes & Levy, 1994). Whole families, including children, work in the fields in order to earn enough to feed the family. When ill, migrant workers often delay seeking care because they are generally uninsured and because they cannot afford to take a day off from the fields. Even with Medicaid coverage, migrants travel through many states for the harvest and benefits do not necessarily transfer from one state to another. Often, by the time the paperwork is completed to establish Medicaid eligibility in a state, the family has moved on. The cultural, language, and transportation barriers to health care are also difficult for migrants to overcome. Migrants frequently do not have their own transportation. Access to the health care delivery system often requires a drive of many miles without any system of public transportation. Providers in the clinics may not speak Spanish or have knowledge of the special health problems of migrants. Hispanic women are frequently uneasy about physical examination by male health care providers; thus, they may delay essential screening and prenatal care.

A large portion of farm work is done by children; therefore, the education of children becomes intermittent. Children as young as four or five work in the fields (Durnan, 1995). Working and living conditions are generally poor with limited access to toilet facilities, safe drinking water, and bathing facilities. Environmental exposure to pesticides is routine. While education about pesticide spraying is now required, migrant workers cannot afford to wait to enter fields until it is safe (Stehney, Guzman, Barnes & Levy, 1994).

EDUCATIONAL STRATEGIES TO IMPROVE PROVIDER DISTRIBUTION

During the 1960s and 1970s the U.S. federal government began initiatives to improve the provision of rural health care. The National Health Service Corps (NHSC) and the Area Health Education Centers (AHECs) were created in 1970 and 1972, respectively, to improve the supply of health professionals in rural areas. The availability of facilities was to be strongly influenced by the implementation of the Migrant Health Centers (1962); Community Health Centers (1965); Rural Health Initiative, and Rural Health Clinics Act of 1975. A variety of other U.S. federally supported educational strategies to promote the recruitment and retention of health care providers has continued to be initiated over the years. In addition to the AHECs and NHSC, these include, but are not limited to, the Health Education Training Centers (HETCs), interdisciplinary grants, and maternal and child health grants.

The National Health Service Corps recruits students in the health professions—such as physicians, mid-level providers, and dentists—who will agree to serve in HPSAs in exchange for financial assistance for educational expenses. The scholarship program requires one year payback for each year of educational support with a minimum of two years in the underserved area. Federal financial support for this program was nearly phased out during the

1980s, but the NHSC is currently being viewed as a necessary factor in an overall strategy to improve health care in underserved areas.

Other federal and state loans are available for students in the health professions who are willing to serve in underserved areas. Nearly all states have loan-for-service and loan repayment programs.

AHEC was begun in the 1970s as a federal program to address issues of maldistribution of health care providers. The AHECs' mission is to improve the supply and distribution of health care professionals, with an emphasis on primary care, through community/academic educational partnerships to increase access to care. The AHEC provides community-based education and training for health care professionals, students, and residents. AHECs engage in activities that encourage students from minority and underserved communities to enter the health professions and support interdisciplinary training that is responsive to community needs.

The Health Education and Training Center (HETC) program was added as a separate section of the AHEC authorization in 1988 to provide special support for health professions shortages along the U.S.-Mexico border. Arizona, California, New Mexico, and Texas all have border HETC programs. HETC programs have engaged in community needs assessment, health education projects, and continuing education of health professionals around border health concerns, among others. AHECs and HETCs support off-campus primary-care residency programs in an attempt to encourage residents who participate to remain in underserved areas after their training is completed.

Interdisciplinary grants from the Health Resources and Services Administration (HRSA), part of the U.S. Department of Health and Human Services, have encouraged health sciences centers to educate students in the health professions together so that they learn to function as a health care team. Students are encouraged to serve in rural clinics in underserved areas.

U.S. federal- and state-supported maternal and child health grants have focused on improving access to care. Many projects along the border are using community health workers (CHWs), also called lay health advisors, to provide basic health education and support to families who would not normally access the health care system. (See Chapter 7 for more on the use of the CHW model in health promotion/education efforts.) These CHWs are indigenous "natural leaders" in their communities who are trained in a core content area such as perinatal care or diabetes education. They learn the core content and go on to do outreach service and advocacy for health in their communities. A majority of the clients of CHWs either do not know how to access the health care delivery system or would not because of cultural and language barriers. Shannon and Gellert (1994) have reported that CHWs can have a large impact on access in a community. Currently, all U.S. border states are using CHWs in a variety of programs. Mexico has trained CHW "promotores" in basic primary care techniques to act as the first contact for primary health care in villages that may be remote from physicians and hospitals. Mexico's immunization rates for children are very high primarily because of the promotores. Both U.S. and Mexican promotores interact for a more comprehensive approach to health care along the border.

SUMMARY

Approximately nine million people live along the U.S.-Mexico border, and the population is growing rapidly. Most live in poverty and substandard living conditions. Environmental health concerns include severe air and water pollution. Millions of gallons of raw sewage enter the Rio Grande and Tijuana rivers daily. This untreated sewage and the chemical contaminants from the maquiladora plants mix with ground water to create a threat to aquifers underlying the entire length of the border. Colonias flourish illegally in counties too poor to remedy the problems (Warner, 1991b).

Air pollution has become a serious threat to health in most border cities. El Paso and Juárez remain below the Environmental Protection Agency's air quality standards in particulates, ozone, and carbon dioxide. Mexico's lax environmental standards and enforcement contribute to the problem while the U.S.-owned maquiladoras take advantage of it. Dumping of hazardous waste has become a serious problem for border communities (Warner, 1991b).

Worsening conditions along the border represent a public health "time bomb" which has severe implications for the future. Solutions to these complex problems depend upon a collective will on the part of both Mexico and the United States to act. In a time of burgeoning populations and reduced resources, economic recession and budget cutting, solving the extraordinary problems along the border will be very difficult.

Solutions must include binational environmental controls to ensure access to clean air and safe drinking water as well as affordable health care. A financially viable and effective public health system for the border must act as one agency with the understanding that no solutions are possible if they are not implemented on both sides. (See Chapter 6 for more information on border environmental health issues.)

More providers and clinical facilities are badly needed on both sides of the border to provide basic, culturally appropriate primary care services. Strategies such as the U.S. National Health Service Corps and loans for service must be expanded to specifically target and increase the number of providers in border underserved areas. These efforts must include recruitment of local minority students into primary care health professions.

Continued federal and state funding for Community and Migrant Health Centers is essential. Any plan to increase the number of these clinics must include federal and state funding for capital expenditures for new clinics and to modernize older facilities.

High levels of uncompensated care will continue to adversely affect any attempts to strengthen the health care infrastructure. Therefore, financial incentives that encourage providers to locate in border areas should be implemented. A system of financing health care services must have the flexibility to cross the border and improve access for the people of both countries.

A system to monitor the quality of care and the licensing and certification that allows verification of provider competence should be implemented. Most importantly, a reciprocal financing system must be instituted that allows U.S. and Mexican people living along the border the freedom to seek care on both sides of the border.

REFERENCES

Beil, L. & Rivas, M. (1994, December 3). Health menace grows along border. *Albuquerque Journal*, A2.

Berchem, S. & Dankmyer, T. (1994). Are rural independent pharmacies an endangered species? *Rural Health News*, 1(3), 1.

Blane, D. (1995). Social determinants of health: Socio-economic status, social class and ethnicity. *American Journal of Public Health*, 85(7) 903–904.

Dever, G.E.A.(1991). Migrant health status: Profile of a population with complex health problems. National Migrant Resource Program, Austin, Texas.

Diehl, A.K. & Stern, M.P. (1989). Special health problems of Mexican-Americans: Obesity, gallbladder disease, diabetes mellitus, and cardiovascular disease. *Advances in Internal Medicine*, 34, 73–96.

Durnan, K. (1995, June 4). Earth angels. *Albuquerque Journal*, E 10.

Eggebeen, D.J. & Lighter, D.T. (1993). Health and well-being among rural Americans: Variations across the life course. *Journal of Rural Health*, 9(2), 86–98.

Five colonias illegal. (1994, June 18). *Albuquerque Journal*, D3.

Frenk, J., Gomez-Dantes, O., Cruz, C., Chacon, C., Hernandez, P., & Freeman, P. (1994). Consequences of the North American Free Trade Agreement for health services: A perspective from Mexico. *American Journal of Public Health*, 84(10), 1591–1597.

Furino, A. & Munoz, E. (1991). Health status among Hispanics: Major themes and new priorities. *Journal of the American Medical Association*, 265(2), 255–257.

Guendelman, S. (1991a). Cross border utilization of health services: The case of Tijuana residents. *Border Health*, 7(4), 2–9.

Guendelman, S. (1991b). The impact on women's health of the maquiladoras: The Tijuana case. *Carnegie Quarterly*, 36(1–4), 11–15.

Hilts, P. (1992, November 23). Quality and low cost of medical care lure Americans on border to Mexico. *New York Times National*, A8.

La Botz, D. (1994). Manufacturing poverty: The maquiladorization of Mexico. *International Journal of Health Services, 24*(3), 403–498.

Lutz, S. (1990). Hospitals struggle to survive along U.S. Mexican border. *Modern Healthcare*, August 6, 28–31.

McCoy, J. & Brown, D. (1978). Health status among low-income elderly persons: Rural/urban differences. *Social Security Bulletin, 41*, 14–26.

Nichols, A.W., LaBrec, P.A., Homedes, N., & Geller, S.E. (1991). Perceptions and preparations for free trade—The use of Arizona physician services by residents of Mexico. *Border Health, 1*(4), 13–28.

Ortega, H. (1991). Promoting bi-national cooperation to improve health along the U.S.-Mexico border. *Carnegie Quarterly, 36*(1–4), 1–8.

Perry, T. (1995, October 22). Gingrich: Pay for illegals. *Albuquerque Journal*, A2.

Primary Care Bureau. (1995). *New Mexico health professional shortage areas.* Santa Fe, NM: New Mexico Department of Health. Unpublished.

Shannon, P.D. & Gellert, G.A. (1994). Enhancing health education and Medicaid access in a U.S.-Mexico border community. *Border Health, 4*, 12–22.

Short, P.F., Monheit A., & Beauregard K. (1989). *National Medical Expenditures Survey: A profile of uninsured Americans.* Rockville, MD: National Center for Health Services Research and Health Care Technology.

Stehney, M., Guzman, J., Barnes, M., Levy, C., & Myers, J. (1994). *Working group on farm workers and health care reform.* New Mexico Border Health Council. Unpublished.

Straub, L.A. & Walzer, N. (1992). *Rural health care: Innovation in a changing environment.* Westport, CT: Praeger.

Syme, S.L. and Berkman, L.F. (1994). Social class, susceptibility, and sickness. *Sociology of Health and Illness*, New York: St. Martin's Press, 29–35.

Texas Governor's Office (1993). *Health and human services issue: U.S. (Texas)-Mexico border.* Austin, TX: State of Texas, Governor's Report.

U. S. Office of Technology Assessment. (1986). Nurse practitioners, physician assistants, and certified nurse midwives: A policy analysis. U.S. Congress, Washington D.C., 39.

Warner, D.C. (1991a). Financing rural border health. *Border Health, 1*(4), 29–40.

Warner, D.C. (1991b). Health issues at the U.S.-Mexican border. *Journal of the American Medical Association, 265*(2), 242–247.

5   HISPANICS, HIV, AND AIDS ALONG THE U.S.-MEXICO BORDER

DISTINCTIVE TRANSMISSION TRENDS AND PREVENTION STRATEGIES

Michael D. Barnes, Robert W. Buckingham, and Allison M. Wesley

INTRODUCTION

The purpose of this chapter is to discuss how HIV transmission and AIDS incidence rates of Hispanics vary along the U.S.-Mexico border compared to groups of Hispanics in other geographic regions in the United States and Mexico. The unique risks and characteristics of adult Hispanic women, adult Hispanic men, and Hispanic youth along the border will be addressed so that culture- and border-specific strategies for prevention can be better utilized.

There is a need to focus on the distinct risk factors and transmission trends along the border since the human immunodeficiency virus (HIV) epidemic increasingly threatens Hispanic communities (Carrillo & Uranga-McKane, 1994). Hispanics account for 9 percent of the U.S. population, but represent 17 percent of all reported AIDS cases—82,910 as of June 1995 (CDCP, 1995c; Carrillo & Uranga-McKane, 1994). The AIDS case rate in the U.S. is at least 2.5 times higher among Hispanics than among non-Hispanic whites (Diaz, Buehler, Castro & Ward, 1993). Unfortunately these trends do not appear to be changing. From January 1994 through mid-1995, the proportion of AIDS cases increased among Hispanics from 15 percent to 18 percent, whereas decreases were noted among U.S. men and among white (Anglo) populations, 85 percent to 83 percent, and 47 percent to 43 percent, respectively. Although the rate of increase is slowing among the general population, increases among Hispanics and Blacks are not (CDCP, 1995b).

U.S.-MEXICO BORDER AND NATIONAL HISPANIC AIDS COMPARISONS

In 1992, the prevalence rate of AIDS cases in the Mexican border states was 9.1 cases per 100,000, and in the American border states 14.6 cases per 100,000 persons. This number has increased significantly in the last few years due primarily to increased cases in the American border states (Magis et al., 1992). In terms of cumulative AIDS cases (all age groups), two of the four border states, California and Texas, are among the highest in the United States (CDCP, 1995b). Along the U.S. side of the U.S.-Mexico border, HIV infection leading to AIDS is one of the principal causes of death (seventh), particularly apparent in the 25–44 age group among Hispanics. The Mexican side of the border reports that the same age group (25–44) exhibits AIDS-related deaths, but AIDS is the sixth leading cause of death (Ortega, 1995). Among all ages in the U.S., HIV infection/AIDS was the eighth leading cause of death (CDCP, 1995b).

"Hispanic" is an umbrella descriptor applied to groups with distinct historical, political, economic, and racial differences (Amaro, 1988). Most Hispanic-related research on the knowledge, attitudes, beliefs, and behaviors regarding HIV/AIDS have been drawn from many small samples of Hispanics in different parts of the country and from various ethnic and socioeconomic groups. Unfortunately, the conclusions from these studies are often inappropriately generalized to the greater Hispanic population. This problem has resulted in readers not being aware of the population's heterogeneity, and the unique characteristics of Hispanics throughout the United States (Carrillo & Uranga-McKane, 1994).

Although Mexicans (Hispanics from Mexican descent, who live primarily in the western and southwestern portion of the United States) are numerically the largest Hispanic group in the United States, they generally have lower incidence rates of AIDS compared to other Hispanic groups (Carrillo & Uranga-McKane, 1994). However, these rates are expected to gradually reverse if the rate of exposure continues to increase among Hispanics along the border. Diaz and colleagues (1993) have claimed that the incidence of AIDS appears lower along sections of the U.S.-Mexico border than in the northeast and southeast portions of the country (Hispanics in the Northeast, Puerto Rico, and Florida). The comparable rate of AIDS cases in 1992 still showed that non-Hispanic whites along the U.S.-Mexico border had rates 1.5 to 2 times higher than Hispanics (Diaz et al., 1993). Many HIV prevention efforts and large-scale AIDS research projects have been funded and carried out primarily in geographic sections of the country where AIDS rates appear highest. Unfortunately, comparisons such as these may thwart or misdirect effective and unique prevention efforts away from the specific needs of reducing HIV infection among Hispanics along both sides of the U.S.-Mexico border region.

Seven percent of all women in the U.S. are Hispanic, but more than 21 percent of U.S. women with AIDS are Hispanic. Distinct geographic variations in the epidemiology of AIDS among Hispanic women are noteworthy. Most Hispanic women with AIDS in the U.S. (52 percent) report a history of intravenous drug use (IVDU), or sex with an intravenous drug user. However, only 19 percent of Hispanic women in the southwest present with AIDS cases from IVDU; instead 71 percent of AIDS cases among these women along the U.S.-Mexico border report a history of heterosexual contact from a partner, an intravenous drug user, or a blood transfusion recipient (Rapkin & Erickson, 1990). Rapkin and Erickson (1990) further clarify that the heterosexual infection of HIV occurs in many cases because of bisexual relationships among Hispanic men. Hispanic men, unlike most other groups of men who have sex with other men, are bisexual but classify themselves as heterosexual as long as they play the insertor role in same-sex relationships (Diaz et al., 1993; Rapkin & Erickson, 1990). Additionally, Hispanic men were reported by Rapkin and Erickson (1990) as being unlikely to wear condoms during intercourse, having a low income, and being less well educated. Hispanic women, who were primarily Spanish speaking, were also found to be less well educated, and were less likely to receive, pursue, or fully understand the information currently available for HIV prevention.

Clearly, the greatest risk associated with HIV/AIDS among Hispanic adult males along the U.S.-Mexico border region is sexual contact, not IVDU as is the case among Hispanics in other geographic sections of the country. Guerena and colleagues (1991) identified homosexual/bisexual men (11.6 percent) as the leading transmission risk factor for HIV, with the distant second, third, and fourth risk factors including intravenous drug users (1.9 percent), prisoners (1.2 percent), and prostitutes (0.5 percent).

Carrillo and Uranga-McKane (1994) have more recently confirmed several distinctions between Hispanics of Mexican or South American (MSA) descent and Hispanics of Puerto Rican and Cuban (PRC) descent that are important to differentiate regarding the mode of HIV infection. First, among men born in MSA countries, the vast majority of AIDS cases are associated with homosexual and bisexual contact, while among PRC men, most cases are attributable to IVDU. Second, transfusion-related AIDS among Hispanics has been reported predominantly from MSA descent. For example, approximately 35 percent of Mexican-born women with AIDS were reported as being infected by transfusion, compared with fewer than 15 percent of other Hispanic women. Third, however, Hispanic AIDS cases from eastern states are related to IVDU, or having sex with an IVDU; whereas Hispanics from Mexican descent have fewer than 10 percent of AIDS cases occurring from IVDU. Fourth, Hispanics with AIDS from MSA descent are exposed through homosexual or bisexual contact (65 percent), whereas only 22 percent of men from mainland Puerto Rican descent acquire AIDS through homosexual or bisexual contact. Fifth, Hispanics in the Northeast and Southeast, primarily of PRC descent, traditionally have had the highest HIV seroprevalence rates, while Hispanics in the South and West, primarily of MSA descent, have the lowest seroprevalence rates. Sixth, more Hispanic men than white men (20 percent vs. 13 percent) with AIDS identify themselves as bisexual (Carrillo & Uranga-McKane, 1994).

Finally among Hispanic adolescents, recent studies have demonstrated that sexual experimentation is starting at earlier ages (Trad, 1994; Romer et al., 1994; Boyer & Kegeles, 1991). With the onset of AIDS and the increasing prevalence of other STDs, this behavior poses new threats for young persons in their teens. However, many teens (including Hispanic adolescents) perceive these risks as insignificant. Langer and colleagues (1993) report that only about 10 percent of teenagers are regular condom users. Research has confirmed that along the U.S.-Mexico border region, there is earlier experimentation and less regular condom use among Hispanic teens than among many other populations and locations throughout the country. Thus, with all these differences comes the need to understand why, and to identify unique cultural- and language-appropriate prevention materials that address these HIV/AIDS issues among Hispanics along the border. The following discussions will describe the unique characteristics of Hispanic risk factors along the U.S.-Mexico border by addressing HIV/AIDS from the perspective of adult women, adult men, and adolescents, respectively.

Hispanic Women and HIV/AIDS Risks

Minority women have become the fastest-growing group likely to contract HIV/AIDS (Nyamathi, Bennett, Leake, Lewis & Flaskerud, 1993). Hispanic women are 11.1 times more likely to contract AIDS than white women (Alonso & Koreck, 1989). AIDS is the fourth leading cause of death among American women ages 25–44, and the leading cause of death among U.S. men ages 25–44. Almost one in every five reported cases of AIDS occurs in women. Furthermore, according to the CDCP, the proportion of AIDS cases among women has increased 11 percent in the last 10 years, and 77 percent of the 1994 cases reported to the CDCP were among Black and Hispanic women (CDCP, 1995a).

The escalating risk of heterosexual/bisexual spread of HIV is particularly apparent among Hispanic women, who already bear a disproportionate share of the epidemic (Carrillo & Uranga-McKane, 1994). Furthermore, women are at a significant epidemiological disadvantage since male-to-female HIV transmission is three to five times more efficient than it is from female to male (Diaz et al., 1993). Among the Hispanic male sex partners of Hispanic women along the border region, more than 65 percent of adult Hispanic male AIDS cases are attributable to the homosexual/bisexual transmission category (Diaz et al., 1993). Thus, sexual practices play a more critical role in the epidemiology of AIDS among Hispanics of Mexican origin than other Hispanic groups, especially among Hispanic women (Alonso & Koreck, 1989).

Cultural and sociodemographic factors differ significantly across populations of Hispanic women for HIV–risk reduction intervention programs. Hispanic women of Mexican descent, as compared to Latinos from Puerto Rican descent, had less formal education, but more influential family and acquaintance support networks to foster receptivity to HIV risk reduction (Pares-Avila, Harrold, Ramos & Gonzalez, 1990). Nyamathi (1993) also found that, in general, less acculturated Hispanic women have greater numbers of misconceptions about the casual transmission of AIDS than acculturated Hispanic women along the border region. Hispanic women are overrepresented as heads of households, due to the higher proportions of births to unmarried women. This proportion of women heads of households is slightly over one-fourth among Mexican-American women (Amaro, 1988).

Intravenous drug use does not appear to be a significant source of HIV transmission (fewer than 10 percent) among Hispanics along the U.S.-Mexico border region (Diaz et al., 1993). A nationwide study comparing the risk behaviors among intravenous (IVDU) and non-intravenous (non-IVDU) drug-using women who are sexual partners of IV drug users also identified that these women are primarily from minority populations, unemployed, and with child care responsibilities. Very few of these women report the use of condoms with their partners, yet 42 percent of the IVDU women and 32 percent of the non-IVDU women trade sex for drugs or money. From this study, 72 percent of these groups of women are at high risk for HIV/AIDS through these practices and sexual contacts (Young, Sowder & Weissman, 1990).

Hispanic women rely heavily on television and printed material to learn of HIV and AIDS. This, combined with their lower knowledge level, suggests that more comprehensive education about AIDS in the Spanish media and greater linguistically appropriate outreach efforts are essential for HIV prevention among Hispanic women (Rapkin & Erickson, 1990).

A recent study of knowledge and risk factors pertaining to Hispanic women revealed that Hispanic cultural factors (those less acculturated to Anglo norms) may lower the personal risk of HIV exposure among Hispanic women, but the lack of knowledge about AIDS and partner behavior may increase risk (Rapkin & Erickson, 1990). This protective effect among Hispanic women was confirmed by providing evidence that speaking only Spanish indicates a lower level of U.S. acculturation with an emphasis on a more conservative lifestyle regarding sexual behavior and substance abuse. The researchers caution, however, that there may be a potentially greater hidden risk since Hispanic women, who have conservative natures, resist disclosing intimate behaviors to people they do not know well. They also point out that these women are often aware that their partners engage in homosexual extramarital behavior, but do not report it since they interpret it as their failure to satisfy their partners (Rapkin & Erickson, 1990). Thus, it appears that a more family-, culture-oriented emphasis on education programs that prevent HIV or reduce HIV risk may be more influential among Hispanic women along the U.S.-Mexico border. However, these education/prevention programs should reflect acculturated and less-acculturated Hispanic women's perspectives and accommodate the language and educational deficiencies that may be apparent therein (Nyamathi et al., 1993).

HISPANIC ADULT MEN AND HIV/AIDS RISKS

Sexual transmission, especially through homosexual and bisexual practices, is the leading (more than three-fourths of AIDS cases) cause of HIV/AIDS infection along the Mexican-American border region. In fact, although Hispanics in the U.S. only account for 14 percent of AIDS cases, 45 percent of these cases are associated with Hispanic male homosexual practices (Ramirez, Suarez, de la Rosa, Castro & Zimmerman, 1994). Gay and bisexual men make up 46 percent of all the Hispanic AIDS cases in the U.S. In the southwest region of the U.S. (Texas, New Mexico, Arizona, Colorado, and California) the percentages for gay and bisexual Hispanics are "drastically higher" (i.e., Austin, TX—89 percent, Houston, TX—87 percent, Los Angeles, CA—86 percent, and San Francisco, CA—92 percent) (Rodriguez & Ornelas, 1992). See Table 5.1. Stine (1995) estimates the proportion of persons infected with HIV among homosexual men at between 20 and 25 percent, bisexual men and men with highly infrequent homosexual contacts at 5 percent, and IVDU at 30 percent.

Although transmission through male-to-male sexual contact has steadied among whites (Anglos—31 percent), homosexual or bisexual contact remains the most frequently reported mode of transmission of HIV and has increased among Hispanics (39 percent) and Blacks (31 percent) (CDCP, 1995d). The rates of HIV-infected persons of this classification in 1994 were 6.8/100,000 among blacks, 3.2/100,000 among Hispanics, and 1.1/100,000

TABLE 5.1. Adult AIDS Cases—CDC Data through 12/94; Exposure Category by Region

	Arizona		California		New Mexico		Texas	
	N=	%	N=	%	N=	%	N=	%
Men who have sex with men:	2,446	65.1	57,624	74.2	775	72.7	20,159	66.2
IVDU	375	10.0	6,774	8.7	73	6.8	3,468	11.4
MSM/IVDU	454	12.1	6,731	8.7	108	10.1	2,902	9.5
Hemophilia, etc.	46	1.2	407	0.5	17	1.6	218	0.7
Heterosexual contact	129	3.4	2,290	2.9	30	2.8	1,352	4.4
Transfusion, etc.	117	3.1	1,302	1.7	18	1.7	495	1.6
Other/Undetermined	189	5.0	2,544	3.3	45	4.2	1,866	6.1

	Border Total		Non-Border Total		Total U.S.	
	N=	%	N=	%	N=	%
Men who have sex with men:	81,004	71.7	147,950	45.9	228,954	52.6
IVDU	10,690	9.5	98,703	30.6	109,393	25.1
MSM/IVDU	10,195	9.0	18,326	5.7	28,521	6.6
Hemophilia, etc.	668	0.6	2,954	0.9	3,642	0.8
Heterosexual contact	3,801	3.4	27,862	8.6	31,663	7.3
Transfusion, etc.	1,932	1.7	4,934	1.5	6,866	1.6
Other/Undetermined	4,644	4.1	21,636	6.7	26,280	6.0

Source: Samuel, M. & Espy, D. (1995). *Adult AIDS Cases—CDC Through 12/94*. New Mexico Department of Health, Public Health Division, Bureau of Epidemiology. Santa Fe, NM. Specially created data from Centers of Disease Control Database.

among whites. Regardless of the mode of transmission, AIDS incidence has been higher in Black and Hispanic men, and is very often associated with decreased access to prevention services, higher rates of sexually transmitted diseases, and culturally inappropriate HIV-prevention activities (CDCP, 1995d).

In the U.S.-Mexico border region, 80 percent of Hispanic males diagnosed with AIDS were exclusively homosexual and 20 percent bisexual. Bisexual men are less likely to consider themselves gay, and thus are at an increased risk for HIV infection (Alonso & Koreck, 1989). Geographically, heterosexual contact, which includes bisexual contact, and homosexual contact account for the larger number of cases in the region of the Southwest as compared to Hispanics along the East Coast of the United States (Alonso & Koreck, 1989). More specifically, the most common high-risk sexual practice was mixed behavior between homosexual and bisexual practice (i.e., both insertive and receptive sex). This mixed practice creates the highest risk, especially among partners of bisexual males since this group reports little condom use and practices both vaginal and anal sex with women (Hernandez et al., 1992). "The substantial seroprevalence among bisexuals, their frequent sexual contact with women, and their low rate of condom use imply a continuing role as a bridge of infection to females" (Hernandez, Uribe, Gortmaker & Avila, 1992, p. 892). Other researchers identified the risk for homosexual and bisexual men in cities with a strong Hispanic culture and heritage, stating that "the main sexual risk for HIV-1 infection is not exclusively receptive anal sex, but rather mixed behaviors (mostly insertive, mixed and mostly receptive) risk practices" (Izazola-Licea, Valdespino, Gortmaker & Townsend, 1991). These researchers also confirmed a low condom use rate on last sexual encounter (30 percent) among these bisexual, homosexual Hispanic males.

South of the U.S.-Mexico border corridor in Latin America, sexual transmission from male to male is the leading cause of HIV infection. Within Mexico, approximately 80 percent of AIDS cases are due to sexual transmission (i.e., 35 percent to homosexual male practices, 24 percent to bisexual behavior, and 21 percent to heterosexual sex.). Ramirez and others (1994) quote Magana and Carrier (1991): "Mexicans . . . are more likely to prefer one role, either receptive or insertive anal sex" (p. 165). The Mexico AIDS Case Registry reported that as of December 1992, the estimated cases of AIDS were 18,680. The male/female ratio was 6:1. Adult male AIDS cases were ranked from the following socioepidemiological perspective: homosexual (39.9 percent), bisexual (27.7 percent), heterosexual (19.9 percent), transfusion (6.2 percent), blood donors (2.7 percent), homosexual/IVDU (1.4 percent), hemophiliacs (1.3 percent), and IVDU (0.8 percent). Comparatively, adult female AIDS cases (13.7 percent) were ranked also from the following socioepidemiological perspective: transfusion recipients (57.6 percent), heterosexuals (39.1 percent), blood donors (2.7 percent), and IVDU (0.6 percent). Children's AIDS cases, finally, were ranked from the following socioepidemiological perspective: perinatal (51.2 percent), transfusion recipient (28.2 percent), hemophiliacs (18.6 percent), and sexual abuse (2.0 percent) (Valdespino, Garcia, Salcedo & Magis, 1993). Along the northern Mexican border, growth rates of the epidemic are stabilizing in metropolitan areas, but are growing exponentially in rural areas where the North American culture coexists with indigenous, traditional cultures. Migration and bisexuality in rural areas were identified as important contributing factors to the AIDS problem in Mexico along the U.S.-Mexico border region. Bisexuality is more frequent than homosexuality in rural areas due to cultural reasons and taboos (Valdespino, Garcia, Salcedo & Magis, 1993).

Hispanic men who would be characterized as homosexual or bisexual by Anglo white definitions do not always identify themselves as such. This suggests that the heterosexual, bisexual, and homosexual terms "fit" Anglo America and are not universally held terms. Instead, these terms are "socioculturally and historically produced categories which cannot be presumed to be applicable" to Hispanics or other U.S. minority groups (Alonso & Koreck, 1989, p. 107). Alonso and Koreck (1989) point to several ethnographers and researchers of Mexican and Mexican American males who explain that these men play the active insertor role (machos) in homosexual encounters and are not generally "conceptualized as homosexuals, and neither is their masculinity diminished nor their identity stigmatized by such practices" (p. 108). The receptor male partners (jotos), however, are stigmatized for their unmanly effeminate behavior and only engage in sexual relations with masculine men. These masculine men (machos), on the other hand, engage in sexual activity with both jotos and women without being stigmatized and without being classified as "homosexual" (Alonso & Koreck, 1989). These researchers conclude that the "active, penetrating role in sexual intercourse is seen as a source of honor and power, an index of the attributes of masculinity, including virility" (p. 111). Thus, it appears that bisexual relations among these Hispanic males (machos) are acceptable and to some degree honorable. However, the increased risk of HIV transmission from these males may be erroneously discounted because of these beliefs and practices, and actually introduce significantly higher risk to their "heterosexual" and "homosexual" partners.

In spite of this unique and alarming 15-year trend, "comprehensive (culturally and linguistically appropriate) education and prevention program[s]" have not been addressed to counter this trend (Rodriguez & Ornelas, 1992, p. 443). Additional concerns among Hispanic gay or bisexual men were identified by Rodriguez and Ornelas (1992), including the lack of information on cultural values or sexuality and the important relationship of these issues to achieving behavior change.

Preventing male-to-male HIV transmission should focus on culturally appropriate programs that provide risk reduction education targeted toward the perspectives of both homosexual and bisexual Hispanic groups (Schilling et al., 1991). Educational strategies for homosexual or bisexual Hispanic males may be most effective at reducing HIV infection if behavioral change and educational strategies target specific groups. For example, Ramirez and colleagues (1994) recommend that outreach work in the "streets" is necessary to learn more about the specific needs of this Hispanic subgroup along the U.S.-Mexico border.

With respect to HIV/AID prevention strategies for "high risk" men along the U.S.-Mexico border, practitioners and educators must realize that Hispanic homosexual men are reluctant to "come out" because they fear ostracism and other familial and social sanctions. As a result, they are not likely to identify with prevention messages designed for the mainstream gay community (Carrillo & Uranga-McKane, 1994). Homosexuality is still not accepted in the Mexican, or to some degree in the Mexican/American, society because of dominant cultural and religious beliefs. Ramirez and others (1994) recommend that HIV prevention efforts must target homosexuals in ways that do not challenge social structure and values. Peer education and small-group sessions may be particularly more effective at delivering prevention with these constructs than community-wide interventions like media and public education. HIV prevention efforts in communities along one side of the U.S.-Mexico border must also take place in counterpart cities across the border, especially in communities where easy contact and access are readily available (Ramirez et al., 1994).

HIV AND AIDS AMONG HISPANIC BORDER YOUTH

Hispanic adolescents are at 2.5 times higher risk for HIV infection than white non-Hispanic adolescents (Smith et al., 1993). Contributing to this risk are numbers of STDs, pregnancy, and drug use among adolescents and young adults (Stine, 1995). Stine (1995) reported that the overall male-to-female ratio of AIDS cases in the U.S. is 9:1, versus a 3:1 ratio in teens aged 13 through 19 years. Of these cases, approximately 60 percent are minority persons of color. Teenage women are leading the next wave of the HIV epidemic worldwide, primarily through heterosexual contact with infected partners.

The AIDS case rates for Hispanic adolescents and children were 2.5 to 7.5 times higher than comparable non-Hispanic white groups. Among these youth, the difference was greatest for females and least for males (Diaz et al., 1993). Approximately 50 percent of HIV-infected teenagers, including a substantial percentage of Hispanic teens, come from five American states—New York, New Jersey, Texas, California, and Florida—several of which are border states to Mexico in the southwestern U.S. (Stine, 1995).

Nationally, Hispanic youth make up only about six percent of the teenage population. However, they account for approximately 20 percent of teenage AIDS cases (OSAP Technical Report #5, 1991). Although the number of reported AIDS cases among adolescents is exceedingly low (1 percent of all AIDS cases), this does not give a realistic measure of the status of HIV infection in teenagers. The estimated incubation period between time of infection and onset of clinical symptoms is as long as five to eleven years. Reliance on AIDS case surveillance data significantly underestimates the severity of this health threat to adolescents (Manoff et al., 1988; DiClemente, 1993). A teenager infected in early adolescence may not experience the impact of the disease in his or her daily life until the mid- to late-twenties (Manoff et al., 1988; DiClemente, 1993).

To obtain a realistic picture of the impact of the AIDS epidemic on teens, it is necessary to have studies of seroprevalence of HIV infection in this population. Until these data are available, it is more sensible to look at the number of AIDS cases in adults in their twenties and early thirties. Researchers have identified that more than 60 percent of all AIDS cases fall between the 20 to 30 age category along the border region. Clearly our teen population is at great risk and must not be overlooked because of "low" incidence rates.

For many, adolescence is a time of sexual experimentation and exploration. This behavior is considered by many to be a part of the developmental process from child to adult. Studies show that sexual experimentation is starting at earlier ages (Trad, 1994; Romer et al., 1994; Boyer & Kegeles, 1991). With the onset of AIDS and the increasing prevalence of other STDs, this behavior poses new threats for young persons in their teens. However, teens perceive these risks as insignificant. Langer and colleagues (1993) report that regular condom use among teenagers is only about 10 percent.

Data from births to teenage mothers indicate that Hispanic adolescents are not using condoms or other contraceptive methods and are at high risk for HIV infection. Acculturated Hispanics—those acculturated to Anglo norms—appear to be at greater risk of HIV infection because of changes in sexual behavior norms as compared to less-acculturated Hispanic populations (Amaro, 1988). Unfortunately, a sparse number of empirical studies exist that describe how the process of acculturation affects sexual behavior, contraceptive norms, and contraceptive behaviors among Mexican American groups.

Other studies point out that psychological barriers render new information inaccessible or misunderstood. Stiffman and colleagues (1992) found that even having acquaintances who are HIV-infected or who have died of AIDS does not alter feelings of invincibility among adolescents. With these attitudes of invincibility, young persons in their teens continue to engage in high-risk behavior, such as unprotected sex and IVDU. Nowhere is this seen more than in minority communities such as the Mexican-American border region (California, Arizona, New Mexico, and Texas) (Stine, 1995).

AIDS has no cure or lasting effective treatment to control its devastation. Education has been targeted as an essential means of control and prevention. Boyer and Kegeles (1991) report that most studies of teenagers have concentrated on transmission, knowledge, perceptions of risk, and to a lesser extent, if at all, on behavior. A study by DiClemente, Boyer, and Mills (1987) showed Hispanic adolescents were likely to harbor erroneous information about risk factors associated with AIDS in contrast to their non-minority counterparts. However, with accurate information, behavior does not necessarily change (Langer, Zimmerman, Warheit & Duncan, 1993). Many recognize that it is a tedious effort to modify entrenched, often pleasurable behaviors (National Commission on AIDS, 1993). It may then be unrealistic to expect that teenagers will change risky behaviors, especially with an information-only approach toward AIDS prevention. Because of these realities, educators and policy makers are faced with a challenge to select an appropriate method for educating Hispanic adolescents to prevent or modify the various risky behaviors associated with HIV transmission. Furthermore, with high-risk behaviors continuing and the number of Hispanic adolescents being infected with HIV rising, current education strategies targeted at Hispanic adolescents are falling short (Stine, 1995).

PREVENTION ALONG THE BORDER MUST INCLUDE COMMUNITY INPUT

Most people agree that education is the first step to preventing HIV infection until a vaccine is also available (Amaro, 1988). The prevention of HIV infection depends on informing individuals to encourage and enable them to alter risky behaviors in order to prevent infection. Effective education efforts must require significant Hispanic involvement so that programming and policies are acceptable and so that the risk of stigma is reduced. Furthermore,

Hispanics must step forward to take a role in mobilizing human and financial resources against the HIV/AIDS epidemic along the border (Carrillo & Uranga-McKane, 1994). Among Hispanic populations, family planning clinics represent an ideal setting for AIDS education, since structured counseling sessions are provided as a part of routine health care (Rapkin & Erickson, 1990).

HIV prevention programs that target Hispanics must address the diverse cultural, economic, and educational backgrounds of this population (Simon & Sorvillo, 1993). These researchers discovered that Hispanics emigrating from Mexico to a large metropolitan border community in the U.S. had fewer financial resources, and were less able to receive support to obtain HIV prevention programs and health care services, than were U.S. native-born Hispanics.

Many researchers or practitioners who have worked with Hispanic populations in the U.S.-Mexico border region report that developing culturally and linguistically appropriate prevention programs is crucial, but that these prevention programs must occur with input and direction from each targeted Hispanic population. Rodriguez and Ornelas (1992) recommend that simply adapting an effective model from another population will likely lead to a lack of "buy-in" and program effectiveness. Additionally, these researchers report that "educational models must take into account the specific cultural, economic, and social circumstances of the target population" that are "adaptable to subgroups within the [Hispanic] population (i.e., first generation, Central Americans, etc.)" (Rodriguez & Ornelas, 1992, p. 443). However, among impoverished Hispanic women, educational outreach and skill building for HIV prevention also must be directed toward meeting their survival needs. Among "acculturated" and "less acculturated" women of various minority groups, vastly different risk behaviors are exhibited for acquiring HIV/AIDS, thus supporting the need for culturally and linguistically appropriate AIDS prevention programs that address specialized areas of concern (Nyamathi et al., 1993). Prevention programs must account for Hispanic characteristics and reflect the social, cultural, and economic contexts that shape the realities of their lives (Amaro, 1988).

Amaro (1988) recommends that an effective education program for preventing HIV/AIDS should focus on general reproductive and AIDS education issues through a "trained community health educator who is of the same gender and cultural and linguistic background as the woman or man who is the target of the prevention effort" (p. 436). Furthermore, since a relative lack of success in traditional health care delivery models has been noted among Hispanic populations, prevention efforts should be innovative and community-born. Community-based organizations such as tenant groups, neighborhood organizations, unions, churches, parent groups, drug treatment programs, local professionals, and indigenous leaders are needed for involvement in HIV/AIDS prevention efforts. Particularly effective methods of education outreach should focus on "alternative communication media" such as telenovelas (soap operas), Spanish radio and television programs, street theater, and bilingual telephone hotlines in addition to traditional written materials (Amaro, 1988).

Romien and colleagues (1991) developed a mathematical model to project the spread of the AIDS epidemic among Hispanics. The researchers calculated that specific behavior change programs would likely decrease the transmission probability by 10–20 percent from all transmissible groups, which would result in a decrease of over 18–31 percent of the number of accumulated cases over a five-year period. Thus, prevention-oriented education programs targeted to high-risk Hispanic groups have the potential for substantially impacting behavior change to decrease the spread of HIV/AIDS (Romien, Sandberg, Mohar & Awerbuch, 1991).

Suggested HIV/AIDS Prevention Strategies along the Border
Foundations of Educational HIV/AIDS Programs

Hispanics, as a whole, are the most medically underinsured of all U.S. ethnic groups, lack an effective primary care health service infrastructure, experience barriers due to issues of language and culture, and experience a wide array of transmissible diseases (including HIV) because of migration patterns to and from countries and regions with a high prevalence of particular diseases (including HIV/AIDS). Powerful sexual taboos about homosexuality and the barriers to communication about sex between men and women further complicate HIV prevention efforts in Hispanic communities (Carrillo & Uranga-McKane, 1994).

The educational level of Hispanics is lower than that of Anglos (Amaro, 1988). The lower educational attainments of Hispanics must be considered when developing and delivering HIV/AIDS prevention educational programs. Amaro (1988) points out that the most common approach used in developing these materials are to develop them first for "mainstream" America, in English, and then to translate them into Spanish. A more desirable alternative would be to develop strategic materials for specific Hispanic populations. School-based programs should be supplemented with out-of-school programs for youth in and out of school. Community programs through social service programs and agencies might offer sources of contact with adult and youth Hispanic populations (Amaro, 1988).

Educational Outlets

Jimenez and Bond (1990) provide a glimpse into effective health education
–oriented HIV/AIDS prevention programs in their assessment of the mass
media treatment of HIV/AIDS in Central and North America. Their results
indicate that "the media tended to limit its function to reporting and discussing disease symptoms, defining the condition in terms of human suffering and societal implications, yet falling short of providing support in prevention by printing guidelines such as the use of prophylactics and
eliminating the use of vague language such as bodily fluids" (Jimenez &
Bond, 1990, p. 474). These researchers conclude that educational messages
sent through the media should involve sensitization training workshops between representatives of the media, health care, and government.

An integral part of AIDS prevention and education programs at the
community, state, and national levels is the use of AIDS hotlines (Saunders,
Helquist, Stein & Coravano, 1989). These researchers suggest that hotlines
in the U.S. provide information dissemination, referral and listening support to callers, and tracking of concerns, misperceptions, and service needs.
In Mexico and Peru, hotlines provide information targeted to gay and bisexual men; in Trinidad and Tobago the hotline serves as a listening support system. Thus, site-specific hotlines may provide a first point of intake
and education for communities and regions with unique prevalence concerns and prevention issues. The U.S.-Mexico border communities or regions would likely benefit significantly from these HIV/AIDS hotlines.

Within large border cities, culturally competent one-on-one street
outreach programs that reach sexual and drug-using partners with information on HIV transmission prevention and access to services are essential.
Particular consideration should be given regarding the sexual modes of HIV
transmission along the border. Oral/anal and oral/genital sex as well as bisexual practices must be addressed (Carrillo & Uranga-McKane, 1994).
High-risk Hispanic men are reluctant to receive or accept HIV/AIDS information when cultural difference, prejudices, machismo homophobia, and
racism are present. Furthermore, prevention materials are often inappropriate
when mainstream sources of information (i.e., gay white male material) are
used among Hispanic populations along the border (Carrillo & Uranga-
McKane, 1994).

Education Materials

A comprehensive AIDS education program utilizes material that will optimize consciousness of the high-risk factors and behaviors related to HIV infection. The materials that will optimize consciousness in teenagers vary with

the diversity of each group. Each group has unique norms and concerns, which should be taken into account in the formulation of prevention efforts. In the Mexican American border region a substantial portion of the population is of Hispanic origin. Many of these young people come from households where English is not spoken regularly; instead, these families speak Spanish. For these areas the use of English-only materials will present an obstacle for understanding to the Hispanic students. The solution is not to simply translate the English into Spanish, which is considered an ineffective shortcut by health professionals. Matiella (1988) suggests that materials should make use of pictures and illustrations rather than be written at a high reading level. This approach will prove much more efficient in reaching the Hispanic youth. The materials (brochures, posters, comic books, etc.) need to show cultural sensitivity and at the same time be able to elicit discussion by the students.

The use of Latin American popular culture provides a wide range of choices to meet the educational needs of the Hispanic adolescents (Matiella, 1988). Matiella proposes the use of novellas, comic book–like books that use illustrations and minimal written material. The only written material is the dialogue used to communicate messages. The OSAP Technical Report #5 (1991) also suggests that comic books be developed for gay persons as well as other Hispanics.

Parent Involvement

Parents play a pivotal role in AIDS education for teenagers. The influence of parents is exceptionally powerful in the Hispanic culture, where there are conservative moral and social values and traditional personal roles (Matiella, 1988). In the Hispanic culture, discussions about sexuality have been traditionally regarded as a private subject that should be dealt with within the family setting. In the age of AIDS, home education may not be enough or reliable in some homes because parents do not typically possess accurate information about AIDS and are typically ambivalent toward the emerging sexuality of teens.

AIDS education in the schools is slowly gaining public acceptance. However, there is still controversy over the content of the information the students receive. As a result, essential pieces of information are left out and students acquire disjointed information.

While the Hispanic culture is beginning to allowp AIDS education in schools, it does not mean that parents should stop educating. Parents are in a position to offer support during the education process and ongoing support after it has concluded. Even though teenagers are normally uneasy about discussing subjects as sensitive as AIDS with their parents, they will react positively when their parents reach out to them. This allows for an open communication line between parents and children. By opening the communication lines, parents can help their children comprehend the seriousness of the disease. Parents can also help their children understand the consequences of making responsible decisions versus irresponsible decisions.

Church Involvement

Another powerful influence in the Hispanic culture is the Catholic Church. While having no difficulty acknowledging the reality and significance of the AIDS crisis, the Catholic Church has faced hard questions regarding education about AIDS (Pickerel, 1988). The most prevalent forms of transmission of HIV are non-monogamous sexual activity and sharing contaminated needles. These two methods of transmission are looked upon by the Catholic Church as immoral. The homosexual and bisexual influence among Hispanics in the border region is also looked upon by the Catholic Church as a lifestyle against the teachings of God. Even the ways in which people are taught to lower their risk of HIV infection, such as using condoms and sterilized needles, are deemed inappropriate by the Church. However, prevention methods such as sexual abstinence or monogamous sexual relations and abstinence from IVDU can still be promoted to prevent HIV while also assisting devout religious persons in living the way they believe. The purpose of this discussion is not meant to be derogatory to the Church or any other religious group with similar teachings. Rather, this discussion is aimed toward reminding HIV prevention experts that Hispanics and other groups with devout religious beliefs deserve respect, with the realization that with this recognized respect may come the opportunity for mutual trust. Obviously, people have always and will likely continue to practice the freedom of moral choice.

EDUCATION MODELS FOR HIV/AIDS PREVENTION APPROPRIATE FOR HISPANICS

The U.S.-Mexico Border Health Commission (1994) advocates that health education along both sides of the border is the best and most economical means of achieving a better quality of health, including the prevention of HIV/AIDS. Many models for AIDS education have been proposed for distinct populations throughout the country. Three models of HIV/AIDS education, in the context of the Mexican-American border region, will be presented (Trad, 1994; Schinke et al., 1990; Boyer & Kegeles, 1991). These models of education go beyond just informing border Hispanic populations about facts and statistics on AIDS and HIV infection. These models propose enhancing cognitive behavior skills and using experiential techniques. These proposed HIV/AIDS models also are ideally suited for adolescent populations because of their potential for primary prevention. However, these models are expected to perform well for other "at risk" groups in a variety of settings. They may be excellent resources since models with a certain degree of adaptability are ideal among Hispanic populations along the U.S.-Mexico border region.

I. Previewing

Trad (1994) introduces a new technique to facilitate the understanding of high-risk behavior and AIDS through an approach called "previewing." This technique is based on the developmental principle that initially emerges between an infant and its caregiver, and reemerges during the identity formation period of adolescence and beyond (Trad, 1994). Although it has been used primarily for school-based settings, its appropriateness in other community settings is encouraged (Trad, 1994).

Previewing is a two-stage technique, involving representation and enactment. Representation involves gathering participants in a group setting to envision significant events in their future (such as the opportunity for sexual encounter) (Trad, 1994). During this stage, members of the group are encouraged to discuss their viewpoint concerning the representation. Enactment is done by having students in the group act out a real-life situation that is significant to them in a traditional role-playing format. Members are selected to participate and role-play the given situation from their own beliefs or point of view. After the given situation is acted out, group members are encouraged to discuss their own perspectives. The value of this activity may be to encourage belief and value clarification, a recommended activity for adolescents and adults alike. These techniques are carried out in a group setting with discussion between participants while providing an opportunity to explore options, practice skills, and understand their peers' opinions. Discussion between all groups is encouraged, emphasizing mutual respect, because opinions and perceptions of individual members will likely be revealed or clarified. By enacting meaningful real-life situations, adolescents have the opportunity to articulate possible repercussions of their behavior from their own perceptions, and to experiment and receive reinforcement or sanctions for behavior in a protected environment. The student can learn about the likely consequences without bringing harm to himself or herself. Romer and colleagues (1994) propose that boundaries for acceptable behavior are more influenced by peer norms than individual norms.

Besides positive peer pressure, enactments can be valuable for group participants for other reasons. By enacting meaningful real-life situations, members also have the opportunity to practice skills that will assist them in the future (Trad, 1994). Because experimentation is an important part of the developmental process, these enactments are a protected manner in which to experiment. Another value of these enactments is the importance of picking situations that are meaningful to the targeted group of participants. Seltzer and others (1989) showed that adolescents tend to gain the most benefit from guided techniques that enable them to confront personal challenges. Thus, this technique may be ideal for them (Trad, 1994).

Even though this model of AIDS education is comprehensive in teaching participants cognitive behavior skills, it does not directly address cultural sensitivity. For persons in the Mexican-American border region, cultural norms and values must be addressed and recognized since these factors are significant in affecting the behaviors and practices that make them more at risk for HIV. However, in an indirect way this model of education can very easily address these issues. The facilitator can select events for the students to preview that they can relate to.

The model has been criticized because it lacks an evaluation component. Continuous evaluation of the program allows educators to identify information gaps and also changes in knowledge, behavior, and attitudes. As is the case with virtually any program, ongoing evaluation from implementation stages through the completion and followup of program outcomes is a priority. Innovative evaluation techniques such as these are encouraged for this model. Another potential deficiency of this model is that it does not directly emphasize the element of teaching basic facts and figures and dispelling myths. While it is essential that participants learn cognitive-behavior skills, they also need to know what is high-risk and what is not. This is critical because many "at-risk" persons, especially minority populations, have incorrect information and myths about HIV transmission.

II. Skills Intervention Model

A second model for AIDS education for Hispanic youth in the border region is recommended by Schinke and colleagues (1990). The skills intervention model builds its instruction on a cognitive-skill intervention. Skills intervention helps participants avoid problems, and promotes their health through a repertoire of cognitive and behavioral techniques (Schinke et al., 1990). This model of education may help Hispanic populations by providing a nurturing environment that will strengthen their self-image and maintain a sense of cultural heritage (Schinke et al., 1990). There are five components to this model:

1. Ethnic Pride
2. HIV Facts
3. Problem Solving
4. Coping
5. Communication

When exploring this model in the context of the U.S.-Mexico border, ethnic pride is an integral element in educating Hispanic populations about AIDS. Ethnic pride can take many forms. Curricula that are sensitive to ethnic pride will emphasize cultural values and language (Schinke et al., 1990). For Hispanic youth, this curriculum should be in Spanish, and cultural, church, and family influences should be considered for incorporation into the model.

The second component to this model is HIV facts. The content of HIV facts comprises known facts about (a) AIDS, (b) HIV infection, and (c) behavioral risks (Schinke et al., 1990). This component is critical because Hispanic youth and less-acculturated adults are more apt to possess false information about AIDS risk factors, myths, and prevention (Schinke et al., 1990). Schinke and colleagues (1990) suggest that facts about HIV be presented through vignettes. Vignettes give participants a means to integrate facts with behaviors.

Problem solving, the third of five components, is similar to previewing, with the variation being that problem solving is more individualized. Hispanic adolescents are taught to approach HIV dilemmas in five steps:

1. Stop
2. Options
3. Decide
4. Act
5. Self-praise

In the first step (stop) adolescents are taught to pause and define the dilemma when confronted with a situation dealing with the risk of HIV infection (Schinke et al., 1990). Once the problem is defined, the participants explore options that lead to resolutions (step 2). This leads into the third step (decide), where participants ponder and choose the most viable option from those outlined in step 2 (Schinke et al., 1990). The fourth step (act) leads into cultivating the best strategy. The final step is where the participant praises himself or herself for working through the problem.

Along with problem solving, another component of the skills intervention model is coping. The adolescent years are a time of peer pressure and temptations. Through this component participants are taught skills that assist them in coping with stress and peer pressures that may put them at risk. These skills include cognitive and behavioral strategies (Schinke et al., 1990). Unlike the problem-solving component, coping is done in group settings where the participants can see the coping skills demonstrated and also have the chance to rehearse these skills (Schinke et al., 1990).

The final component of this AIDS education model is communication. The skills for communication are demonstrated through videotaped scenes. For Hispanics in the U.S.-Mexico border region, these scenes should have Hispanic persons acting in the scenes. This provides participants the opportunity to see similar persons faced with dilemmas and how they successfully handle these dilemmas. In addition to viewing videotapes, the students practice communication skills in role-playing situations that are of relevance to them. The role playing gives the students the opportunity to practice the skills they have observed in the videotapes.

This model of education, unlike the first, directly emphasizes cultural sensitivity. Throughout the components of this model, Hispanic Americans are used as role models. The participants are more likely to identify with the other Hispanics on the videotapes.

There are a variety of exercises in a group format and there is also the potential for small-group or individual exercises done out of the group setting. Unlike the first model, this model includes using a portion of the instruction time to give participants facts and figures about the disease and its transmission. Because many Hispanics are more likely than non-minority persons to possess unfactual beliefs about HIV transmission and to engage in more high-risk behavior, it is imperative that curricula contain the most up-to-date information about the disease (Schinke et al., 1990).

Schinke and colleagues (1990) provide a potential timetable for the instruction to be carried out. The instruction is set up in a weekly or semi-weekly format for about 12–15 meetings. Schinke and colleagues (1990) considered this time frame adequate to provide participants with substantial intensity and detail to learn cognitive behavior skills. After this initial instruction, Schinke and colleagues (1990) suggest that participants partake in semi-annual booster sessions to strengthen what they have learned. However, once again there is no reference to ongoing evaluation of this program.

III. Specificity and Sensitivity Model

The third model for AIDS education targeted at the Hispanic population in the border region (Boyer & Kegeles, 1991) signifies six tactics that may educate toward preventing HIV. As with the other two models discussed, the model by Boyer and Kegeles (1991) shows specificity and cultural sensitivity. The first strategy relates to content of information about AIDS and HIV infection. Besides providing students with information about cause, transmission, and prevention, comprehensive AIDS education should also dispel myths about AIDS and HIV infection. Schinke and colleagues (1990) reported that a significant portion of Hispanics in their study possessed erroneous information about non-risk factors of HIV transmission. An example of misinformation about non-risk factors found was that 35–58 percent of the Hispanic youth believed that using a public toilet was a risk factor. Secondly, in addition to content of information, the context of the information needs to include information on sexuality and sexual intercourse (Boyer & Kegeles, 1991). For this information to be accepted by participants, educators need to keep in mind that scare tactics do not commonly deliver positive results (OSAP Technical Report #5, 1991). Discussion is very much encouraged between students because it assists students in understanding the issues surrounding AIDS and HIV infection.

The third tactic of this model is dissemination of information. To solidify the content and context of the information about cause, transmission, and prevention of AIDS, communication is used. To facilitate communication between participants, many strategies can be used. Examples of the types of strategies include small-group discussions, role playing, videos, and music (Boyer & Kegeles, 1991). By having small group discussions, students will usually be more able to talk openly about anxieties and misconceptions about AIDS and HIV infection. Role playing, on the other hand, enables the students to work on skills that will help prevent them from getting involved in high-risk behavior. Music and videos are used to establish an environment that is favorable for the students to openly discuss AIDS and HIV infection.

A fourth tactic emphasized in this model is sociocultural factors. It is essential to keep in mind that a program approach with one group of participants will not necessarily work with another group of persons. Sociocultural factors such as ethnicity and religion cannot be overlooked. As with the Schinke and colleagues (1990) skills intervention model, culturally sensitive curricula emphasize cultural values, choices and language. Building on the cultural values and strengths of the given group rather than working against the prevailing values or taboos will result in elevated acceptance of the prevention messages (Boyer & Kegeles, 1991).

In addition to methods of providing information and sensitivity to sociocultural factors, this model's element includes program evaluation activities. The evaluation process of an AIDS education program should be ongoing so that information gaps or changes in knowledge, behavior, or attitudes can be identified and the program modified appropriately (Boyer & Kegeles, 1991). Interventions referred to as "booster" interventions should be conducted every three to six months (Boyer & Kegeles, 1991). This method of evaluation will allow educators to follow the impact of the education in the short and long term, in addition to providing a continual forum for participants to integrate new information (Boyer & Kegeles, 1991).

The sixth and final strategy for this model of AIDS education is examining resources. For an AIDS education program to be successful, a cooperative effort has to be made among school districts, community-based organizations, health officials, and local and state governments (Boyer & Kegeles, 1991). To provide the required leadership for the Hispanic participants, health educators, counselors, and researchers need to work together to develop and implement these AIDS intervention programs (Boyer & Kegeles, 1991).

This model of education is the most comprehensive of the three. In addition to addressing cognitive behavior skills and providing students with facts and statistics, this model addresses cultural factors and also suggests the need for continuous evaluation of the program, something the other two models lack. As with the other two models of AIDS education, the cognitive behavior skills are an intricate part of the model. Many "at-risk" Hispanics often lack the skills that are required for decision making and negotiation. Because they lack these skills, phrases like "just say no" will likely prove ineffective. Participants must develop the skills and enhance attitudes and beliefs that will enable them to "just say no."

One element that none of the three models mention is the role of the media. The media are an element that educators should not ignore. Hispanics, like most other ethnic groups, are heavily influenced by what they see in the media. Over and over again the media glamorize sex. Sexuality sells everything from perfume to coffee. Stories depict people in situations that are considered high risk for contracting HIV. What is not depicted in these story lines are people discussing safe sex or the repercussions of not engaging in safe sex or in abstaining from sex. As media consumers see persons depicted in the media engaging in high-risk behavior (for HIV infection) and not suffering any repercussions, they may become ambivalent toward educational and prevention efforts.

Each of the three models presented provides unique strengths and flexibility for a variety of HIV/AIDS prevention audiences. However, the sensitivity and specificity model is the most comprehensive and addresses the needs of culture sensitivity among Hispanics specifically. Thus, any of the models presented could be the valuable prevention resource needed to impact HIV/AIDS among Hispanics, but the final selection of the most appropriate educational model will be dependent on community needs and input and also on the desired outcomes of these efforts.

CONCLUSION

The Centers for Disease Control and Prevention (1995b) estimate that approximately one million people are infected with HIV in the United States, representing nearly 1 in 250 Americans. Although the rate of increase is slowing among the general population, increases among Hispanics and Blacks are not (CDCP, 1995b). The AIDS case rate in the United States is at least two-and-one-half times higher among Hispanics than non-Hispanic whites (Diaz et al., 1993). Unfortunately these trends do not appear to be changing. The number of AIDS cases along the U.S.-Mexico border has increased significantly in the last few years due primarily to the increased cases within the American border states (Magis et al., 1992). In terms of cumulative AIDS cases (all age groups), two of the four border states, California and Texas, are among the highest in the United States (CDCP, 1995b). Thus, among Hispanic populations in general, and among Hispanics of the U.S.-Mexico border region, the threat and increase of HIV/AIDS continues. There also are clear distinctions between the Hispanics of primarily Mexican descent along the southwestern U.S. border region, and Hispanics (Latinos) from other parts of the country. This risk-factor distinction is a significant predictor for developing the unique programs that are needed to prevent HIV/AIDS along the U.S.-Mexico border.

The primary mode of HIV infection and AIDS cases among Hispanic men from the U.S.-Mexico border region is with homosexual and bisexual contact, while among other groups of Hispanic men, most cases are attributable to IVDU. The border region reports much greater transfusion-related AIDS among Hispanics than in other regions (Carrillo & Uranga-McKane, 1994). Among Hispanic women, only 19 percent present with AIDS cases from intravenous drug use from the border; instead, 71 percent of AIDS cases among these women along the U.S.-Mexico border report a history of heterosexual contact from a partner (most often bisexual), a blood transfusion recipient, or an intravenous drug user. Clearly, the greatest risk associated with HIV/AIDS among Hispanic adult males and females along the U.S.-Mexico border region is sexual contact, not IVDU as is the case among Hispanics in other geographic sections of the country. Among U.S.-Mexico border region Hispanic youth, research has confirmed that earlier experimentation and less regular condom use occur among this group more often than among many other populations in locations throughout the country. Thus, with all these differences and unique risks along the border comes the need to identify unique cultural- and language- appropriate prevention materials that address these HIV/AIDS issues.

Undoubtedly, all ethnic groups of all ages and both genders are potentially at risk for acquiring HIV/AIDS. Although the focus of this chapter is almost exclusively Hispanic populations along the U.S.-Mexico border region, the prevalence, transmission, and prevention of HIV/AIDS is not characterized or isolated solely by ethnicity, geography, or borders. The following statement reminds prevention experts that identifying significant risk factors such as those presented in this chapter should be used to direct prevention and funding priorities, and that these problems have not and do not occur in a vacuum.

> While it is clear that AIDS is not a disease of one ethnic or racial group, there must be honesty in describing its impact on minority populations. To send a color-blind message about AIDS would only fog reality, resulting in inappropriate solutions being applied to poorly characterized problems and scarce resources being mistargeted and used ineffectively. (Carrillo & Uranga-McKane, 1994, p. 328)

The HIV/AIDS epidemic is problematic in many areas throughout the country and the world because of many varied risk factors and cultural issues. Hence, it makes sense that education and prevention strategies and health policy issues for the border Hispanic population must be different. Additional research with this population is needed since the sociocultural barriers are complex and not sufficiently understood. Comprehensive AIDS education for this population needs to enable women, men, and children to modify behaviors that could place them in high-risk positions. This chapter has sought to incorporate culture-specific strategies for prevention based on a clearer understanding and contrast of the HIV/AIDS situation among Hispanics along the U.S.-Mexico border region as compared to Hispanic populations in other parts of the country.

Because research has not been able to develop a drug that will arrest the HIV virus, experts continue to look at education as an important means of AIDS prevention. Early methods of education concentrated on high-risk behaviors and modes of transmission. Now experts believe that comprehensive AIDS education needs to involve key members of target communities to assist prevention experts in helping community members modify behaviors that could place them in high-risk positions. This chapter considered several HIV/AIDS prevention strategies and three models of education that may assist unique education and prevention efforts to combat this disease along the border. These strategies and models require community support in order to be implemented into the community, school education curricula, media sources, and other potential prevention education sites.

When developing an AIDS education program for Hispanic men, women, and children, opposition from the community is to be expected. In Hispanic communities, this opposition may emerge from parents and religious groups concerned that this kind of information is a matter to be discussed in the home or not at all (Matiella, 1988).

The first step in developing a comprehensive AIDS education program is creating a community task force that includes school administrators, teachers, medical professionals, clergy, parents, adolescents, and business leaders (Haffner, 1988). Diversity in a task force will allow the community to explore questions and concerns from many angles. The task force should evaluate the community needs and concerns surrounding HIV/AIDS education, evaluate current levels of knowledge and attitudes toward the disease, identify community resources, and review materials and curriculum (Haffner, 1988). Because of the controversy involving HIV/AIDS and the education thereof, certain questions, such as the following, should be answered (Haffner, 1988).

1. How will parents and the community be involved in the program? Will parental permission be required for participation?
2. Who will teach the AIDS unit and how will it be monitored?
3. What reviews and updates of the curriculum will there be? How often will the reviews take place?
4. How will issues like monogamous relationships, homosexuality, bisexuality, condom use, abstinence, anal intercourse, and mutual masturbation be approached?

As the task force develops an AIDS curriculum, it is important to have town meetings. The task force should provide the community with written information and facts about AIDS and HIV infection. At some point during these meetings, the program's content and goals should be introduced. This gives the public the opportunity to ask questions or voice concerns. The general public is both scared and confused about AIDS (Haffner, 1988). By having these town meetings, fears and misconceptions can be alleviated while at the same time developing support for the program.

An ongoing method that can be used to gain support from the community is the media. Television, radio, and newspapers can be useful tools to send out messages that will reinforce program intervention efforts (OSAP Technical Report #5, 1991). Because the media have a heavy influence on young people, they can be used to alleviate fears, prejudice, and stigmatization associated with HIV infection (OSAP Technical Report #5, 1991). For the general public, the media can be used to provide messages that will arouse awareness and interest (OSAP Technical Report #5, 1991).

While developing an AIDS curriculum to be implemented in community prevention sites, program goals must be reasonable. Educators, parents, and others must realize that any comprehensive AIDS education program will not eradicate HIV/AIDS. Comprehensive education will, however, arm the community not just with facts, but also with skills that will assist them in making informed and reasonable resolutions. As a result, the potential of being exposed to the HIV virus should significantly decrease.

Finally, among Hispanic male, female, and adolescent populations, HIV/AIDS is on the rise. As a result, all of these groups could benefit and should participate in education, awareness, and prevention efforts. If an increased understanding of HIV/AIDS were achieved, based on the unique risk factors along the border, individuals would be able to make their own choices concerning how to avoid HIV/AIDS. Much of the success of these efforts will involve the community taking the reins of leadership in establishing educational and prevention opportunities for its citizens. With community support and community input, prevention experts can continue to compile geography-specific research and funding to refine HIV/AIDS education and prevention actions and make a difference in lowering HIV/AIDS rates in the U.S.-Mexico border region.

REFERENCES

Alonso, A.M., & Koreck, M.T. (1989). Silences: Hispanics, AIDS, and sexual practices. *Journal of Feminist Cultural Studies, 1*(4), 101–124.

Amaro, H. (1988). Considerations for prevention of HIV infection among Hispanic women. *Psychology of Women Quarterly, 12,* 429–443.

Boyer, C.B. & Kegeles, S. M. (1991). AIDS risk and prevention among adolescents. *Social Science and Medicine, 33,* 11–23.

Carrillo, E. & Uranga-McKane S. (Eds.). (1994). *Latino health in the U.S.: A growing challenge.* Washington, D.C.: American Public Health Association.

Castro, K.G. & Manoff, S. B. (1988). The epidemiology of AIDS in Hispanic adolescents. In *The AIDS Challenge: Prevention Education for Young People,* Quackenbush, M. Nelson, M. & Clark, K. (Eds.) 321–331.

Centers for Disease Control and Prevention. (1995a). HIV conference spotlights women's concerns. *AIDS Alert, 10*(4), 54–57.

Centers for Disease Control and Prevention. (1995b). CDC facts about recent trends in reported U.S. AIDS cases. *CDC Facts About Trends,* March 29, 1–2.

Centers for Disease Control and Prevention. (1995c). *HIV/AIDS surveillance report,* Part 9. Atlanta, Georgia: Centers for Disease Control and Prevention. On-line Gopher (Internet) site from CDCP.

Centers for Disease Control and Prevention. (1995d). Update: Trends in AIDS among men who have sex with men—U.S., 1989–1994. *Morbidity and Mortality Weekly Report, 44,* 401–404.

Diaz, T., Buehler, J.W., Castro, K.G., & Ward, J.W. (1993). AIDS trends among Hispanics in the United States. *American Journal of Public Health, 83*(4), 504–509.

Di Clemente, R.J. (1993). HIV-related risk behaviors among psychiatrically hospitalized adolescents and school-based adolescents. *American Journal of Psychiatry, 150*(2), 324–325.

DiClemente, R.J., Boyer, C.B. & Mills, S.J. (1987). Prevention of AIDS among adolescents. Strategies for the development of comprehensive risk-reduction health education programs. *Health Education Research, 2* (3), 287–291.

Guerena, B.F., Benenson, A.S., & Sepulveda, A.J. (1991). HIV-1 prevalence in selected Tijuana sub-populations. *American Journal of Public Health, 81*(5), 623–625.

Haffner, D.W. (1988). Developing community support for school-based AIDS education. *The AIDS Challenge* (Prevention Education for Young People), 93–103.

Hernandez, M., Uribe, P., Gortmaker, S., & Avila, C. (1992). Sexual behavior and status for human immunodeficiency virus type 1 among homosexual and bisexual males in Mexico City. *American Journal of Epidemiology, 135*(8), 883–894.

Izazola-Licea, J.A., Valdespino-Gomez, J.L., Gortmaker, S.L., Townsend, J., and others. (1991). HIV-1 seropositivity and behavioral and sociological risks among homosexual and bisexual men in six Mexican cities. Ministry of Health, Mexico City, Mexico. *Journal of Acquired Immune Deficiency Syndrome, 4* (6): 614–622.

Jimenez, M.V. & Bond, L.S. (1990). The media and health education in AIDS prevention. *International Conference on AIDS, 6*(2), 474, Abstract #4083.

Langer, L.M., Zimmerman, R.S., Warheit, G.J., & Duncan, R.C. (1993). Decision-making orientation and AIDS related knowledge, and behaviors of Hispanic, African-American and white adolescents. *Health Psychology, 72,* 227–234.

Magana, J. F. & Carrier, J.M. (1991). Mexican and Mexican American male sexual behavior and spread of AIDS in California. *The Journal of Sex Research, 28,* 425–441.

Magis, C.L., Garcia, M.L., Valdespino, J.L., & Gonzalez, G.M. (1992). AIDS in the Mexico-USA border. *International Conference on AIDS, 8*(3), 168.

Manoff, S.G., Gayle, H.D., Mays, M.A., & Rogers, M.F. (1988). Acquired Immuno-deficiency Syndrome in adolescents: Epidmiology, prevention and public health issues. *Pediatric Infectious Disease Journal, 8*(5), 309–314.

Matiella, A.C. (1988). Developing innovative AIDS prevention programs for latino youth. *The AIDS Challenge* (Prevention Education for Young People), 333–343.

National Commission on AIDS. (1993). *AIDS: an expanding tragedy: The fourth report of the National Commission on AIDS.* The Commission: Washington, D.C.

Nyamathi, A., Bennett, C., Leake, B., Lewis, C., & Flaskerud, J. (1993). AIDS-related knowledge, perceptions, and behaviors among impoverished minority women. *American Journal of Public Health 83*(1), 65–71.

Ortega, H. (1995). *United States-Mexico border: Vital statistics review.* El Paso, Texas: The Interamerica Institute for Border Health and Environment.

OSAP Technical Report #5. (1991). *Prevention of HIV infection among youth.*

Rockville, MD: U.S. Department of Health and Human Services, Public Health Service, Alcohol, Drug Abuse and Mental Health Administration.

Pares-Avila, J., Harrold, L., Ramos, R., & Gonzalez, A. 1990). HIV-related knowledge and attitudes among female prostitutes and sexual partners of IV drug users in San Juan and Juárez. *International Conference on AIDS, 6*(2), 410.

Pickerel, C. (1988). AIDS education in religious setting—a Catholic response. *The AIDS Challenge* (Prevention Education for Young People), 211–218.

Ramirez, J., Suarez, E., de la Rosa, G., Castro, M.A., & Zimmerman, M.A. (1994). AIDS knowledge and sexual behavior among Mexican gay and bisexual men. *AIDS Education Prevention, 6*(2), 163–174.

Rapkin, A.J. & Erickson, P.I. (1990). Differences in knowledge of and risk factors for AIDS between Hispanic and non-Hispanic women attending an urban family planning clinic. *AIDS, 4*(9), 889–899.

Rodriguez, J. & Ornelas, M. (1992). Gay Latino HIV prevention workshop series. *International Conference on AIDS, 8*(2), D443.

Romer, D., Black, M., Ricardo, I., Feigelman, S., Kaljee, L., Galbraith, J., Nesbit, R., Hornik, R., & Stanton, B. (1994). Social influence on the sexual behavior of youth at risk for HIV exposure. *American Journal of Public Health, 84,* 977–985.

Romien, I., Sandberg, S., Mohar, A., & Awerbuch, T. (1991). Modeling the AIDS epidemic in Mexico City. *Human Biology, 63*(5), 683–695.

Saunders, S.G., Helquist, M., Stein, J., & Coravano, K. (1989). Extending the role of AIDS hotlines in AIDS prevention programs in developed and developing countries. *International Conference on AIDS, 5,* 870.

Schilling, R.F., El-Bassel, N., Schinke, S.P., Gordon, K., & Nichols, S. (1991). Building skills of recovering women drug users to reduce heterosexual AIDS transmission. *Public Health Report, 106,* 297–304.

Schinke, S.P., Botvin, G.J., Orlandi, M.A., Schilling, R.F., & Gordon, A.N. (1990). African-American and Hispanic American adolescents, with HIV infection, and preventive intervention. *AIDS Education and Prevention, 2*(4), 305–312.

Seltzer, V.L. Rabin, J., & Benjamin, F. (1989). Teenagers' awareness of the acquired immunodeficiency Syndrome and the imact on their sexual behavior. *Journal of Obstetric Gynecology, 74* (1), 55–59.

Simon, P. & Sorvillo, F. (1993). Socioeconomic differences between native-born and immigrant Latinos with AIDS in Los Angeles county. *International Conference on AIDS, 9*(2), 879.

Smith, K.W., McGraw, S.A., Crawford, S.L., Costa, L.A., & McKinlay, J.B. (1993). HIV risk among Latino adolescents in two New England cities. *American Journal of Public Health, 83,* 1395–1399.

Stiffman, A.R., Earls, F., Dore, P., & Cunningham, R. (1992). Changes in acquired immunodeficiency syndrome-related risk experience concerning human immunodeficiency virus infection. *Pediatrics, 89* (5), 950–956.

Stine, G.J. (1995). *AIDS update 1994–1995: An annual overview of Acquired Immune Deficiency Syndrome.* Englewood Cliffs, NJ: Prentice Hall.

Trad, P.V. (1994). A developmental model for risk avoidance in adolescents confronting AIDS. *AIDS Education and Prevention, 6*(4), 322–338.

U.S.-Mexico Border Health Commission. (1994). *Committee on health and social impacts of increased trade along the border region: Recommendations for the 1994 border governors' conference.* Arizona-Mexico Border Health Foundation, The University of Arizona College of Medicine Rural Health Office, and The Arizona-Mexico Commission.

Valdespino, J. L., Garcia, M. L., Salcedo, R. A., & Magis, C. (1993). AIDS epidemic in Mexico: The result of socioepidemiological mosaicism. *International Conference on AIDS, 9*(2), 756.

Valdespino, J.L., Garcia, M.L., Loo, E., & Salcedo, R.A. (1992). HIV-1 and STD sentinel surveillance among homosexual men and female prostitutes in Mexico. *International Conference on AIDS, 8*(2), c253.

Young, P., Sowder, B., & Weissman, G. (1990). Risk factors among women IV and non-IV drug users in a national AIDS prevention program—U.S., Puerto Rico, and Mexico. *International Conference on AIDS, 6*(2), 267.

6 OUR BORDER ENVIRONMENT

PUBLIC HEALTH, PRACTICE, AND POLICY PERSPECTIVES

Michael D. Barnes, Carleton H. Morrison, Jr.,

and Kitty Richards

INTRODUCTION—NATURE OF THE BORDER

The border region faces an enormous challenge in attempting to protect the environment and health of its residents. Along the 2,000 miles of international border between the United States and Mexico, air and water pollution, illegal hazardous waste dumping, poverty, substandard housing, and increased infectious and other diseases are the norm. Unprecedented demographic growth and regional economic activity along the U.S.-Mexico border are placing stress on an environmental health system already overburdened with air and water pollution, waste management issues, water shortages, and their related public health problems. An estimated nine million people live along the 2,000-mile Mexico-United States border. By the year 2,003, population growth to nearly 10.5 million people is expected, with 45 percent projected to reside in Mexico, and 55 percent in the United States (Good Neighbor Environmental Board, 1995; Taylor, 1992). (Refer to the U.S.-Mexico border map at the frontispiece of this book.)

The border region is generally characterized by low incomes and corresponding inadequate infrastructure and services. In fact, a deficient investment in public works is cited as one reason why the environmental health situation may be worse in Mexico than the U.S. (Espinoza-Torres, Hernandez-Avila & Lopez-Carrillo, 1994). The number of persons living at or below the poverty line on the U.S. side of the border is nearly twice the national average (12.4 percent). Mirroring issues of poverty are the 1,200 colonias (unincorporated settlements that lack safe drinking water and adequate waste water treatment and solid waste disposal) scattered along the Texas, New Mexico, and Arizona borders with more than 250,000 residents. Many of these colonias lack adequate plumbing (13 percent in Texas, as compared to 5.4 percent in the U.S. overall) and add to the public health problems and diseases already associated with the environment. Many communities along the border, including colonias, have rates of gastrointestinal diseases (e.g., cholera, hepatitis A) that are significantly higher than anywhere in the United States, and are associated with human-waste-polluted water supplies through inadequate sewers. Toxic wastes, pesticides, and profound air quality problems are also glaring environmental health problems. Over the last 10 years there has been an explosion of industrial development in the border area, especially in Mexico, driven by the low wages for Mexican workers (and less-stringent and less-enforced environmental policies). Obviously a public health crisis exists along the border (Taylor, 1992, p. 55; Good Neighbor Environmental Board, 1995).

In addition to the unusual environmental conditions existing along the border, the border area also has an extremely mobile population due to the immigrant status and the migrant farm-work lifestyle of many residents. Because of this mobility, it is often difficult to identify potential population exposures resulting from existing environmental pollution. Also, because of the nature of exposure to toxic substances, it is often difficult to determine when a person may have been exposed to a particular contaminant. Frequently, adverse health effects resulting from an environmental exposure do not show up until long after the initial exposure. In addition, there are sometimes multiple exposures to contaminants across time periods. Therefore, it is difficult to track an illness to a specific exposure incident.

National and state political boundaries become extremely superficial when viewed from an environmental health perspective. Most of the natural or environmental resources such as surface water, ground water, air, and wildlife species are common pool resources, shared by more than one nation or state. Thus, to manage environmental health problems, binational, multi-state, multi-agency communication and coordination is crucial for progress to occur in the avoidance, management, or resolution of current and anticipated environmental problems along the border region (New Mexico Environment Department, 1994).

ENVIRONMENTAL HEALTH DEFINED

Environmental health is a term that is often used in two ways. First, it is used to represent the effects of environmental agents on human health. Second, it is used in regard to the health status of the environment. A combination of both views might be stated as the "pollution status of the environment and how ecological systems are withstanding the onslaught" (Hook, 1995, p. 2). The term "environmental health" creates a perspective of the interrelations and effects of toxic agents on human health and the toxicological status of the environment.

"Environmental health is that aspect of public health that is concerned with those forms of life, substances, forces, and conditions in the surroundings of man that may exert an influence on human health and well-being" (Graber & Johnson, 1995, p. 66). The U.S. Agency for International Development (USAID) views environmental health as "a branch of public health devoted to preventing illness through managing the environment and changing people's behavior to reduce exposure to biological and non-biological agents of disease and injury" (Murphy & Tomaro, 1995, p. 1). In essence, environmental health seeks to prevent disease agents from causing ill health by interrupting the production and transmission of these problem agents and reducing exposure to them, for example by destroying mosquito breeding sites (production), using more efficient stoves (transmission), and using bed nets to keep off mosquitoes (exposure) (Murphy & Tomaro, 1995). Thus, the ultimate goal of environmental health is to prevent needless morbidity and mortality by protecting people from unnecessary exposure to environmental hazards through epidemiological approaches (Schwartz & Corvalan, 1995).

Environmental Diseases and Health Risks along the Border

Human health and environmental quality are inextricably linked, and must be viewed as a high priority along the U.S.-Mexico border. "Public health concerns are heightened by the border region's demographic and economic characteristics, including the lack of planning for industrial and residential zones, difficulties in monitoring or tracking the spread of contagious diseases, the generally lower level of ability to pay for medical care, and the lack of basic water and wastewater treatment in many Mexican border communities and U.S. colonias" (Good Neighbor Environmental Board, 1995, p. 7).

More industrialized societies may generally view environmental health as ozone depletion and toxic wastes, and a less industrialized society may view environmental health as problems of water and sanitation. In less industrialized regions of the world the greatest health burden is infectious agents causing diarrheal diseases, cholera, malaria, and other vector-borne diseases such as dengue fever or onchocerciasis (Murphy & Tomaro, 1995). In more industrialized societies, noninfectious toxic agents from industrialized living create deleterious health effects that are often insidious in producing clinical effects over a period of time. The U.S.-Mexico border region, like that of India and central Mexico, faces a combination of both problems (Murphy & Tomaro, 1995).

Contaminants of Concern along the Border

All of the contaminants existing on the border can create adverse health effects for border residents if they come in contact with these compounds. Xylene, an aromatic hydrocarbon, can be dangerous to life and health. Exposure to xylene causes dizziness, drowsiness, and eye, nose, throat, and skin irritation. Nausea, vomiting, and abdominal pain can also occur. Exposure to heavy metals, such as lead, can adversely affect the gastrointestinal tract. Low levels of exposure to compounds such as xylene and lead may hinder a physician's diagnosis and treatment of gastrointestinal illnesses. This is especially true in environments where humans are exposed to multiple infectious, parasitic, and chemical agents, all of which cause, mimic, or enhance gastrointestinal disease. Neuromuscular symptoms of lead exposure include muscle weakness, pain, and cramping. Lead and other metals such as nickel and mercury can adversely affect the central and peripheral nervous systems. Chronic lead exposure can cause lead encephalopathy and degenerative brain disease (Rothwell, Hamilton & Leaverton, 1991; Shy, Greenburg & Winn, 1994).

Air pollutants such as carbon monoxide and ozone irritate eyes and the respiratory tract. Carbon monoxide also affects the central nervous systems, causing dizziness, headaches, sleep disturbances, and memory impairment. Tetrachloroethylene and trichloroethylene have also been discovered in border water samples. These compounds affect the respiratory and central nervous systems and can affect the liver and kidneys (Rothwell, Hamilton & Leaverton, 1991; Shy, Greenburg & Winn, 1994).

Only recently have professionals begun to study the range of health effects resulting from exposure to environmental agents. Unfortunately, only a small percentage of the thousands of commonly used chemicals have been tested for the ability to cause or promote cancer. Even fewer have been evaluated for effects on critical organs, such as the neurologic, immunologic, and reproductive systems. Sensitive toxicologic methods must be developed and validated for use in screening this huge backlog of substances and hundreds of new substances introduced each year. There are significant gaps in knowledge about exposures to environmental agents in both indoor and outdoor air, ground and surface water, in the atmosphere, in soils, wetlands, and in plants and animals (United States Department of Health and Human Services, 1990).

Health problems identified as having a relationship to border environmental pollutants include gastrointestinal diseases (cholera, shigella, amebiasis, salmonella, hepatitis A, B, and C); tuberculosis; respiratory diseases; multiple myeloma and systemic lupus erythematosus (SLE); zoonotic diseases (i.e., rabies); vector-borne diseases (i.e., dengue and malaria); occupational health exposures; childhood lead exposure from ceramics, candy wrappers, and toys; anencephalic births and other neural tube defects; and exposures to lead, arsenic, PCBs, pesticides, and other hazardous chemicals (Good Neighbor Environmental Board, 1995; Espinoza-Torres, Hernandez-Avila & Lopez-Carrillo, 1994).

THE BORDER'S "AT-RISK" POPULATIONS

Calderon and colleagues (1993) state that environmental inequities exist among minority populations in general. In their report from a national survey, they found that race is the single most important factor in locating toxic waste sites across the nation, and that microbial and chemical water contaminant exposure is greater than in non-minority counterparts. The environmental picture is no different among the large number of minority groups along the U.S.-Mexico border. Hispanics in general, and their children specifically, face a disproportionate risk of exposure to environmental hazards through (1) ambient air pollution, (2) worker exposure to chemicals, (3) indoor air pollution, and (4) poor drinking water quality. These environmental conditions are the four leading threats to the environmental health status of Hispanic populations along the border (Metzger, Delgado & Herrell, 1995).

Children are more uniquely vulnerable to environmental exposures in the air, water, food, their homes, and their schools than adults. "Pound for pound of body weight, children drink more water, eat more food, and breathe more air than adults" (Landrigan & Carlson, 1995). In fact, infants in their first six months consume seven times as much water per pound as average adults, and children one through five eat three to four times more food per pound than the average adult (Landrigan & Carlson, 1995). The obvious environmental health implication is that children will have substantially greater exposures pound for pound as compared to exposed adults. Children's hand-to-mouth behaviors and playing close to the ground (soil, carpets, etc.) only compound the risk of child environmental exposures. Another significant problem is that environmental risk assessments do not usually consider children's unique risks so that if regulations or other policy steps are taken to control risk, children's interests are often left out of the process (Landrigan & Carlson, 1995; Lubin & Lewis, 1995).

The following example shows children's health disparities as they exist between two border communities in Mexico and the United States. In Laredo, Texas, there were 75 infant deaths between 1980–1982 with an average of 7,951 births. In Nuevo Laredo, there were 567 deaths with 15,268 births during the same time period. Deaths occuring among persons 30 years of age or greater are seven times greater in Nuevo Laredo as compared to national rates. Over 180 of these deaths are attributed to bronchitis, pneumonia, infectious enteritis, and non-infectious gastroenteritis—environmentally related etiologies. Only two children died of these illnesses on the U.S. side of the border (Espinoza-Torres, Hernandez-Avila & Lopez-Carrillo, 1994). Thus as stated above, children of color are generally the most exposed and least protected from environmental health threats than all other children or populations along the border and in the United States (Mott, 1995; Landrigan & Carlson, 1995).

WATER POLLUTION: OUR GREATEST ENVIRONMENTAL CONCERN

The major factors affecting the environmental health of U.S.-Mexico border residents are water and air pollution, although hazardous/toxic waste, pesticide pollution, and other factors also contribute to serious environmental problems for humans. Air and water quality problems have been persistent along the U.S.-Mexico border, but in a recent poll of public health officials, 82 percent responded that safe drinking water was most important or a very important factor in increasing life expectancy and quality of life along both sides of the border (Metzger, Delgado, & Herrell, 1995). The growth of the populations along both sides of the border as well as the historic problems of building urban-area infrastructure have contributed to the negative environmental impacts on this region (Espinoza-Torres, Hernandez-Avila & Lopez-Carrillo, 1994).

The Tijuana and New rivers of California, the Colorado River of California and Arizona, and the Rio Grande River of New Mexico and Texas are polluted with sewage, pesticide runoff, and industrial discharge (Council on Scientific Affairs, 1990). The aquifers and streams flow across one international boundary and many state boundaries. For example, the Hueco Bolson located in southern Texas and southeastern New Mexico flows south into the country of Mexico. The Rio Grande, with tributaries of southern Colorado leading into it, flows across New Mexico, and enters Texas and Mexico. In fact, the Rio Grande acts as a boundary line between Mexico and Texas.

The Rio Grande Compact introduced water quantity delivery provisions, though at the time water quality restrictions were not a concern. In recent times, with the passage of the La Paz Agreement in 1983, the International Boundary and Water Commission introduced some water quality requirements in which the Rio Grande's water quality must be of a good quality for Mexico and Texas users. The aquifers of Mexico, New Mexico, and Texas flow in both southward and northward directions (Ellis, 1993).

As a result of the billions of gallons of waste water that are discharged to our streams and onto our lands, together with the millions of tons of solid and gaseous wastes that are discharged to the environment, the safety and quality of our water supplies are threatened in a manner not previously considered significant. Our water resources, more perhaps than any other, illustrate the interaction of all parts of the environment and particularly the recycling process that characterizes every resource of the ecosystem. Everything that we inject into the biosphere—chemical, biological, or physical—can ultimately find its way into the earth's water. These contaminants must be removed by nature or by technology before that water is again potable. It is easily recognized that, while it may vary in degree, there is a direct relationship between the water we waste and the water we drink. Water pollution can never be considered separately from water supply. (Calderon et al., 1993, p. 880)

The quantity, availability, and quality of water affects many facets of daily living, from health and hygiene to cultural lifestyles, occupation choices, and geographic locations. Three key water management issues can be classified by (1) quality (microbial, chemical, and physical characteristics), (2) quantity (availability of water supply), and (3) sewerage (water and waste removal) (Varady & Mack, 1995; Calderon et al., 1993). All three have inseparable connections to human health and public health concerns. In fact, "there can probably be no improvement in general health unless the more basic problems of the environment, sanitation, and safe drinking water are resolved" (Varady & Mack, 1995, p. 9).

Water Quality

Many health professionals recently have vocalized fear that binationally shared water supplies (rivers and relatively shallow aquifers) are increasingly threatened or contaminated by sewage and other wastes (dairies, mines, industrial operations) along much of the U.S.-Mexico border region (Cech & Essman, 1992; New Mexico Environment Department, 1994; Shields, 1991). More specifically, shallow water supply aquifers are increasingly subject to contamination from cesspools/septic tanks in rural areas along the border area because of inadequate installation and maintenance or other problems (Southwest Center for Environmental Research and Policy, 1991).

Currently, about 50 percent of the contamination in water wells in New Mexico is caused by poorly functioning septic tanks (New Mexico Environment Department, 1994). In New Mexico's three border counties, for example, nitrate contamination of ground water, generally due to dairy operations and improper disposal of domestic waste at individual homes, trailer parks, and small communities, is the leading water contaminant. Petroleum facilities caused ten water contamination sites, and pesticides and solvents have been found in three respective water contamination sites (New Mexico Environment Department, 1994).

In some areas of the border region, the waters that cross the boundary, or those that drain into or from international rivers, have inadequate sanitary conditions caused by wastewater that flows into these rivers. There is the related risk of pollution of transboundary ground waters if proper management and treatment of wastewater and hazardous waste are not carried out. The Rio Grande River is currently the recipient of raw sewage and industrial wastes along many portions, from both sides of the border. Mexico and the United States are concerned about the adverse public health and environmental impacts associated with pollution of transboundary water supplies. Such concern has been heightened by the approach of cholera, a waterborne intestinal disease. Among other factors, this disease has spread because of inadequate wastewater treatment in the border area. Both governments are closely monitoring the incidence of this disease.

Calderon and colleagues (1993) report that among minority populations, American Indians, Hispanics, and migrant farm workers (the majority of these workers are either Hispanic or Native American) are exposed to much higher rates of gastrointestinal diseases and diarrheal diseases due to the poor microbial quality of water and the lack of adequate facilities that maintain adequate water quality. Coincidentally, these populations and disease conditions abound significantly along the U.S.-Mexico border region.

Colonias Threaten Border Water Quality

Another of the greatest threats to U.S.-Mexico residents, primarily among the poorest of Hispanics, is the existence of shanty developments called "colonias." Most colonias originated in the early 1950s when developers began creating subdivisions outside city boundaries. There are approximately 1,200 unincorporated subdivisions found in Texas, New Mexico, and Arizona. For example, Texas has over 800 separate colonias with over 200,000 persons living in them, but only three (less than 1 percent) have public sewage disposal systems; and only 7 percent of New Mexico's colonias (40,000 residents) are served by sewer systems (Metzger, Delgado & Herrell, 1995; New Mexico Environment Department, 1994; Good Neighbor Environmental Board, 1995). Approximately 20 percent of the colonias in New Mexico have no water systems (New Mexico Environment Department, 1994). These colonias are characterized by the absence of adequate sewage treatment, the lack of safe drinking water, substandard housing, inadequate roads and drainage, and inadequate environmental infrastructure—if such systems exist at all. This lack of safe potable water and lack of adequate sanitation is reported to be partially responsible for the threefold increase in the rates of waterborne diseases (typhoid, cholera, and dysentery) and hepatitis A in Texas and New Mexico (Calderon et al., 1993). These types of outbreaks in colonias are considered "third world diseases" since these waterborne afflictions are rare occurrences in the rest of the United States (Metzger, Delgado & Herrell, 1995). Finally, due to the implementation of the North America Free Trade Agreement (NAFTA) and the economic incentives promoted by such activities, environmental and public health officials anticipate greater numbers of persons immigrating to colonias, and thus increasingly serious public health problems are expected (Good Neighbor Environmental Board, 1995).

Housing developments similar to colonias have also emerged in Arizona and California. In Arizona, lots are often split into three parcels (the maximum allowed by state law) and then subdivided further, creating unregulated developments. These developments are similar to colonias with respect to their lack of a potable water supply, although the sewage systems of individual housing units must be approved by state authorities in Arizona. In areas of California, such as San Diego, the lack of affordable housing for legal and illegal immigrants has resulted in the unauthorized occupation of land owned by others. Such "settlements" in California are not, therefore, like the Texas and New Mexico colonias in which unincorporated subdivisions are built on parcels of land that are reportedly subleased. However, they are characterized by the presence of little or no shelter, water, or sewage facilities (Environmental Protection Agency [EPA], 1992b).

Migrant Farm Work Camps and Water Pollution

The residents of migrant labor camps face health threats similar to those of colonias, but they also contend with biological and chemical contamination of water supplies. Based on sketchy and anecdotal evidence many professionals anticipate that serious drinking water quality problems are a persistent part of the migrant farm worker's life. Additionally, agricultural workers may be exposed to pesticides in the fields where they work and also expose their children to these chemicals through tainted clothing or harvested foods taken home after each working day (Metzger, Delgado & Herrell, 1995).

Water Quantity

Maintaining or improving water quality is vital to improving environmental health along the border, but a quality-only discussion that does not include water quantity issues in the arid Southwest would be significantly shortsighted. Water is being drawn from the ground at a rate faster than rain can replenish most areas of the arid desert of the U.S.-Mexico border region. In fact, the annual recharge is estimated to be only 5 percent of what is being drawn from these underground aquifers (Cech & Essman, 1992). Additionally, overgrazing is widespread on both sides of the border, so that when it rains, the soil erodes downstream, and so the rain cannot soak into the compacted earth to replenish the groundwater aquifers (Steffans, 1994). The lack of available water not only affects the quality of water, but also directly affects daily living practices such as standards of hygiene and cleanliness, which all have a direct effect on health (Calderon et al., 1993). Unfortunately, water quantity problems have led to water quality tradeoffs in the border region. Among Navajo communities along the Puerco River, industrial development and population expansion led these communities to decide to trade off water quality in order to have enough water to meet their basic needs. This tradeoff has threatened to contaminate the sole sources of water that are used for drinking, watering livestock, and irrigation (Calderon et al., 1993). In the Nogales and Sonora area, chronic water shortages seriously compromise household sanitation and personal hygiene. These hygiene issues have led to a number of health problems, most notably gastrointestinal diseases and parasitic infestations. Such water shortages may also affect community members' (usually the very poor) health in another way by causing water users to seek substitutes for household water delivery. These practices often result in microorganism or chemical contamination from the vessels used for storage or transfer (e.g., 55-gallon drums scavenged from local industries) (Varady & Mack, 1995).

Improvements in both water supply and sanitation systems in developing countries (not unlike many areas along the U.S.-Mexico border) found a reduction of diarrheal morbidity by 25 percent, and even greater reductions (60 percent) in mortality from diarrheal diseases (Varady & Mack, 1995). These results are especially relevant to the border region since Varady and Mack (1995) observed that "gastrointestinal diseases are among the leading causes of morbidity and mortality" (p. 13).

Sewerage/Wastewater Treatment

The quantity and quality of water can easily become jeopardized when appropriate attention is not given to sewerage and wastewater treatment issues. Sewerage, as opposed to sewage (liquid and solid waste), is a system for the removal of sewage, and implies the collection and removal of waste.

The issue of water protection from sewage and other wastes also has not been addressed aggressively. In some border areas, waters that cross the border or flow into rivers that form the international boundary between Mexico and the United States may be unsanitary because of wastewater discharges into these water bodies. Inadequate management and treatment of wastewater and industrial wastes also pose a risk to transboundary ground water resources (EPA, 1992b).

The urgency of maintaining adequate sewerage and wastewater treatment infrastructure and practices is that fecal coliform (resulting from human sewage polluting drinking water) are observable in several shared aquifers between metropolitan areas along the U.S.-Mexico border (i.e., Tijuana-San Diego; El Paso-Juárez; and Brownsville-Matamoros). As discussed earlier, fecal coliform in drinking water is responsible for a host of gastrointestinal diseases and corresponding increased morbidity and mortality rates. Groundwater pollution is equally if not more troublesome than surface water sources for sewage-contamination. Obviously, the amount of exposable water is usually much greater in groundwater sources (aquifers) as compared to surface water sources. In any event, sewage-contaminated water can spread parasites, including pathogenic bacteria, protozoa, gastrointestinal helminths, and enteric viruses. Gastrointestinal disease is the leading cause of death in the six Mexican border states among children. On the U.S. side in the El Paso area, the rate of hepatitis A was 18.3/100,000 compared with 9.7/100,000 for the United States on the whole. The unspecified hepatitis rate was 13.3/100,000 compared with 2.0/100,000 for the United States as a whole. Type A hepatitis and likely non-A and non-B are transmitted by water and sewage. The problem on both sides of the border is real (Cech & Essman, 1992).

Local health officials in the El Paso area reported in one border community that by age 8, approximately 35 percent had been infected with hepatitis A, and by age 35, 85–90 percent of the residents had been infected. The frightening reality is that these are only the reported (known) cases (Cech & Essman, 1992). A Mexican study in the Mezquital Valley sought to determine the health problems associated with irrigating fodder and cereal crops with sewage-contaminated surface water. Exposed children (children who consumed produce grown from sewage-contaminated water) were at as much as twice the risk for diarrheal diseases as compared to children in control groups who were not exposed to produce grown from sewage-contaminated water (Cifuentes et al., 1993).

Water quality and health concerns along the Mexican side of the border are extensive problems. In the border area of Mexico, 85.5 percent of communities have potable water, 68.1 percent have some sewage disposal, and 90.1 percent have electricity. Three factors increase the health risks of contaminated water along the border in Mexico (and throughout Mexico): (1) open ditch sewers in the streets of some cities that contain not only sewage, but also high levels of volatile toxic residues; (2) the lack of a domestic water supply that necessitates residents storing their water inadequately in tanks; and (3) the inadequate or nonexistent wastewater treatment facilities and infrastructure (Espinoza-Torres, Hernandez-Avila & Lopez-Carrillo, 1994).

Wastewater being discharged into rivers, canals, and streams (including the Gulf of Mexico and Pacific Ocean) is not treated for the most part in Mexico. In Tijuana for example, industrial wastes that include untreated wastewater (e.g., sewage) have forced a quarantine of the Mexican and U.S. beaches. The aquatic ecosystems in the Tijuana estuary also have been damaged. In Nuevo Laredo, as another example, 27 million gallons a day of untreated wastewater are discharged in the Rio Bravo (Rio Grande). It contains high levels of mercury and aluminum, as well as a high level of fecal contamination. This has limited the use of the river for drinking water. However, the water is used for irrigation purposes, and 60 kilometers downstream for drinking water, thus causing serious potential health risks in the area. Yet another example is that Ciudad Juárez (home of over 1,000,000 residents) has no wastewater treatment at all. Wastewater is discharged into the Rio Bravo (Rio Grande). Furthermore, industrial wastes from maquiladoras (U.S.-owned industries within the Mexican border) and other industries are virtually unmonitored by the Mexican government. The industrial discharge contains lead, mercury, nickel, chrome, and other metals. It is estimated that up to 40 percent of the maquiladoras in the area illegally discharge their dangerous wastes into the nearby river or canals (Espinoza-Torres, Hernandez-Avila & Lopez-Carrillo, 1994).

Thus, there is a direct relationship between the water we waste and the water we drink. Water pollution can never be considered separately from the quantity and quality of a community's water supply.

AIR POLLUTION ALONG THE BORDER

Air pollution problems, the second most-cited factor affecting the environmental health of U.S.-Mexico border residents, are most severe in major metropolitan areas along the border. The sister cities of these areas suffer from poor air quality because of the shared airshed. Traffic congestion, compounded by long border crossing waits, adds to vehicle emissions. The main air pollutants in these major metropolitan areas along both sides of the border are carbon monoxide, nitrogen oxide, ozone, and particulate matter (Espinoza-Torres, Hernandez-Avila & Lopez-Carrillo, 1994). El Paso and Ciudad Juárez, for example, share an airshed where meteorologic conditions often fail to sweep the atmosphere of pollutants. El Paso regularly fails to meet EPA ozone, carbon monoxide, and inhalable particulate standards from within its own U.S. boundary, and increasingly fails such air quality standards from the larger and more polluted neighboring city, Ciudad Juárez, Mexico. Thus, like water, air pollution knows no boundaries.

The levels of U.S. criteria air pollutants (ozone, carbon monoxide, particulate matter less than 10 microns [PM-10], nitrogen dioxide, sulphur dioxide, and lead) are monitored in several of the larger U.S. border area communities. U.S. border communities currently not attaining one or more of the pollutant standards include San Diego (ozone, carbon monoxide); Imperial County (PM-10); El Paso County (ozone, carbon monoxide, PM-10); and Yuma, Pima, Santa Cruz, and Cochise counties, Arizona (PM-10) (EPA, 1992b).

In spite of the formation of many groups and agencies over the past 100 years, the public and environmental health along the border continues to deteriorate. As mentioned earlier, this is a result of uncontrolled air and water pollution, and the lack of appropriate disease vector control. As a result, the future health and economic vitality on both sides of the border is increasingly in jeopardy (Council on Scientific Affairs, 1990).

PESTICIDE POLLUTION AND EXPOSURE ALONG THE BORDER

Chronic effects in pesticide-exposed populations include cancer, birth defects, neurotoxicity, and adverse effects on reproduction and fertility. Most farm workers have chronic exposure to low levels of many different pesticides over a lifetime. The extent and magnitude of health problems from occupational and environmental exposure to pesticides is not known because few such studies have been performed.

Recent epidemiological studies suggest an increased risk of cancer in humans who are occupationally and environmentally exposed to pesticides. There are reports of statistically significant increased risks for lymphoma, leukemia, multiple myeloma, liver cancer, testicle cancer, brain cancer, and lung cancer in those exposed to pesticides. In addition, several men working in pesticide chemical companies discovered they were not capable of fathering children. Sperm tests showed them to be either completely lacking in sperm or as having sperm counts of less than 20 million. The fumigant

1,1-Dibromo,3-Choloropropane was found responsible for the sterility. A California study showed that birth defects, the leading cause of infant mortality, are highly prevalent among agricultural farm workers' infants, in particular limb reduction defects. Pesticide-induced delayed neuropathy has been attributed to organophosphate pesticides, causing long and large diameter fibers in the spinal cord and peripheral nervous system. Onset is typically two to four weeks after the acute exposure. Other studies have shown that organophosphate pesticides can cause profound mental and psychological changes resulting in acute psychosis in previously stable patients. Other behavioral changes include anxiety, difficulties in concentration, memory deficits, and other effects.

One area of concern for importing produce from Mexico into the United States is that differences in the use of agricultural chemicals in Mexico may result in higher levels of pesticide residues than are permitted on crops produced and sold in the United States (Vandermeer, 1993).

Control over pesticides is important to the border area where their use may create health or environmental problems if there is worker exposure or contamination of air or water. Both the Mexican and U.S. agricultural growers use significant quantities of pesticides in the production of fruits and vegetables. Generally, the pesticides used in both countries are the same or at least closely related. One major difference is that there are a few pesticides used in Mexico that do not have the same registered agricultural uses in the United States, although they are most often USDA- or FDA-approved for other food uses in the United States. Officials from Mexico and the United States have met to begin a project to identify Mexican or U.S. pesticide uses that do not have corresponding tolerances in the two countries, and to determine whether alternative pesticides with appropriate tolerances could be substituted or new tolerance levels developed (EPA, 1992b).

Hazardous/Toxic Waste along the Border

According to the Environmental Protection Agency (EPA), toxic pollutants are one of today's most serious emerging problems. Despite low concentrations, toxic chemicals emitted into the air may have short-term and long-term effects on health. More than 300 chemicals released by manufacturers into the air, soil, and water are tracked by the EPA Toxic Chemical Release Inventory. Once released, toxic substances are available for human intake (EPA, 1992a).

Historically, hazardous waste dump sites have been a serious problem for the U.S.-Mexico border region. Yet the practice is expected to continue and possibly increase since more than 32 million tons of toxic waste are produced annually by 150 industrial facilities in the border region (Good Neighbor Environmental Board, 1995). Examples of mishandling include unauthorized disposal of many types of hazardous wastes in abandoned dump yard or sites, in river beds, or estuaries. The control and management of transportation and disposal of toxic and hazardous substances is crucial for short-term and long-term environmental health practices since inappropriate handling and disposal of these substances often have long-lasting health implications (Serrano, 1995; Good Neighbor Environmental Board, 1995).

ECONOMIC GROWTH AND INDUSTRIALIZATION: THREATS TO THE BORDER ENVIRONMENT?

"Good economic policy protects the environment and good environmental policy strengthens the economy" (Worrest, 1994, p. 2). Economic development should not be detrimental to the environment or human health (Espinoza-Torres, Hernandez-Avila & Lopez-Carrillo, 1994). The issue of trade to boost binational economies is not should we or should we not, but rather, how do we conduct such commerce without jeopardizing the environment and health of populations along the border (Cech & Essman, 1992).

Besides just the commercial aspects, NAFTA affects the economic, social, and cultural lives of Mexico, Canada, and the U.S. (Espinoza-Torres, Hernandez-Avila & Lopez-Carrillo, 1994). The environmental health aspects have received great attention in all three countries. In all three there is manifested the preoccupation with reducing the environmental and health dangers. However, it is logical to suppose that Mexico will experience a greater impact from NAFTA than the other countries since it will require the most changes to meet the new environmental challenges and opportunities (Espinoza-Torres, Hernandez-Avila & Lopez-Carrillo, 1994).

Critics of NAFTA continue to argue that existing environmental contamination problems along the U.S.-Mexico border will only be increased and exacerbated unless the environment, economy, and physical welfare of people on both sides of the border are equally addressed. These critics propose that NAFTA will accomplish the goal of freer trade and economic prosperity for certain industries, but it will also increase the already present serious environmental problems that exist along both sides of the border. "No free trade economic program will ultimately succeed without protecting the environment and citizen health, because sooner or later, unaddressed environmental and health problems become economic problems—as already evidenced in the border region" (Taylor, 1992, p. 50).

The competitive system of industrial development and the doctrine of private property, while fueling economic growth unparalleled in history, have diminished the quality of life and increased the health threats to those persons having little private property or having property of low market value. To those areas of low market value and communities with little wealth have come the processes and industries that seek minimum investment in order to compete. Unfortunately for the residents, many of the industries tend to be those with greater amounts of environmental liabilities. The resultant inequities constitute a justifiable and timely concern for agencies mandated to protect the environmental health of all citizens (New Mexico Environment Department, 1994).

Many sources document that environmental liabilities and threats to health from environmental factors are unevenly distributed among the members of society; people of color and the poor inherit a disproportionate amount of the environmental price of industrialized growth. The growing disparity between the general populace and those living in substandard border areas demonstrates that all border states are not immune to this occurrence. Making efforts to address this problem by increasing public outreach, increasing a proactive assessment of environmental impacts, and promoting greater access to the political/regulatory process for those entities affected by these disparities are important (New Mexico Environment Department, 1994).

INDUSTRIALIZATION THROUGH BORDER MAQUILADORAS

U.S. companies, from Fortune 500 giants to small entrepreneurs, began relocating to the northern Mexico border region to cut costs 30 years ago (1965) under a program called maquiladora (from an ancient tradition of trading raw for finished goods), after the United States cancelled the Bracero program in which Mexicans could enter the United States to work because of the scarcity of the labor force created by WWII. Most of the population increase in Mexico along its northern border is due to growth of maquiladora plants. Mexico created this program to attract business that could introduce capital, raw materials, and other components without paying taxes, while also having to pay much lower wages for Mexican employees. After production and assembly of these materials, they were exported to the U.S., with companies paying only the tax for increased valuation resulting from the Mexican labor (Espinoza-Torres, Hernandez-Avila & Lopez-Carrillo, 1994).

Over a 10-year period of time, Mexico experienced a 16 percent increase in plants and workers, while the U.S. has experienced only a 2 percent increase on its side of the border. Maquiladoras are the second most important external source of resources for Mexico. In 1991 there were 1,739 plants and 380,000 workers, with half the plants (977) in Tijuana and

Ciudad Juárez, employing 265,000 workers. Two of three workers in maquiladoras are women in Mexico, while in non-maquila Mexican industries, only 28 percent of the work force is female. However, lately the demand for workers has surpassed the supply so the number of male workers has increased nearly 140 percent from 56,000 in 1986 to 133,500 in 1989. Men are employed mostly in metal and wood industries. Women are employed mainly in electronics companies, with corresponding poor effects on the reproductive and infant health of these female workers (Espinoza-Torres, Hernandez-Avila & Lopez-Carrillo, 1994).

Today, many American-owned maquiladora factories in Mexico are fouling the environment while their workers are still not prospering (Satchell, 1991). Economic benefit, however, appears to be directed primarily to the owners and operators of these facilities, with the environment and Mexican workers least benefited. The larger, U.S.-owned plants have the greater health and environmental risk because of the nature of the maquiladora industries along the border (Espinoza-Torres, Hernandez-Avila & Lopez-Carrillo, 1994). The price to be paid on the U.S. side of the border is that as the Mexican-based firms (both U.S.- and Mexican-owned) continue to be able to operate beyond the limits of the EPA, U.S. industries and communities will be accountable to correct these pollution excesses. As a result they are contributing to the pollution produced along the border to a greater extent than they would if they operated in the U.S. under more strict and expensive environmental requirements (Satchell, 1991).

Maquiladoras (multinational industrial and commercial plants) continue to flourish along the border in Mexico and perpetuate environmental and occupational health problems, as evidenced by local newspaper briefs (Moure-Eraso et al., 1994, p. 315):

Two waste haulers indicted for transporting toxic wastes from California to Tijuana (*Los Angeles Times*, 5/11/90).

Furniture manufacturers in Southern California planning to leave for Mexico in anticipation of the new U.S. Clean Air Act requirements (*Los Angeles Times,* 5/14/90).

Dr. Isabel de la O. Alonso has identified 20 retarded children whose mothers worked with toxic chemicals at Mallory Capacitators, a closed maquiladora in Matamoros, Mexico (*The Buffalo News*, 3/11/87).

A 1988 survey of maquiladora managers in Agua Prieta (Mexico) showed that none had ever seen an environmental health inspector (*Wall Street Journal*, 9/22/89).

A fire at a Deltronics plant that supplies parts to General Motors sends 76 workers to a hospital emergency room in Matamoros, some from smoke inhalation, others panicked by the fear of toxic chemicals (*Brownsville Herald and El Bravo*, 5/29/90).

Some of the most explosive maquiladora growth occurred in border areas proximate to New Mexico. Ciudad Juárez and surrounding communities, for example, experienced the most intensive development of the maquiladora industry in terms of employment of any city in Mexico. The city's population nearly doubled during the 1980s. A similar although less dramatic pattern of growth occurred in the counties of El Paso, Texas, and Doña Ana, New Mexico. The overall average annual rate of growth of employment during 1980–1988 in New Mexico's three border counties (Doña Ana, Luna, Hidalgo) exceeded that experienced in the comparably situated counties of the other three U.S. border states (Texas, California, Arizona) (New Mexico Environment Department, 1994).

Present working conditions in one of the most active maquiladora areas along the U.S.-Mexico border are expressed by Moure-Eraso and colleagues (1994) as "reminiscent of nineteenth-century U.S. sweatshops" (p. 311). Environmentally related occupational health concerns are also of significant concern in many maquiladoras along the Mexican border. They include inadequate lighting and ventilation, little or no education or job training (resulting in greater incidence of inappropriate toxic exposures or accidents), excessive noise levels, lack of hygiene and security measures, deficient rest periods, microscopic particles (montaje) in the air after long periods of time, exposure to toxic and dangerous substances (three main types of toxic substances include solvents, acidic and alkaline substances, and heavy metals), and insufficient information about the toxicity of the materials with which the laborers work (Espinoza-Torres, Hernandez-Avila & Lopez-Carrillo, 1994). Sanford Lewis characterizes the border area as "a 2,000 mile-long Love Canal" as a result of maquiladora contamination (Taylor, 1992, p. 59). Taylor (1992) further characterizes these industrial facilities as an immediate public health threat to Mexican citizens. These threats are clearly visualized when the downstream effluent (chemical wastes and sewage) from many of these maquiladoras flows along Mexican streets in open canals near people's homes, where children play and fish and from which livestock and agricultural products are nourished and raised (Taylor,

1992). The conclusion is that, even with economic, social, and environmental differences, there needs to be an integrated plan to deal with these public health and environmental health issues along the border.

SHARED ACCOUNTABILITY AND RESPONSIBILITY FOR BOTH NATIONS NEEDED FOR ECONOMIC GROWTH

The brunt of the blame for environmental problems of the maquiladoras and other environmental polluters is often most directed at the Mexican government. However, as is often the case, responsibility for solutions and environmental accountability should be a shared, cooperative venture. Many of Mexico's environmental rules exist and are similar to, and sometimes more stringent than, those of the United States, but they lack enforcement by SEDUE (Mexico's environmental protection agency) (Taylor, 1992).

Mexican government officials report that "we won't let our current economic situation lower our standards," and "Mexico has one of the strictest sets of norms and standards in the world. The trouble is we lack the capacity to enforce them. We must stop cheating ourselves about what we can do and what we can afford to do" (Mader, 1995a, p. 1). Thus, Mexico reports "no intention of going backward in environmental regulations, but that it may slow down its schedule of environmental improvements" (Mader, 1995a, p. 1).

Many groups have recently voiced fears that U.S. border citizens will experience downgraded environmental and health standards because of the U.S. government. Unfortunately a mechanism is in place to weaken environmental standards in certain sections of the U.S. border region. According to Taylor (1992), Section 179B of the 1990 Clean Air Act Amendment allows lower health protection for U.S. citizens to "protect" these communities from economic sanctions due to environmental violations. For example, when the border city "El Paso is declared non-attainment and has taken steps to reduce emissions under federal mandates but pollution from across the border affects its ability to comply, it does not have to invoke additional clean air programs as would other U.S. cities with similar pollution" (p. 58). While this exemption may help El Paso avoid economic sanctions and avoid additional pollution control costs, it promotes a precedent that the health of its citizens takes a back seat to the "uncontrollable" pollution from Mexico. A more favorable solution to this dilemma is to enforce more stringent pollution-control standards that take into consideration the citizens' health along both sides of the border (Taylor, 1992).

Significant border environmental health findings and recommendations were developed by the Good Neighbor Environmental Board (non-partisan) to advise the President of the United States and the U.S. Congress concerning environmental needs of the states contiguous to Mexico. The following select results were recommended for the development and implementation of border environmental programs (Good Neighbor Environmental Board, 1995, p. 2).

Findings:

- Border environmental issues are not separate from such topics as preservation of natural resources, health, housing, and transportation.
- A long-term, comprehensive, integrated, and binational approach is the only satisfactory approach to developing a sustainable environment and viable economy in the border region.
- Border environmental issues involve both sides of the border and can only be solved through binational cooperation on federal, state, and local levels.
- Emphasis on pollution prevention is crucial to minimize long-term degradation to the environment and the economy of the region.
- Community capacity-building is the key to sustaining efforts to resolve binational and community-specific environmental problems.
- Increased coordination among all governmental levels is needed to effectively use limited public resources.
- Promoting public-private partnerships encourages the most cost-effective uses of limited resources and can create incentives for private sector compliance and cooperation.
- Native American community representatives must be included in planning efforts to ensure equity in allocation of funds, projects, and other resources.
- Binational cooperation requires that local communities and state agencies have access to reliable planning data.

Recommendations:

- Focusing on pollution prevention, remediation, public health, and infrastructure development through greater community input, and improved federal and state programs and resources coordination.
- The United States (and Mexico) should focus on the water and wastewater sectors as most critical for improving environmental quality,

public health, and standards of living on both sides of the border. Specifically, expanded funding for wastewater treatment facilities and sewer lines, and drinking water treatment construction needs.

- Infrastructure efforts should be focused on colonias and small communities to ensure that the poorest neighborhoods have the necessary infrastructure to profit from increased economic opportunities through trade agreements.
- Improved notification and monitoring processes for cross-border transportation of hazardous materials.
- U.S. federal agencies need to establish more effective collaboration with their Mexican counterparts to focus on the unique public health needs along the border.
- Community-based, electronic, binational, environmental and health surveillance systems should be strengthened and expanded to strengthen and link preventative interventions to environmental border needs. Training is especially needed in surveillance, epidemiology, and environmental health.
- The train-the-trainer format is recommended to develop and empower leaders who can train others to build the much-needed local capacity required to address environmental health issues on an ongoing basis. "The promotora concept, used on both sides of the border, shows considerable promise in training local community leaders to teach others and in developing community-based expertise and leadership." (p. 9)

Therefore, the border environmental health efforts must emphasize not only environmental issues, but also other topics that affect healthy living (a more holistic public health view) and involve comprehensive, integrated efforts between nations, contiguous states, and local communities. Traditional public health efforts that involve community development and capacity-building are important to long-term success, and must also involve more emphasis on prevention and education. Improved coordination and partnerships between agencies and groups are also important for built-in incentives, compliance, and cooperation.

Coordinated monitoring and health surveillance should have as their aim to link preventative interventions to border environmental needs. Finally, a train-the-trainer model of empowering local key persons with the capacity to address their own local needs on an ongoing basis is essential.

Public Health's Emerging Roles in Environmental Health
Recently, there has been growing concern that current national policies are

not adequately addressing the most important risks to the environment and public health. According to Burke, Shalauta, and Tran (1995), there has been a steady decline in public health agencies' role in environmental protection over the last 25 years because of the establishment of the Environmental Protection Agency and the subsequent proliferation of related federal and state agencies. Fragmented responsibility, a lack of coordination, and inadequate attention to public health dimensions account for much of the effect we see today. Furthermore, funding priorities are now allocated primarily for enforcement, monitoring, and cleanup activities, with very little aimed at evaluating and preventing adverse public health impacts (Burke, Shalauta & Tran, 1995).

An ongoing dilemma making the connection between environmental pollutants and ill health is the lack of systematic, binational environmental studies on health. The current animal study experiments (i.e., rats exposed to toxins and tested for incidence of cancer) and the risk assessment approach have been criticized recently for their narrowness in scope. Public health's environmental epidemiology is claimed to show great promise to correct this problem. However, in the meantime, quantifying the different sources of pollution that contribute to exposing border residents to environmental risks is difficult since the existing data are highly variable in quality and character. This problem is serious for the border since existing undocumented and unabated problems could translate into economic losses through poorer health, fewer jobs, and a degenerating and depleted environment (Worrest, 1994).

Burke, Shalauta, and Tran (1995, p. 80) outline in Table 6.1 how the current risk assessment approach may not be ideal for current environmental health needs along the border as compared to the public health approach. In fact, risk assessments often are limiting and contrary to public health practices. For example, public health focuses more on public-based, grass-roots intervention, while traditional risk assessments focus on a specific pollutant and are top-down oriented with the development of regulations and permits. Burke and colleagues (1995) argue that incorporating more public health perspectives will aid in successfully making short-term and long-term environmental health decisions. Thus, cooperation between the two entities is necessary and potentially very beneficial. Finally, the community focus of public health is a natural mechanism for improving public participation and buy-in to specific environmental health activities (Burke, Shalauta & Tran, 1995; Graber & Johnson, 1995).

Therefore, based on current border recommendations and the suggestions of environmental health specialists, environmental health strategies

TABLE 6.1. Comparison of the Risk Assessment and Public Health Approaches. Goal: The Protection of Public Health

	Risk Assessment	Public Health
Driver:	single hazard	population health impact
Approach:	pollutant-specific	population-based assessment
Process:	hazard ID dose response exposure assessment risk characterization risk management	policy-development assurance
Health Endpoint:	limited (cancer)	diverse/multiple
Tools:	toxicology, modeling	epidemiology, surveillance
Agencies:	federal/state	local/community
Outputs:	standards/regulations	intervention strategies
Actions:	permits, enforcement, monitoring	outreach, screening, treatment
Solution:	high tech/pollutant-specific	low tech/broad-based
Public Values:	no mechanism for inclusion	essential part of intervention strategy
Decision-making:	top-down	bottom-up (grass-roots)
Success:	regulatory compliance	improvement in health-related outcome

Modified from Burke, T.A., Shalauta, N.M., & Tran, N.L. (1995). Strengthening the role of public health in environmental policy. *Policy Studies Journal, 23*(1), 76–84.

along the U.S.-Mexico border could be strengthened, longer lasting, and more effective if a better integration of public health-oriented strategies were implemented with those that currently exist.

Example of Strategies Needed for Border Environmental Health Assessment

A discussion of the complexity and process of performing an environmental health assessment for the Nogales, Arizona, and Nogales, Sonora (Mexico), border population will aid environmental health professionals in performing such assessments. A description of geological, environmental, and health conditions is an important variable for any community in an environmental health assessment. Thus, the following paragraphs will serve as a literal example of select items that may require consideration for a comprehensive environmental health assessment.

Nogales-Nogales are twin cities located on the Arizona-Mexico border. The issues of concern include a landfill located in Nogales, Sonora, and illegal sewage disposal resulting in a contaminated wash that runs north through Nogales, Arizona. A recent study of the area suggests a lupus (a type of cancer) cluster existing in Nogales, Arizona. The hydrology of the region is quite complex, with the underlying aquifer flowing from Nogales, Sonora, north toward Nogales, Arizona. The chemicals existing in the ground water are above Environmental Protection Agency maximum contaminant levels and consist of the following: nitrate, trichloroethylene, and tetrachloroethylene (Varady & Mack, 1995).

Residents of Nogales, Sonora, live near a dump known for catching fire and spouting plumes of noxious white smoke. Most of the residents purchase their drinking water from a well source that rests below an abandoned plating shop named "La Tomatera." Metals from the shop, particularly chromium, leach into the well and contaminate the area surrounding the shop. Effluent from the Nogales dump and a local maquiladora park drains into the Nogales Wash. Currently, streets and neighborhoods surrounding the Nogales Wash area are partitioned off to prevent the effects of flash flooding during the monsoon season. Several studies indicate this waterway is heavily polluted.

> The Nogales Wash, which flows north from Mexico into the United States, regularly contains such toxins as mercury, nitrates, lead, and cyanide. So contaminated is the waterway that in 1991 it exploded, lighting a city block on fire in Nogales, Sonora. . . . Water testing has revealed the existence of a ten-mile underground plume of chemical

contamination flowing north into Arizona. (Varady & Mack, 1995, p. 11)

Prior analyses of Nogales' air and water samples indicate the presence of trichlorethylene and tetrachloroethylene. Residents suspect the chemicals come from solvents found in the local electronics manufacturing industry and disposed of improperly. In addition, improperly treated sewage also flows north along the Wash in Nogales. Downstream in Arizona, the hepatitis A rate is estimated to be 20 times the United States national average. In addition, an investigation of death certificates for Arizona residents suggests the local death rate from cancer is twice the national average. Aside from the Nogales-specific elements for conducting an environmental health assessment, a generic process will be described below to further aid environmental specialists in conducting environmental health assessments.

Environmental Health Assessment Process

Environmental health assessments should include a site evaluation of communities in question (as outlined above in the Nogales-Nogales example), including information on community health concerns and demographic data as well as land use information (to determine the potential routes for environmental contaminant exposure and potential health outcomes). Oftentimes, aerial photography is useful in determining historical land use patterns. In addition, the U.S. Census Bureau provides digitized tiger line files that provide a wealth of demographic data by tract, block, and sub-block designations.

An environmental health assessment must include key environmental contaminants existing in the community, and a review and evaluation of existing sample-analysis data results. The data results should be compared with both health advisory levels and background sample analysis data. Researching community health concerns (perceptions), human exposures, and cumulative risks is important to evaluate the public health impact associated with environmental hazards. Exposure pathways can be determined by identifying sources of contamination, ease of contamination rate and transport, physical properties of the contaminant of concern, and potential points of exposure, for example, food, air, soil, and/or water. Finally, toxicological information, health outcome data, and community health concerns must be evaluated (Aldrich & Leaverton, 1993).

Data gathering for environmental health assessments involves either or both the epidemiological approach (public-health model) and the traditional hazard-driven risk assessment. An epidemiological approach to environmental health, rather than the hazard-driven risk assessment, will involve a larger context of disease prevention and public health concerns. According to Silbergeld (1994), the environmental epidemiological approach would evaluate such concerns as "What are the major types of diseases or disabilities in the U.S. population for which environmental factors could reasonably be proposed as significant or important causes or contributing factors?" (p. 4). Risk assessments would instead be concerned with identifying and characterizing a pollutant for its potential to cause harm.

Environmental epidemiological studies assessing the environmental impact on human health are highly recommended to counterbalance lifetime rodent toxicity studies and other traditional environmental health assessment protocols (hazard-driven risk assessment). However, epidemiological studies, no matter how carefully constructed, can rarely prove an *a priori* hypothesis, and can often only infer a cause-effect relationship with repeated studies. Nevertheless, they are the most powerful method available to translate suspicions drawn from animal studies to human populations that are potentially at risk (Draper, 1995).

The survey instrument, if implemented, should consist of population characteristics, site characteristics, and community health and environmental concerns and perceptions. Along the border, the instrument's design must account for the literacy level of border populations and provide both English and Spanish translations. Furthermore, a determination should be made regarding the sample population, whether it consists of a cross-sectional population or a prospective cohort population. Depending on the need for high confidence levels, most surveys should have sample sizes large enough for a 95 percent confidence interval. Confounding variables (i.e., health risks that may be attributed to smoking, nutritional habits, or occupational health hazard exposures) must be accounted for in the survey instrument to provide non-biased results.

Community outreach, an essential part of community assessment and building community buy-in, consists of organizing meetings with concerned citizens, local public health officials, and environmental scientists in the area of concern. Typically during the pre-project meeting, anecdotal and factual reports are obtained on adverse health outcomes in the community. Next, a determination of the initial health concerns and contaminants of concern to residents is made based on a review of environmental and health-related data. Agencies such as the EPA, state environmental agencies, and nonprofit environmental organizations are contacted for this information. During the mid-project stage, an examination should be made to identify gaps in data. Then, a determination is made of the priorities for closing data gaps. Priorities can consist of sampling more environmental media to obtain a better idea of existing environmental contaminants as well as developing a better understanding of the hydrology of the area. In addition, a toxicity study can be arranged to identify potential environmental exposures and their consequent health impacts on people of all age groups. The toxicity study would incorporate information on the "biologically plausible" hypotheses regarding adverse health outcomes that may be associated with known or potential environmental contaminants present in the community.

A database should be developed for the new data collected. A mechanism for establishing quality assurance and quality control should be in place to ensure data reliability. Next, a statistical or descriptive analysis is performed on the data results including chi square, risk/odds ratio determination, means comparisons, confidence intervals, ANOVA, and/or multiple logistic regression. Following these data collection and data analysis activities, the development of priority needs can be identified and interventions and policies developed or better enforced. Finally, as discussed earlier, the outputs of such assessments should incorporate pollution prevention and other preventive activities to reduce or remove the risk of environmentally induced illness or disease.

Geographic Information System (GIS) and Environmental Health

An increasingly valuable and popular tool used in environmental health assessments is the geographic information system (GIS) computer database. Researchers use statistical analysis to forecast disease distribution trends based on existing environmental contaminant and health data. The latest innovation to aid in this forecasting is new computer technology that has enabled researchers to create a database that allows a researcher to spatially plot data points based on health and environmental data. For example, by using GIS, a researcher can plot cases of lupus, as in the Nogales, Arizona, example, in locations where volatile organic compounds exceed the EPA maximum contaminant levels. Furthermore, the GIS can use statistical analysis in its database management system to forecast disease distribution trends. A visual representation of the spatial distribution of disease and contaminants can provide citizens of communities and agency representatives with an aid in policy decision-making.

GIS also enables a researcher to assess the vulnerability of an area to contamination. In the case of ground water, the researcher can input information on depth to ground water, vadose zone geology, soils, recharge, hydraulic conductivity, slope, and aquifer media. Additional parameters that may be input include land use practices (i.e., aerial application of pesticides and herbicides), locations of underground storage tanks based on locations of gas stations, existing or abandoned landfills, and existing or abandoned industrial sites. In essence, areas of high vulnerability with potential or existing contamination sites have a greater probability of contributing to an environmentally linked disease such as leukemia. Populations within a specified radius of these sites also have a greater probability of becoming exposed to contaminants in the air, water, or soil.

An additional benefit of the GIS is that instead of relying on the 1983 La Paz Agreement (100 kilometers on either side of the borderland constitutes the U.S.-Mexico border) to designate environmental problem areas, the GIS can explore the shared airsheds and watersheds and common species along the border region without the limitations of manmade boundaries. This will allow a more precise method for identifying health problems and environmental solutions without the restraints of the political border.

PUBLIC HEALTH SURVEILLANCE

GIS plays a beneficial role in the planning of a public health surveillance system. Components of disease surveillance include collection, analysis, and dissemination of data on specific diseases. The process of disease surveillance can only be understood in the context of specific health outcomes. Any surveillance system should incorporate information on the objectives of the system, methodology, case definition, data collection, standardization of data collection instruments, field testing, data analysis, interpretation and dissemination, evaluation, and involvement of interested parties in the surveillance itself.

Sentinel Health Event

A component of public health surveillances is the documentation of sentinel health events. The definition of a sentinel health event (SHE) is a "preventable disease, disability or untimely death whose occurrence serves as a warning signal" (Rothwell, Hamilton, & Leaverton, 1991, p. 263). The occurrence of a SHE is considered an indication that an environmentally induced health effect may have occurred and implies some action should be considered. The action may consist of further investigation or analysis or a reduction or cessation of exposure. Answering the question of environmental contamination and the possible adverse health effects caused is complicated by several factors, including the difficulty in defining the potential exposure, the measurement of dose, the long and variable latency period for effects associated with most environmental exposure, the relative rarity of most environmentally related diseases, the nonspecificity of most potential outcomes, the possibility of multiple factors that may interact, and the inadequate health data systems that exist. Environmentally caused SHEs include poisoning (pesticide, toxic gases, heavy metals, solvents, and chemical spills) that produces short latency effects from high-dose exposures. Methemoglobinemia, a subacute chronic condition—also a SHE—usually found in infants, results from excessive nitrate levels in drinking water. Identification requires access to medical records in hospitals or through physicians. Mesothelioma, a rare form of cancer of the lining membranes of the thoracic or abdominal cavity, is largely caused by asbestos exposure. The tumor can be identified through existing tumor registries and medical records. Hepatic angiosarcoma is a rare liver cancer in humans attributable to vinyl chloride monomer exposure. Angiosarcoma can be identified in tumor registries. Potential signs of population exposure to environmental contaminants include low birth weights, birth defects, spontaneous abortions, chronic respiratory disease in children, active leukemia in children, acute granulocytic leukemia in adults, aplastic anemia, asthma in children, dermatoses, skin cancer, malignant melanoma, lung cancer in nonsmokers, bladder cancer in nonsmokers, primary liver cancer in nondrinkers, acute sensory irritation, developmental defects, hearing loss in children, chromosome defects, neurological function, immunological function, renal function, cardiac function, hematologic function, respiratory function, reproductive function, liver function, and auditory function (Shy, Greenberg & Winn, 1994, pp. 316–317).

Data Sources for Disease Surveillance

Sources of data for disease surveillance include death certificates, cancer registries, hospital outpatient records, laboratory data, birth defects registries, and poison centers. The United States has been criticized for having a medical care delivery system that impedes public health surveillance and detection of SHEs. This is because no universal identifiers exist, thus health records on events are fragmented across the health care delivery system. This problem is further complicated when looking at SHEs across an international boundary. For example, Mexico's health system is centralized at a statewide level while many states in the United States have health care delivery systems at a county, state, or district level. Because of the differences existing in disease surveillance across states and countries, comparisons in disease distribution across boundaries becomes difficult.

Thus, the discussion of conducting an environmental health assessment, utilizing the new GIS, and public health surveillance techniques is intended to assist environmental health professionals in performing border-specific environmental health assessments. Using the practical experience of an environmental health assessment will provide the professional with the information needed to conduct prevention strategies and interventions to improve the border's environmental health.

PREVENTION STRATEGIES TO IMPROVE BORDER ENVIRONMENTAL HEALTH

Benjamin Franklin's long-remembered message, that an ounce of prevention is truly worth a pound of cure, has direct application to the environmental health of the U.S.-Mexico border. Preventative environmental health control is important to managing the etiological agents of disease before they get to people. Morgan (1993) outlined a human being's four lines of defense against disease applying the public health practice model to environmental health problems. Controlling manmade and naturally occurring environmental conditions by environmental health practice ("environmental management") provides a people's "first line of defense against disease" (pp. 24–25). This includes water quality management, proper human waste disposal, rodent control, land use management, and many other health protective actions. In other words, this fundamental line of defense seeks to prevent people being exposed to harmful environmental pollutants or conditions (primary prevention). The "second line of defense against disease" is maintaining and improving the human body's own defense mechanisms (skin, mucous membranes, cilia, perspiration, etc.) through general health promotion practices that include proper nutrition, good personal health practice, routine health checkups, and health education activities (primary prevention). Humans' "third line of defense against disease" includes strengthening the body's immune system through public health and preventative medicine activities that include active and passive immunity through immunizations (primary and secondary prevention). "The fourth line of defense against disease" is curative medicine techniques to help prevent a disease from becoming more serious, such as surgery, medication, radiation, laboratory testing, or corrective therapy (secondary or tertiary prevention). Obviously, the first two lines of defense (primary prevention) are most effective since environmental problems are reduced or prevented through appropriate public health action.

According to USAID's experience, environmental health interventions, such as environmental management and behavior change, need not be costly if a consumer demand–driven approach is used. Three elements are essential to such an approach: (a) involvement of the community in identifying its environmental hazards and needs; (b) responsiveness to the community's needs for development and information appropriate to its environmental conditions and resources; and (c) participation of the community in managing, financing, and sustaining accountable services (Murphy & Tomaro, 1995).

Pollution Prevention

Pollution prevention is an innovative approach to environmental protection that promises substantial benefits in the border area. It is a relatively inexpensive way to protect the environment; the costs involved in preventing pollution often are dramatically lower than the costs of treatment and disposal. At least equally important, prevention eliminates that much more potential pollution. Because privately owned businesses often have an incentive to develop ways of minimizing waste, they sometimes are willing to apply their own technical expertise in voluntary programs, thus reducing the need for government expenditures. Furthermore, pollution prevention efforts lessen the possibility of hazardous spills or accidents occurring either within or outside a facility's boundaries because less hazardous material needs to be handled, transported, and disposed (EPA, 1992a).

AN EXAMPLE OF A SUCCESSFUL POLLUTION PREVENTION PROGRAM

One successful example of a pollution-prevention program is a simple yet effective binational, cooperative, community-based pollution prevention program with integrated public health education. This program is located in the El Paso-Juárez-Sunland Park area and focuses on cleaning up the air.

Nowhere along the U.S.-Mexico border is the air more polluted than this region, largely because of poorly maintained vehicles, open trash burning, mazes of dirt roads, ill-controlled brick making, auto painting, and manufacturing in Juárez. Levels of carbon monoxide, ozone, and PM-10 regularly are beyond regulatory standards. This binational community-based effort began by teaming local environmental groups, universities, governmental agencies, and industry on both sides of the border to teach brick makers, auto painters, and vehicle mechanics in Juárez pollution-control practices. The program's success is reportedly due to these solutions being drafted and implemented by local people who live there and know the problem (the "bottom-up approach"), thus helping them be more creative than "outsiders" from Washington, D.C., or Mexico City. In the United States, bricks are made in modern plants, but in Mexico, bricks are made by some of the poorest of the poor. The act of making brick itself by sun-drying the clay-water mixture formed in wooden forms is not the pollution problem. Rather, it is because of the day-long firing of the bricks in kilns (400 of the 2,300 kilns in Mexico are in Juárez) fueled largely by pesticide-treated lumber, glue-bearing particle board, other wood sources, and tire scraps. This burning process releases black smoke and dangerous cancer-causing chemicals and particulates into the shared airshed of this region. Through the efforts of this pollution-prevention program, over 300 brick makers in Juárez have honed their techniques in improving their brick making quality and have learned to use cleaner fuels such as sawdust from untreated lumber, natural gas, or liquid petroleum gas (Hauritz, 1995).

Prevention through Environmental Health Education

Aside from preventing the creation of hazardous waste, an essential step in preventing exposure to environmental problems is to enhance public awareness and participation through environmental health education, effective health-risk communication, and community development efforts (Lichtveld & Johnson, 1993; Good Neighbor Environmental Board, 1995).

Community health education activities are essential to responsive environmental health activities along the U.S.-Mexico border region (Lichtveld & Johnson, 1993). A public education campaign from community and governmental sources should be targeted to residents of the U.S.-Mexico border, particularly those at most risk (Metzger, Delgado & Herrell, 1995). Further, an environmental health education program should not be perceived by local people along the U.S.-Mexico border region as a scheme imposed from afar, but as something they have helped to create (El-Katsha & Watts, 1994).

Although expanded environmental education campaigns are recommended for individuals in their formative years, significant audiences, including minority and multiethnic communities, senior citizens, the illiterate public, and other adult populations, are being left out of environmental health education campaigns (EPA, 1992b). It is recommended that such programs be developed cooperatively by each border state's department of education and department of the environment, as well as private sector and nongovernmental organizations (Good Neighbor Environmental Board, 1995).

Economic development in the border region suggests the need to promote environmental health education and public participation to raise the population's consciousness and motivation regarding environmental problems. Furthermore, in many cases, the insufficient level of environmental health education contributes to increased environmental degradation due to inappropriate natural resource use. Because the border populations are heterogenous and have diverse cultures, it will be necessary to develop both formal and informal environmental health education programs. Such programs will foster diverse alternatives for the solution of environmental problems, promote better conduct toward the environment, and train specialists capable of suggesting technical solutions to minimize adverse environmental impacts. Furthermore, educational efforts will need to address the multilingual (at least Spanish and English) characteristics of the border region (EPA, 1992b). Judging from mass media efforts in other areas of the country and in third world countries throughout the world, TV and newspapers, including printed leaflets, may not be the most effective or sufficient ways for reaching the largely poor Hispanic communities and cities along the U.S.-Mexico border. Rather, door-to-door contact and a "networking" of public health promoters may be necessary (Cech & Essman, 1992).

Environmental Law and Policy: Opportunities and Challenges for the Future

This chapter so far has pointed out the significant public health and related problems that exist along the U.S.-Mexico border because of the general failure to protect the quality of water, air, and other aspects of the environment. One should never think, however, that this is because of the lack of strict environmental regulations on either side of the border. In fact, environmental regulations along the border are just as strict, if not more so in some cases, than in other parts of the respective nations. As will be seen, the North American Free Trade Agreement (NAFTA), which became law in January 1994, has brought with it many regulations designed to improve environmental conditions as the border area grows from increased economic activity. Francisco Giner de los Ríos, chief of environmental regulations for the Mexican National Institute of Ecology, stated it succinctly when he said that the problem is enforcement (Mader, 1995a). He was, of course, speaking for Mexico. But all one has to do is visit the U.S. side of the border to see that the same can be said of the United States.

It is true that the rapidly increasing population along the border, mostly as a result of the maquiladora industries in Mexico, has presented challenges. These include enforcing regulations designed to protect workers and the environment from hazardous materials and other industrial wastes. In addition, public services such as water and sewers have been hard pressed to keep up with the growth. Nevertheless, there are many examples in other communities, especially in the United States, where rapid growth has occurred without any relaxing of environmental standards.

A key question, then, is why haven't environmental regulations been enforced along the border? For Mexico, which is not the primary focus of this chapter, the answers are simpler. First, even with strict environmental laws on the books, it is not surprising that there does not seem to be the general public or government interest in such laws as there is in the United States as there are insufficient funds and manpower to enforce laws. Second, the economic crisis in which Mexico presently finds itself has taken away resources originally intended for environmental programs. An example is the 50 percent cut in funding to the Coahuila Department of Ecology that oversees the "Clean Coahuila" program, which includes pollution prevention and control, environmental education, tree planting, and water clean-up projects in Tamaulipas (Mader, 1995a). Other projects, such as a $72.2 million wastewater treatment plant in Ciudad Juárez that was to be operational a year ago and two other plants in Mexican border cities, are on hold pending foreign grants (Nusser, 1996).

In the United States, the reasons for not enforcing environmental regulations are more complex. Bullard and Wright (1993) suggest that the United States is guilty of practicing environmental injustice. They point out that some African American, Latino American and Native American communities are the unhealthiest places to live in the country. This, they say, is because they are seen as the paths of least resistance for the siting of landfills, incinerators, chemical plants, lead smelters, abandoned toxic waste sites, and a host of other polluting industries. Of course, it should be remembered that industries along the border that are taking advantage of trade-related benefits are there necessarily because of the ethnicity of the population.

Kraft and Scheberle (1995) point out in a case study on lead poisoning that environmental justice requires more than equitable enforcement of environmental laws. They suggest that environmental justice includes giving priority treatment to communities that have suffered disproportionately in the past (Kraft & Scheberle, 1995). This position is supported by the name change of the U.S. Environmental Protection Agency's Office of Environmental Equity in 1994 to the Office on Environmental Justice. Of course, the U.S.-Mexico border clearly could be included in this category of communities that have suffered disproportionately in the past.

Even many environmental groups have lost interest in the border, says Ron Mader, a journalist specializing in border environmental issues (Mader, 1995b). The Sierra Club, which opposed NAFTA, moved on to put its efforts into opposing the General Agreement of Tariffs and Trade (GATT). Mader says even pro-NAFTA groups such as the World Wildlife Fund and National Wildlife Federation maintain little presence on the border.

Mader states that there was great media interest in environmental issues during the NAFTA debate. But it has fallen off too, he says, as mainstream reporting has reverted back to more "sexy" immigration and drug issues. Mader also suggests that the U.S. side of the border is viewed as at the periphery of two cultures, therefore perhaps getting treated differently than if viewed as clearly within the U.S.

Another point that Mader makes is that border environmental issues are often piecemealed. There are four U.S. states and six Mexican states along the border. Each, of course, is primarily interested in issues affecting its own border. Even studies by state universities tend to focus on the state in which the campus is located.

There also is the difference in laws, even in the United States (Mader, 1994b). New Mexico law, for example, provides that groundwater is a public resource. Texas, on the other hand, follows the English common law approach that groundwater belongs to the property owner.

Even though it may seem to be the case, the intent so far of this chapter has not been to discourage the public health professional from trying to improve environmental conditions along the border. The intent has been merely to point out the challenges facing any effort to bring about such improvements. A great deal can be done to improve the environment along the border, as was cited earlier in the case of El Paso community leaders and activists helping reduce emissions from brick kilns in Ciudad Juárez.

Of course, it should not be forgotten that the economic benefits of development along the border, whether it be industrial, commercial, or residential, are being balanced with the enforcement of environmental regulations. In tough economic times for both countries, it is not hard to see why enforcement of environmental laws may well be taking a back seat.

Border Environmental Laws and Regulations

There are many Mexican laws that deal with the environment, including the environment along the border. Except through diplomatic and economic pressure, which may be unlikely, and perhaps via some nongovernmental organizations working in specific communities as will be discussed later, there is little the U.S. health professional can do to seek enforcement of Mexican environmental laws. This section, therefore, will give a very cursory view of laws and regulations in the U.S. that may be employed in efforts to improve border public health conditions at least on the northern side of the border.

Environmental laws and regulations can be found at all levels of the United States government—federal, state, and local. Federal laws include those administered by the Environmental Protection Agency, various resource agencies (such as the U.S. Fish and Wildlife Service), safety-related agencies (such as the Occupational Safety and Health Administration and the Interstate Commerce Commission) and those laws developed by treaty or other type of international agreement (such as NAFTA).

State laws include those administered by agencies with functions similar to those of the federal agencies mentioned above. States also have regional boards that oversee water and air quality. Health departments exist at the state, county, and city levels.

It should be obvious that many of the laws and regulations administered by these agencies are violated every day along the U.S.-Mexico border. Those interested in the public health impacts of these violations should remember the old adage that "the squeaky wheel gets the grease." In other words, where the populations themselves may not complain because of their economic or social status, others can draw attention to the failure to enforce environmental laws before an assortment of panels, boards, councils, and other elected and appointed officials. With some professional public relations help, great pressure may be brought to bear on decision makers and other officials responsible for enforcing environmental laws and regulations.

FEDERAL LAWS

Executive Order 12898, February 1995, requires all federal agencies to develop comprehensive strategies for achieving environmental justice. This means, as was discussed earlier, that the agencies must exercise measures to help population areas disproportionately affected in the past to remedy harmful environmental conditions. Notwithstanding a conservative Congress that is demanding a credible risk assessment and a cogent economic argument for environmental policy actions, agencies clearly have to move toward remedying blatant instances of environmental injustice.

Once considered to be among the most effective tools in improving border public health is the North American Free Trade Agreement (NAFTA) and its related documents. NAFTA's companion document is the North American Agreement on Environmental Cooperation. It also is referred to as "NAFTA's Environmental Side Agreement," "Supplemental Agreement on the Environment," or "Environmental Agreement."

Amanda Atkinson says that NAFTA with its side agreement has the potential to affect public health and environmental issues in border states in many ways (Atkinson, 1994):

1. A challenge could be brought against a state environmental law alleging that the law violates NAFTA and if successful, the challenge would necessitate a series of negotiations and possibly result in the law's demise.
2. A state environmental law could be changed through the course of NAFTA-mandated negotiations to harmonize environmental laws.
3. A state's non-enforcement of its environmental laws could be chal-

lenged under NAFTA's Environmental Side Agreement.

4.   Increased trade resulting from NAFTA could further burden the already over-burdened environmental infrastructure in the border region.

NAFTA's preamble explicitly identifies environmental protection as a priority and states that the agreement will be enforced "in a manner consistent with environmental protection and conservation," and in a manner that will "strengthen the development and enforcement of environmental laws and regulations. . . ."

Two chapters in the NAFTA document itself address compliance with environmental laws. Chapter 7, Part B deals with Sanitary and Phytosanitary Measures (S&Ps).

A NAFTA party may adopt, maintain, and apply S&Ps to achieve an appropriate level of protection in its own territory to protect human, animal, and plant life. It also may protect against health from risks of plant- and animal-borne pests and diseases, and additives and contaminants in foods and feedstuffs.

These measures must be based on scientific principles, including a risk assessment, as appropriate to the circumstances, and may be applied only to the extent necessary to achieve a NAFTA party's appropriate level of protection.

A party may choose any level of protection it considers appropriate, as long as it doesn't make arbitrary or unjustifiable distinctions that result in arbitrary or unjustifiable discrimination against goods of another party.

In summary, Chapter 7B essentially relies on whether a measure has a basis in science and is based on a risk assessment. Discrimination is allowed as long as it is not arbitrary or unjustifiable.

Chapter 9 of NAFTA deals with Technical and Standard-Related Measures (SRMs). SRMs include voluntary and mandatory product or service standards and the procedures used to determine whether a particular product or service meets the standard. An example is motor vehicle operation standards.

These standards are subject to nondiscrimination tests, not to whether they are scientifically based. A NAFTA party may set appropriate levels of protection. It should, however, avoid arbitrary or unjustifiable discrimination against those that provide goods and services of another NAFTA party.

As in Chapter 7B, a party may adopt, maintain, and apply standards-related measures to reach its chosen level of protection. They are, however, subject to the requirements that they (1) not discriminate against the goods or services of another party, or (2) create an unnecessary obstacle to trade.

In summary, an SRM may be maintained if the purpose is to achieve a legitimate objective (such as a level of protection), and if it does not exclude the goods of another party that meet that objective.

Both Chapter 7B and Chapter 9 contain compatibility and equivalency provisions. Parties are instructed to use "relevant international standards" as a basis for their measures to pursue the objective of making the measures equivalent or identical to those of the other parties without reducing the level of protection of human, animal, or plant life or health.

It should be noted that NAFTA parties do have the right to adopt measures that result in higher levels of protection than the international measure.

Also, two committees were formed to pursue the equivalence and compatibility of measures: The Committee on Sanitary and Phytosanitary Measures and the Committee on Standard-Related Measures.

The Environmental Agreement, or Side Agreement, created the Commission for Environmental Cooperation (CEC). It comprises top environmental officials from the three parties to NAFTA. The Agreement includes a secretariat and an advisory council that meets annually in a public setting. The council is required to develop recommendations for the assessment and review of transboundary environmental impacts. The Secretariat, says the Environmental Agreement, will be a standing body located in one office and managed by an executive director with a staff appointed and retained on the basis of efficiency, competency, and integrity.

The CEC is authorized to deal with disputes over alleged failure to enforce environmental laws. It may receive from any persons or nongovernmental organizations allegations that a party to NAFTA is not effectively enforcing its environmental laws. It will review such allegations and, subject to a two-thirds vote of the advisory council, develop a fact-finding report on the complaint.

In addition, the Secretariat may request that the advisory council consider any issue unless at least two parties to NAFTA object within 30 days.

A dispute resolution enforcement action can only be initiated if a NAFTA party alleges that there has been "a persistent pattern of failure by another NAFTA party to effectively enforce its environmental law" and two-thirds of the council votes to convene a panel.

If the panel determines that there has been a persistent failure to enforce the law effectively, the disputing parties must try to agree on a satisfactory "action plan" to address the problem. If negotiations are not successful, there can be more negotiations, further review by the panel, and escalating penalties, including monetary enforcement penalties. The alleging party also may suspend benefits under NAFTA in an amount no greater than the amount of the monetary penalty assessed at the earlier stage of the process.

This approach to seeking compliance with environmental laws is pretty drastic, and the political realities probably make it not the most effective tool for individuals and nongovernmental entities to improve border public health.

Nevertheless, the United States' intentions that environmental safeguards and compliance are important matters are underscored in several NAFTA-related documents. These will not be discussed in detail, but suffice to say that they may be consulted to understand the Administration's and Congress' intent of various NAFTA provisions, including environmental provisions.

One document is the "North American Free Trade Agreement Implementation Act," also called the "Implementing Legislation" (Pub. L. No. 103–182, 107 Stat. 2057, 1993). It has a binding effect on the U.S. government.

Another is called the "Waxman letter." It was sent by U.S. Trade Representative Michael Kantor to Congressman Henry A. Waxman, chair of House Sub-Committee on Health and the Environment. The letter contained some of President Clinton's initial environmental concerns with NAFTA.

A second piece of correspondence is called the "Adams letter." This was a similar letter sent by Mr. Kantor, but this time to John Adams, executive director of the Natural Resources Defense Council.

Then there is the "Statement of Administrative Action." This statement, which was reviewed and passed by Congress, contains the Administration's interpretations of NAFTA.

The letters and the Statement address two primary areas of concern relating to adverse interpretations of several clauses. The first concern is that a NAFTA party could apply the GATT definition of "necessary," or "least trade restrictive," to the S&P measures "only to the extent necessary" to achieve an appropriate level of protection. The Statement and Adams letter both make it clear that the less-strict GATT interpretation is not controlling.

The second concern is that regulations adopted without extensive risk assessments and other laws passed for policy reasons could be subject to challenge under NAFTA's Article 712.3, which requires that S&P measures be based on scientific principles and risk assessment. The Statement clarifies that this requirement does not permit a dispute settlement panel to substitute its scientific judgment for that of the government. Instead, the panel must determine whether a government has a scientific basis, defined as "a reason based on data or information derived using scientific methods," for the law.

It should be remembered that only the NAFTA parties may initiate an action to enforce environmental laws under NAFTA. The private recourse is to influence the NAFTA party, in this case the U.S. Government, to take action. Private entities, however, may initiate action under the provisions of the Commission for Environmental Cooperation.

As was stated earlier, NAFTA and its accompanying documents were once considered to be among the most effective tools in improving border public health. Environmentalists on both sides of the border now dispute that contention, pointing, for example, to increasing numbers of pollution-creating maquiladoras being constructed south of the border. In 1995, 300 permits were issued by the Mexican government, an increase of 80 percent over 1994. NAFTA, was supposed to take away many of the maquiladora advantages, and reduce the number of factories south of the border. It clearly hasn't worked (Nusser, 1996).

STATE AND LOCAL LAWS
Even with the plethora of federal laws and regulations, from a practical point of view it may be easier to effect change through state and local laws because of the greater ability to influence local officials. It was stated earlier that a good public relations effort may be the "squeak" that gets the wheel "greased." Nowhere more than at the local level is this the case, where all the elected or appointed officials of an agency may be subject to the same media coverage and political pressure.

Greater public involvement and resultant media attention can force resource agencies to adhere more closely to existing laws and regulations. If nothing else, limiting discretionary actions, such as waivers, that may result in relaxed standards will improve to some degree environmental conditions along the border. For example, air boards should be publicly encouraged not to issue permits unless strict air quality regulations are met. Water boards should require strict industrial wastewater pretreatment programs so discharges will not cause harm or overburden the wastewater treatment process.

Health departments at the state, county, and city levels can be encouraged to crack down on those violating local public health regulations. This includes the disposal of solid waste and sanitary conditions in homes, public buildings, and commercial establishments.

BINATIONAL COMMISSIONS
There also are several binational commissions that have some authority and power over border environmental issues. Some are more effective than oth-

ers. The International Boundary and Water Commission (IBWC), for example, which can make recommendations on how to improve the quality of groundwater basins shared by the United States and Mexico, has been criticized for being reluctant to proceed in managing and conserving groundwater resources (Mader, 1994a).

The Border Environmental Cooperation Commission (BECC), on the other hand, appears to be accomplishing its goals after a slow start. The BECC and its lender North American Development Bank (NAD Bank) were created by the governments of the United States and Mexico in November 1993 to give financial assistance to public agencies and private enterprises within 100 kilometers of either side of the border that are engaged in developing projects dealing with environmental issues affecting the two countries. Eligible projects include water pollution control (water supply quality), wastewater treatment, and municipal solid waste disposal. In 1995, three projects were approved. The first is an $8 million wastewater treatment plant in Ensenada, Baja California, that will help improve the water quality of Ensenada Bay. The second project is a 15-million-gallon-per-day wastewater treatment plant in Brawley, California. The third is an $11.7 million reclaimed water project for El Paso, Texas. At least eight more projects are expected to be certified in early 1996.

The United States and Mexico will contribute a total of $3 billion to the program to the NAD Bank, where the BECC forwards projects for financing. It is still uncertain just what the financing arrangements will be.

NONGOVERNMENTAL ORGANIZATIONS

Nongovernmental organizations (NGOs) are playing an increasing role in effecting actual change along the border. One example is the Environmental Committee of the San Diego-Tijuana Region, which has helped push the IBWC to step up plans to construct a wastewater treatment plant in Tijuana where for 20 years the system has been overburdened (Mader, 1994b).

Other examples can be found in El Paso, where air pollution is being addressed, and Arizona, where local citizens are helping industries to inventory hazardous wastes and toxic materials for emergency planning purposes.

CONCLUSION

Both sides of the U.S.-Mexico border are rapidly growing as NAFTA encourages even more the economic ties between the two nations that began in earnest as a result of the creation of the maquiladora program. Not only Mexico, but also the United States, is having difficulty keeping up adequate public services such as water, sewers, roads, and public health facilities. Because of the economic benefits to both countries resulting from growth and economic development, enforcing environmental regulations may not be given the priority that it merits on either side of the border. Public health professionals, however, can take advantage of existing U.S. federal, state, and local laws, as well as the services of binational commissions and nongovernmental organizations, to seek greater compliance with environmental laws and regulations.

The fundamental intent of public health and environmental law should be to prevent disease by reducing exposures to potential problems before human health is affected. Thus, "human evidence linking hazardous exposures and health should not be required to establish social policies of control" (Davis & Poore, 1994, p. 7). Moure-Eraso and colleagues (1994) echo stronger conclusions and recommendations from their study that border industrial and community problems are alarming enough to "invoke conservative public health principles: public health action in the face of scientific uncertainty" (p. 323). They continue by recommending that community leaders' accounts of environmental hazards warrant action by government, by companies, by unions, and by community and citizen organizations. Action to improve environmental health along the U.S.-Mexico border must involve as many key persons, communities, agencies, state and federal governments, and governmental agencies as possible to make a difference. The sooner environmental health issues are addressed comprehensively and cooperatively, the greater the potential for border residents to live longer and healthier lives.

> Over 2,000 years ago a Chinese philosopher wrote, "In the end, we will conserve only what we love . . . we will love only what we understand . . . we will understand only what we are taught." (EPA, 1992b, p. 38)

REFERENCES

Atkinson, A. (1994). Public health and environmental issues in border states. *Natural Resources and Environment, 9*(1), 23–59.

Aldrich, T.E. & Leaverton, P.E. (1993). Sentinel event strategies in environmental health. *Annual Reviews of Public Health, 14,* 205–217.

Bullard, R.D. & Wright, B.H. (1993). Environmental justice for all: Community perspectives on health and research needs. *Toxicology and Industrial Health, 9*(5), 821–833.

Burke, T.A., Shalauta, N.M., & Tran, L.N. (1995). Strengthening the role of public health in environmental policy. *Policy Studies Journal, 23*(1), 76–84.

Calderon, R.L., Johnson, C.C., Craun, G.F., Dufour, A.P., Karlin, R.J., Sinks, T., & Valentine, J.L. (1993). Health risks from contaminated water: Do class and race matter? *Toxicology and Industrial Health, 9*(5), 879–900.

Cech, I. & Essman, A. (1992). Water sanitation practices on the Texas-Mexico border: Implications for physicians on both sides. *Southern Medical Journal, 85*(11), 1053–1064.

Cifuentes, E., Blumenthal, U., Ruiz-Palacios, G., Bennett, S., Quigley, M., Peasy, A., & Romero-Alvarez, H. (1993). The health problems associated with irrigation with wastewater in Mexico. *Salud Publica de Mexico, 35*(6), 614–619.

Council on Scientific Affairs (1990). A permanent U.S.-Mexico border environmental health commission. *Journal of the American Medical Association, 263*(24), 3319–3321.

Davis, D.L., & Poore, L.M. (1994). *Policy issues in environmental epidemiology: Making the connection between exposure and human disease.* Hazardous Waste and Public Health: International Congress on the health effects of hazardous waste, 1993; Atlanta: Agency for Toxic Substances and Disease Registry, Public Health Services, U.S. Department of Health and Human Services.

Draper, W.M. (1995). *Environmental epidemiology: Effects of environmental chemicals on human health.* Washington, DC: American Chemical Society. Baltimore, MD: United Book Press.

El-Katsha, S. & Watts, S. (1994). A model for health education. *World Health Forum, 15*(1), 29–33.

Ellis, M. (1993). *Analysis of investment process in health and the environment in the U.S.-Mexico border states.* Washington, DC.: Regional Plan for Investment in the Environment and Health, Pan American Health Organization, World Health Organization.

Environmental Protection Agency. (1992a). *Integrated environmental plan for the Mexican-U.S. border area: First stage, 1992–1994.* Washington, DC.: U.S. Environmental Protection Agency, Office of Communications, Education and Public Affairs.

Environmental Protection Agency. (1992b). *Building a shared vision for environmental education: A conference sponsored by the federal task force on environmental education.*Washington, DC.: U.S. Environmental Protection Agency, Office of Communications, Education and Public Affairs.

Espinoza-Torres, F., Hernandez-Avila, M., & Lopez-Carrillo, L. (1994). NAFTA, a challenge and an opportunity for environmental health: The case of maquila industry. *Salud Publica de Mexico, 36*(6), 597–616.

Good Neighbor Environmental Board (1995). *First annual report.* A presidential and congressional advisory committee on U.S.-Mexico border environmental and infrastructure issues.

Graber, D.R. & Johnson, J.J. (1995). Perspectives on environmental health policy: Symposium introduction. *Policy Studies Journal, 23*(1), 66–69.

Hauritz, R.K.M. (1995). El Paso, Juarez, Sunland focus on cleaning up air. *Las Cruces Sun-News,* December 25, 1995, A-8.

Hook, G.E.R. (1995). Ramazzini: Father of environmental health? *Environmental Health Perspectives, 103*(11), 2–4.

Kraft, M.E. & Scheberle, D. (1995). Environmental justice and the allocation of risk: The case of lead and public health. *Policy Studies Journal, 23*(1), 113–122.

Landrigan, P.J. & Carlson, J.E. (1995). Environmental policy and children's health. *Critical Issues for Children and Youths, 5*(2), 34–52.

Lichtveld, M.Y. & Johnson, B.L. (1994). *Public health implications of hazardous waste sites in the United States.* Hazardous Waste and Public Health: International Congress on the health effects of hazardous waste, 1993; Atlanta: Agency for Toxic Substances and Disease Registry, Public Health Services, U.S. Department of Health and Human Services.

Lubin, B. & Lewis, R. (1995). Biomarkers and pediatric environmental health. *Environmental Health Perspectives, 103*(6), 99–104.

Mader, R. (1994a). Call for Mexico-U.S. groundwater law. *El Planeta Platica/US Mexico Borderlands*, July 22, 1994 newsletter, Austin, Texas.

Mader, R. (1994b). Cross border environmental cooperation. *El Planeta Platica/US Mexico Borderlands*, August 8, 1994 newsletter, Austin, Texas.

Mader, R. (1995a). Mexico explores new paradigms. *El Planeta Platica/US Mexico Borderlands*, April 5, 1995 newsletter, Austin, Texas.

Mader, R. (1995b). Unknown border: Post NAFTA Apathy. *El Planeta Platica/US Mexico Borderlands*. July 23, 1995 newsletter, Austin, Texas.

Metzger, R., Delgado, J.L., & Herrell, R. (1995). Environmental health and Hispanic children. *Environmental Health Perspectives, 103*(6), 25–32.

Morgan, M.T. (1993). *Environmental health*. Dubuque, IA: Brown & Benchmark, A Division of Wm. C. Brown Communications, Inc.

Mott, L. (1995). The disproportionate impact of environmental health threats on children of color. *Environmental Health Perspectives, 103*(6), 33–35.

Moure-Eraso, R., Wilcox, M., Punnett, L., Copeland, L., & Levenstein, C. (1994). Back to the future: Sweatshop conditions on the Mexico-U.S. border: Community health impact of maquiladora industrial activity. *American Journal of Industrial Medicine, 25*, 311–324.

Murphy, H. & Tomaro, J. (1995). Environment, health & people; An update from ASAID's environmental health project. *Environmental Health Perspectives, 103*(11), 5–6.

New Mexico Environment Department. (1994). *New Mexico's border area: Environmental considerations*. Santa Fe, NM: New Mexico Environment Department.

Nusser, N. (1996). NAFTA appears to be no solution for dirty U.S.-Mexico border. *Las Cruces Sun-News*, Jan. 1, 1996.

Rothwell, C.B., Hamilton, C.B., & Leaverton, P.E. (1991). Identification of sentinel health events as indicators of environmental contamination. *Environmental Health Perspectives, 94*(3), 261–263.

Satchell, M. (1991). Poisoning the border. *U.S. News and World Report, 110*(17), 33–41.

Schwartz, E. & Corvalan, C. (1995). Decision-making in environmental health. *World Health Statistics Quarterly, 48*(2), 164–171.

Serrano, O.R. (1995). Fate, transport, and interactions of heavy metals. *Environmental Health Perspectives, 103*(Suppl. 1), 7–8.

Shields, J. (1991). Ambient air arsenic levels along the Texas-Mexico border. *Journal of Air and Waste Management Association, 41*(6), 827–831.

Shy, C., Greenburg, R., & Winn, D. (1994). Sentinel health events of environmental contamination: A consensus statement. *Environmental Health Perspectives, 102*(3), 316–317.

Silbergeld, E.K. (1994). *Evaluating the success of environmental health programs in protecting the public's health*. Hazardous Waste and Public Health: International Congress on the Health Effects of Hazardous Waste, 1993. Atlanta: Agency for Toxic Substances and Disease Registry, Public Health Services, U.S. Department of Health and Human Services.

Southwest Center for Environmental Research and Policy. (1991). *United States/Mexico borderwide environmental problems, needs, and action priorities: Hazardous wastes and soils, air quality, water quality*. April 25–26, 1991, workshop summary, University of Texas at El Paso.

Steffans, R. (1994). Bridging the border. *National Parks, 68*(7–8), 36–41.

Taylor, L. (1992). The fast track trade agreement: Help or hurt for the U.S.-Mexico border environment? *Environmental-Social Change Quarterly, The Workbook, 17*(2), 50–69.

United States Department of Health and Human Services. (1990). *Healthy people 2000: Priorities for the nation*. Washington, DC: United States Department of Health and Human Services, General Accounting Office.

United States Department of Health and Human Services. (1990). *Healthy people 2000: Priorities for the nation.* Washington, DC: United States Department of Health and Human Services, General Accounting Office.

Vandermeer, D.C. (1993). NAFTA prompts health concerns across the border. *Environmental Health Perspectives, 101*(3), 230– 231.

Varady, R.G. & Mack, M.D. (1995). Transboundary water resources and public health in the U.S.-Mexico border region. *Journal of Environmental Health, 57*(8), 8– 14.

Worrest, R.C. (1994). *The U.S.-Mexico border area regional environmental information system.* Salt Lake City, Utah: Southwest Center for Environmental Research and Policy (SCERP), University of Utah. WWW URL:http://www.civil.utah.edu/scerp/.

Health Promotion Efforts along the U.S.-Mexico Border

Jeffrey E. Brandon

Health promotion has been defined as "the combination of educational and environmental supports for actions and conditions of living conducive to health" (Green & Kreuter, 1991, p. 4). These same authors (1991) described the purpose of health promotion efforts as enabling persons or communities to gain more control over the determinants of their health and pointed out that the target of the interventions could be individuals, groups, or communities. This broader view of health promotion/education reflects the fact that such intervention strategies are increasingly directed toward promoting societal change rather than taking an exclusive individual focus. While individual behavior-change strategies may have relevance for motivating health-promoting behaviors for individuals from the predominant culture, the same strategies may have little, if any, impact on individuals whose cultural values and experiences are quite different, or for those with unmet needs for food, clothing, and shelter. Thus, those from different cultures and subcultures, including those who may not use English as their principal language, may find it difficult to understand or relate to media messages targeting society's dominant groups. Culturally appropriate strategies are needed to better relate health promotion messages to such underserved groups.

At its broader level, health promotion includes social action for health. Such societal-based interventions must be acceptable and accessible to underserved population groups. This is true as well for health promotion efforts that focus on populations along the U.S.-Mexico border. According to H.S. Dhillon (1991), director of the World Health Organization's Division of Health Education:

> Knowledge alone, without adequate supportive systems and facilities, is not enough to lead people to action. Environments and policies supportive of health are essential to make it feasible for people to live

a healthy way of life. Good health depends upon the enlightened involvement of individuals and communities. But there is much that the individual and the community cannot do alone. All societal forces, local communities, and entire nations must be mobilized and work together to solve common problems and achieve health goals. Indeed, a major challenge in health promotion will be to influence the thinking of those who are influential in shaping public policies. Messages must reach policy-makers, legislators, and decision-makers that investment in health is not only a social imperative, but also a political asset and sound economics. (p. 6)

Dhillon (1991) described health promotion and social mobilization as inseparable and indispensable for fostering social, political, and community action for health. In his discussion of health promotion issues for developing countries, Dhillon states that the field of health education must clearly define its benefits and proclaim them widely to such groups as politicians, professionals, the press, trade associations, social and religious institutions, and private and public health care organizations. The active support of community groups is deemed essential to success in such efforts. He also recommended preparing community health workers (CHWs) from the local culture who can speak the common language of the people and share common values and beliefs. Fostering a harmonious relationship between such individuals and traditional practitioners is essential. This same strategy has been applied along the U.S.-Mexico border. Dhillon (1991) ends his article with a challenge to action that includes the following:

> Health promotion is an integral element of the primary health care strategy for the attainment of health for all people, in developing as well as developed countries. It synthesizes education for health and social mobilization through strategies based on advocacy, development of support systems, and empowerment of people for wise individual and collective health choices. (p. 11)

This chapter will focus on culturally appropriate health promotion/education strategies that have been used with Mexican Americans, especially among groups living along the U.S.-Mexico border. It will include a description of health program planning techniques and will focus on three related health promotion intervention strategies: community organization, community empowerment, and the CHW approach. Examples of these approaches will also be included.

Recently, there has been growing interest concerning the development of health education services that are more culturally appropriate to different ethnic groups. According to Steckler (1993), "the significance of health education is rooted in the recognition that the culture of a community has a deep and abiding influence on its health" (p. S29). There is a tendency among health professionals, including health educators, from one culture to attempt to impose their own beliefs and values on those from another culture. In order to avoid this dilemma, the health educator must first learn about the client's or target community's cultural context and gain an appreciation for the close link between culture and health.

In one effort to better prepare students to confront this tendency, the Bachelor of Community Health and the Master of Public Health programs at New Mexico State University, which is located in a county directly on the U.S.-Mexico border, seeks to prepare its graduates to practice in the multicultural context of the American Southwest. An interdisciplinary seminar course on border health issues appears to be particularly successful in working toward the goal of preparing more culturally sensitive health professionals. It utilizes a student-centered, problem-based learning approach to analyzing carefully developed border health cases. This course involves having students analyze and work through the hypothesized causes and possible solutions to case situations involving both individual and community health needs. In doing so, it helps to illustrate the connection between health and culture. For example, a curandero, or native folk healer from the Mexican and Native American tradition, might be invited to speak to the group to describe how he/she works alongside a traditional, allopathic care provider in helping treat a Mexican American diabetic patient. Alternatively, to demonstrate a community-level case, the use of community health workers (CHWs) in providing prenatal care throughout northern Mexico might be incorporated into a case study. Students gain from such learning experiences a greater appreciation of the role culture has in health practices and beliefs, and of the need to be more sensitive to its role in developing culturally appropriate health education interventions.

Marin, Burhansstipanov, Connell, Gielen, Helitzer-Allen, Lorig, Morisky, Tenney, and Thomas (1995) summarized the outcome of health education efforts among underserved populations and argued for the design of culturally appropriate health education interventions. They stated that endogenous characteristics (knowledge, attitudes, beliefs, and cultural influences); sociological factors (family and peer influence and the environment); and social inequity (racism, poverty, less access to and availability of health care) must be considered in designing health education interventions for different underserved groups.

> Research has begun to show that some of the traditional approaches to health education have not reached or have not been as effective with members of these underserved groups as with the rest of the population. Finally, basic research in the social sciences has shown that there are group-specific predictors and correlates of health behaviors that must be taken into consideration if an intervention is going to be effective. . . . In summary, the unique conditions experienced by members of underserved groups can best be addressed by targeted health education programs. (pp. 348–349)

This quote further reinforces the need for greater attention to be given to the development of group-specific health promotion/education interventions. In describing a developing consensus regarding appropriate characteristics of such programs, Marin and colleagues (1995) suggest that a more culturally or group appropriate health promotion/education program should be based upon, and incorporate, the cultural values and characteristics of the targeted group and that "the components that make up the strategies reflect the behavioral preferences and expectations of the members of the group" (p. 350).

Perhaps one approach which best incorporates these recommended elements is the CHW approach. Programs that have been developed with and for underserved populations often have used a self-help or peer counseling model (Marin et al., 1995), and the CHW model appears to be widely used among Mexican American groups and along the U.S.-Mexico border. The community organization and community empowerment approaches are other models that incorporate these culturally specific characteristics. Prior to the implementation of any intervention strategy, however, the health educator must ensure that the health program planning process incorporates an understanding of the cultural context. Unfortunately, there is a relative lack of research on planning group-specific interventions.

HEALTH PROMOTION/EDUCATION PLANNING

Some investigators have proposed adapting familiar and often-used health promotion/education planning models, such as the PRECEDE-PROCEED and its related PATCH (Planned Approaches to Community Health) model, to populations along the U.S. border with Mexico (Villas & Williams, 1993). Others have proposed using grassroots consensus-building activities among local health care providers and policy makers. Two examples of such efforts include the Pan American Health Organization's Project Consenso (U.S.-Mexico Border Health Association, 1991) and the World Health Organization's (WHO) Primary Health Care Review (Ortega, 1991; Selwyn, Loe & Moore, 1992).

Project Consenso, funded by the U.S. Public Health Service, was conducted by the U.S.-Mexico Border Health Association. This program held a series of border conferences that helped develop consensus among local providers regarding the formulation of state and local health priorities for border communities. The six health priority areas identified through these four border state conferences included: (1) environmental health, (2) health promotion/disease prevention, (3) maternal and child health, (4) occupational health, (5) primary health care, and (6) substance abuse. Examples of the recommendations made within the health promotion/disease prevention priority area included: (1) promoting the use of media to inform border populations about public health and environmental issues and their causes and prevention steps, (2) developing binational health promotion programs to educate adolescents and women of reproductive age on prenatal care, family planning, and overall reproductive health, and (3) introducing health education in the health professions curricula and at the elementary and secondary school levels. The overall recommendations for this area included a focus on the promotion of healthier lifestyles, community health education, and legislative action. Within the community health education recommendation, the use of volunteer CHWs or promoters was suggested for aggressive outreach programs. Included in Ortega's contribution to the *Carnegie Quarterly*'s (Ortega, 1991) special issue on promoting binational cooperation was the recommendation to use volunteer CHWs in local communities to improve health along the U.S.-Mexico border. Again, studies that have used this approach will be discussed later in this chapter.

In this same report, Ortega (1991) further recommended involving the community in research and public health planning using the World Health Organization's Primary Health Care Review (PHCR) approach. This approach to research and public health planning has been used by the Pan American Health Organization (PAHO) to conduct needs assessments of at-risk women, children, and adolescents along the border. The first PHCR in the U.S. was headed by Loe and colleagues at the University of Texas School of Public Health in collaboration with the Lower Rio Grande Valley Regional Development Council (Ortega, 1991). A local review team and steering committee was formed to assess the health status of indigent people and the barriers to services; the committee recommended the formation of a nonprofit corporation to ensure that the group's recommendations were followed. Ortega (1991) also reported a larger PHCR project which was PAHO-sponsored and involved multiple universities and research teams binationally. The five study areas were: (1) maternal and child health, (2) adolescent health, (3) working women's health, (4) utilization of health services, and (5) environmental health. The consortium collected data between 1989 and 1990 in paired sites along the border. Community workers were trained to conduct household surveys in their neighborhoods and youth focus groups for 11–17-year-olds were held to identify and recommend solutions to identified problems. Their findings were integrated and shared with the respective local review committees, which were then used to develop recommendations. The use of CHWs (promotoras) and the expansion of school-based social and health services for adolescents were among their recommendations. Selwyn, Loe, and Moore (1992) report on the specific methodology for this study in greater detail.

This discussion of planning models was not meant to be inclusive, but was designed to highlight approaches which seem particularly useful for implementation with populations along the U.S.-Mexico border. The two approaches cited are not unique to the border region, but are examples of planning models which incorporate a high degree of community orientation and cultural awareness of local health problems. The remainder of this chapter will highlight three related health promotion/education intervention strategies/models.

HEALTH PROMOTION/EDUCATION INTERVENTION STRATEGIES/MODELS

Health promotion/education strategies that have recently been utilized with underserved populations include mass media (Romer & Kim, 1995); social marketing (Williams & Flora, 1995), including health behavior segmentation (Belcazar, Castro, & Krull, 1995); and the use of culturally specific educational interventions (LeMaster & Connell, 1994). The three strategies/models most frequently cited in health promotion/education programs in communities sharing the border between the U.S. and Mexico include: (1) community organization, (2) community empowerment, and (3) the CHW model.

Community Organization

Glanz, Lewis, and Rimer (1990) defined community organization as:

> the process by which community groups are helped to identify common problems or goals, mobilize resources, and in other ways develop and implement strategies for reaching the goals they have set. (p. 257)

Such community-based programs are well suited for addressing health problems of underserved populations living along the U.S.-Mexico border. According to Braithwaite and Lythcott (1989):

> Because health behaviors are culture-bound, primary prevention efforts that address preventable disease and illness must emerge from a knowledge of and a respect for the culture of the target community to ensure that both the community organization and development effort and any interventions that emerge are culturally sensitive and linguistically appropriate. (p. 283)

According to Bracht (1990), community residents must be involved early in the health promotion/education planning efforts and in collaborative decision making. He recommended several principles for guiding the community organization work, including the caution to remember that not all members of a minority group are homogenous and thus avoid assuming that one health promotion message should appeal to the entire group.

The A Su Salud (To Your Health) program is one illustration of use of the community organization method in a border community. This community organization effort is based in Eagle Pass in southwest Texas, where 93 percent of the population is of Mexican American descent. Amezcua, McAlister, Ramirez, and Espinoza (1990) described this program as beginning with the identification of health concerns through the use of focus group meetings, the membership of which was composed of persons from the community at large. The program included the training of CHWs as volunteers. The volunteers served as healthy models and encouraged and reinforced positive health behaviors among others in their social network (Amezcua et al., 1990). The media component consisted of television programs that utilized well-known community health professionals as role models. Almost 400 volunteers were trained overall during the entire program. Networks included commercial/worksite settings, neighborhoods, and religious organizations. In Amezcua and colleagues' assessment of the first summer of the program's operation, 7,860 contacts (an average of 20 each) were made by the volunteers. According to a related evaluation of 43 volunteers in the Eagle Pass program presented by Gonzales and colleagues (1994), the interviewed volunteers reported that 25 people stopped smoking, 880 made dietary changes, 143 had a mammogram, and 810 received a pap smear. The authors concluded that "these results indicate that volunteers can effectively stimulate initiation of health promoting behavior changes presented by role models in a media campaign" (p. 3).

Modern health promotion/education intervention strategies have developed beyond the almost exclusive focus on individual responsibility and accountability to a broader appreciation of exogenous social factors. While specific individual behaviors continue to be recognized as important, external environmental and social factors are likewise being viewed as predisposing, reinforcing, and enabling factors affecting a community's health status. The dominant health education theories today are often based on social psychology, such as Bandura's social learning or self-efficacy theories, self-regulation theory, attribution theory, or the theory of reasoned action (Freudenberg, Eng, Flay, Parcel, Rogers & Wallerstein, 1995). Community empowerment is another approach that builds upon the community organization model.

Community Empowerment

The original health promotion application of community enpowerment, as described by Steuart (Steckler, Dawson, Israel & Eng, 1993), encourages the development of individual and community competence that could then be directed toward solving health and social problems. The community empowerment approach is based on the literacy programs developed by the Brazilian educator Paulo Freire (Freire, 1973). According to Wallerstein and Bernstein (1994), since powerlessness is recognized as a risk factor for disease, community empowerment is seen as a health-enhancing strategy. They define it as embodying "an interactive process of change, where institutions and communities become transformed as people who participate in changing them become transformed" (p. 142). Empowerment education was described by Freudenberg and colleagues (1995) as a strategy that involves people in assuming control and mastery over their lives and in their social and political contacts. The authors suggested certain principles to guide the use of this approach in health education practice. Included in their recommendations were that health education interventions should (1) be tailored to a specific population within a particular setting, (2) involve participants in the program planning, implementation, and evaluation, (3) integrate efforts aimed at changing individuals, social and physical environments, communities, and policies, (4) link participants' concerns about health to broader life concerns, (5) use existing resources within the environment, (6) build on strengths found among participants and their communities, and (7) advocate for the resources and policy changes needed to achieve the community's goals. The use of such principles requires of a professional health educator the ability to use a variety of health education theories, and to take a multidisciplinary approach in planning community-wide health education interventions.

The various meanings of the community empowerment or participation movement have been explored by Robertson and Minkler (1994), who stated that:

> This new health promotion movement has resulted in a fundamental shift in the way many health professionals think, talk, and write about health, the determinants of health, and strategies for achieving health. . . . The new health promotion movement has given birth to a new group of experts with new knowledge bases, new language, and new skills. . . . Some of the prominent features of this new health promotion movement include: (1) broadening the definition of health and its determinants to include the social and economic context within which health—or, more precisely, non-health—is produced; (2) going beyond the earlier emphasis on individual lifestyle strategies to achieve health to broader social and political strategies; (3) embracing the concept of empowerment—individual and collective—as a key health promotion strategy; (4) advocating the participation of the community in identifying health problems and strategies for addressing those problems. (p. 296)

Health educators who utilize the empowerment approach serve as resources to assist individuals and communities to identify and prioritize their health problems, to develop action plans to address the priority areas identified, and also assist in locating funding sources and in grant writing efforts. The goal is to assist the community's indigenous leadership with accessing information and in developing its own problem-solving skills or community competence. In addition to serving as resources for the community, another role for health educators in this model is to be actively involved "in the empowerment process as partners, plunging ourselves equally into the learning process" (Wallerstein & Bernstein, 1994, p. 144).

Application examples of this model include the Alcohol and Substance Abuse Prevention (ASAP) program and the Casa en Casa (House to House) program. Both programs are ongoing attempts to blend community organizing with Freire's empowerment approach.

Wallerstein (1994) described the ASAP as a community-based program aimed to reduce morbidity and mortality among high-risk, low-income middle and high school students from multiethnic communities. The program is designed to empower these students to make health-promoting choices in their lives and to encourage them to be active leaders in their schools and communities. The program brings together small groups of students in both hospital and correctional settings. Students meet with patients and inmates who have suffered from the consequences of alcohol and/or drug abuse and who may have been involved in interpersonal violence. This approach to experiential learning is designed to increase students' motivation to avoid such destructive behaviors while increasing their self-efficacy and coping skills. Decision-making discussions and instruction in coping skills conclude each site visit. After four such visits, students are trained at their home schools as peer educators to carry their message to their fellow students. According to Wallerstein (1994):

> The coping skills curriculum, linked with additional training in peer education techniques back at their school sites, assists the students in becoming leaders in their schools and communities. The action stage of ASAP has included many student projects, such as peer teaching with students in lower grades, developing videos on their own communities, writing a rap song to play on a local radio station, or testifying at tribal council meetings. . . . The pre- and post-test data collected on individuals and the participant observations of youth actions suggest that the program is having an effect on psychological empowerment variables, as well as community competence dimensions, such as the youths' ability to articulate themselves as political actors in their worlds. In sum, the ASAP program incorporates Freire's underlying philosophy of personal and social transformation with youth who often experience societal inequalities, cultural conflicts or powerlessness. The educational problem-posing approach with triggers and dialogue helps people move beyond barriers to learning and involves them in a group process to change their lives as learners and as emerging teachers in their communities. (pp. 172–173)

A second example of a community empowerment program, the Casa en Casa program, is the mental health outreach program of La Clinica de la Raza in Oakland, California. This program also includes use of the CHW model. Meredith (1994), who presents both the results and weaknesses of this program, described the project goals as: (1) to promote grassroots leadership within Oakland's Latino community (via the CHWs), and (2) for these promoters to become organized and to plan and direct community health education projects. The project began by recruiting group members through community health education presentations and by inviting neighbors to health discussions held in participant homes. These discussions included steps to becoming involved in community action. Monthly meetings and annual community workshops were held to increase the promoters' knowledge of such topics as sexuality and reproductive health, gang violence, and immigration rights. According to Meredith, the professional staff continued to collaborate with the CHWs on the planning and implementation of these workshops.

One criticism staff had about the program was the continued dependence of the promoters on the staff. As the staff began investigating this problem, several limitations were found to the methods as utilized by their program. Meredith described these as including: (1) no orientation of promoters to the purpose of the program or to their role in it, and (2) an excessive focus on content areas without educating promoters on process skills such as how to facilitate meetings, set goals and objectives, and manage group dynamics. The program staff lacked a consensus regarding both their understanding of the nature of community organization and also a common definition of the empowerment process. While these limitations were common to at least one such program, it would be prudent to attempt to address them in future community empowerment efforts.

Community Health Workers

The Casa en Casa model just described included the use of trained CHWs to plan, organize, and deliver community health education workshops. CHWs (also referred to as lay health advisors, promotoras, or promoters) have often been used in addressing the needs of underserved populations (Gagnon, 1991; Giblin, 1989; Gokcay, Bulut & Neyzi, 1993; Hubbard, 1989; National Migrant Resource Program, 1994; and Warrick, Wood, Meister & de Zapien, 1992). CHWs are respected lay health workers who provide information and community-based health promotion/education services. In a recent annotation of the CHW literature, conducted by the Centers for Disease Control and Prevention (CDCP, 1994), such volunteer workers were described as:

> conducting community-level activities and interventions that promote health and prevent diseases. These advisors are trusted, respected members of the community who serve as a bridge between their peers and health professionals. Their informal, but direct, involvement enhances the delivery of health-related services to diverse populations, including minority, rural, and underserved populations. They provide a vital service by establishing and maintaining relationships with health care professionals in local public health departments and laypersons in the community. As health advocates, community health

advisors promote and encourage positive, healthful behaviors among their peers. (p. vi)

Such workers increase both the accessibility and acceptability of health promotion/education and health care services by serving as a bridge between traditional or organized health professionals and their local communities. They are viewed as local friends rather than outside providers, yet as residents of their local communities they are also the most knowledgeable about a community's cultural and social traditions. With adequate training, CHWs can provide basic health promotion/education and referral services. This approach seems particularly useful in working with "hard-to-reach" Hispanic groups and border populations.

Barnes (1995) stated that in the American Southwest, CHWs "focus almost exclusively on maternal-child-health-related areas, prenatal care, adolescent sexual behavior, and nutrition" (p. 3). He added that half of all CHW programs in the U.S. are funded through public support and that three-quarters of CHW programs compensate their workers. Training is a component of most programs, with workers most frequently being supervised by a CHW coordinator (typically a public health educator, social worker, or nurse). According to Barnes (1995), training for CHWs:

> should include (1) health/need assessments; (2) client recruitment; (3) health promotion/education—inform target population of available services and how to access them, educating through multilingual, multifaceted modes of communication (home visits, radio, TV, written materials), interpreting and advocating; and (4) coordination — effective referral and follow-up. (p. 4)

One such example of how CHWs function as educators is through the Institute for Border Community Health Education (1994). The duties of CHWs in this program were described as recruiting and training volunteer health workers from the area to inform other residents about center services, organizing community development projects, and promoting self-care and preventive health care among residents in El Paso County, Texas. Trainees completed 65 hours of study with health professionals and then completed on-the-job training through area health centers.

Watkins and colleagues (1994) investigated use of a CHW model with Latino migrant farm workers and infants. The program was conducted through selected community migrant health centers in North Carolina. In recent years there has been a major shift in Latino ethnic representation among East Coast migrant workers. The percentage of Latino women receiving care at one such center increased from 45 percent in 1982 to 85 percent in 1988. Staff reported that most of the migrant Latinos were from Mexico and central America. The purpose of their study was to determine the extent to which assistance from CHWs was associated with improved health practices and status among Latino migrant farm workers enrolled in prenatal and child health care services at the selected community migrant health centers (Watkins et al., 1994). Results showed that 66 percent of their sample population had interacted with CHWs, with 22 percent indicating that they had received CHW help. Though involvement with CHWs had no statistically significant effect on health status, mothers who were exposed to CHWs were more likely to bring their children in for sick child care and had greater knowledge about health practices. At those sites where the CHW programs had been active for more than a year, a higher number of pregnant women made the recommended number of prenatal visits (Watkins et al., 1994). These results suggest that while the CHW approach may be a useful extension of community empowerment efforts, further outcomes-based research is needed.

The widespread support for the CHW model for community-based health promotion/education has led at least one international group to call for its continued support and growth. The XII Border Governors' Conference held in May, 1994, in Phoenix, Arizona, focused on health issues along the border. One of the governors' six policy recommendations included support for a border volunteer corps.

> The development of the border volunteer corps in both countries will provide opportunities for border residents to serve as volunteers along both sides of the border, within public and private institutions, to better meet health and other social needs along the border. (Committee on Health and Social Implications of Increased Trade along the Border Region, 1994, p. 6)

According to Sanders (1994), the U.S. Congress has stated that the work of CHWs should include: (1) collaboration with health care providers to facilitate the provision of health services, (2) instruction in public education on health promotion and disease prevention to facilitate the use of preventive health care services, (3) education in health-related counseling and referrals to available health and social services, and (4) training in the provision of outreach services to inform the community of their program.

All three of the health promotion/education strategies/models addressed in this chapter share a concern for cultural sensitivity, individual or community empowerment, and the belief that appropriately trained individuals from the local community are the ideal promoters of culturally appropriate health education messages. These approaches hold promise in enabling public health educators to design more culturally appropriate programs. Unfortunately, they also have in common a general lack of outcome studies to support many of their claims. Designing such program evaluation studies may be more difficult at the larger community/societal level than at the individual level of behavior change. Yet such studies are needed in order to validate the usefulness of these approaches.

Academic programs preparing public health educators must include a more significant programmatic focus on instilling a greater appreciation for the role such cultural themes have in determining the health practices of a population group, and in designing more culturally appropriate interventions. They must do more than this, however, to better meet the health promotion/education needs of disadvantaged groups in the U.S. and along the border region. As the CHW model suggests, the best individuals for promoting health in their local neighborhoods are those from the local communities. For academic programs, an extension of this suggests the need for greater recruitment efforts targeting minority and disadvantaged students for their degree programs. According to Ginzberg (1991):

> One of the reasons for the difficulties Hispanics experience in obtaining adequate health care is the fact that they are seriously under-represented in the health occupations, particularly those requiring higher levels of skill . . . a continuing gross deficiency of Hispanic health professionals threatens the level of access of this large and growing minority to the health care system. However, to increase significantly the flow of Hispanics into health professional schools is not an easy undertaking and the resources required far exceed those currently available. Such an effort requires early interventions to direct capable students to precollege programs that offer special educational guidance, counseling, and tutoring; the availability of financial assistance; and the provision of a variety of other supports. (p. 240)

According to *Healthy People 2000* (U.S. Department of Health and Human Services, 1990), greater numbers of minority public health practitioners and culturally appropriate interventions are needed to better address several health disparities among minority groups. One of the report's objectives (item 21.8) emphasized the need to increase the proportion of all degrees in the health professions awarded to members of underrepresented racial and ethnic minority groups. The report added that in the 1985–1986 academic year, all underrepresented minorities combined made up 8.3 percent of the graduates from schools of public health, demonstrating the need to recruit more students from the rural and border areas into public health programs.

In one effort to address this need, the community/public health degree programs at New Mexico State University obtained federal funding from the Health Resources and Services Administration's Bureau of Health Professions to establish an Allied Health Careers Opportunity Program (AHCOP). This initiative recruits high school seniors and college pre-matriculants to participate in a six-week summer enrichment program. The objective of this summer experience is to enhance the skills of such students so that they may better compete for admission to the university's community/public health degree programs. The program also includes financial aid information and, for those admitted to the academic programs, provides for ongoing retention programming. Since this is only the fourth year of participating in the AHCOP effort, evaluation results will not be available for several more years. An immediate result, however, has been an increase in the minority student enrollment within the academic programs. Already its minority graduates have assumed leadership positions in their local border communities, leading grassroots efforts in community organizing and empowerment to address some of the serious environmental issues confronting their neighborhoods. This approach to targeting increased recruitment of minority and educationally disadvantaged students may be among the more effective models for addressing the numerous public health needs of the border region.

REFERENCES

Amezcua, C., McAlister, A., Ramirez, A., & Espinoza, R. (1990). A Su Salud: Health promotion in a Mexican-American border community. In N. Bracht (Ed.), *Health promotion at the community level*. Newbury Park, CA: Sage.

Barnes, M.D. (1995). *The development of recommendations for a community health worker (promotora) education and training program*. New Mexico Border Health Office No. 95/665.42.136. Santa Fe, NM: Public Health Division, New Mexico Department of Health.

Belcazar, H., Castro, F.G., & Krull, J.L. (1995). Cancer risk reduction in Mexican American women: The role of acculturation, education, and health risk factors. *Health Education Quarterly, 22*(1), 61–84.

Bracht, N. (Ed.). (1990). *Health promotion at the community level*. Newbury Park, CA: Sage, 253–356.

Braithwaite, R. & Lythcott, N. (1989). Community empowerment as a strategy for health promotion for black and other minority populations. *Journal of the American Medical Association, 261*(2), 183–184.

Centers for Disease Control and Prevention, National Center for Chronic Disease Prevention and Health Promotion. (1994). *Community health advisors: Models, research, and practice—selected annotations—United States.* (Vol. 1). Atlanta, GA: U.S. Department of Health and Human Services, Public Health Service.

Committee on Health and Social Implications of Increased Trade along the Border Region. (1994). *Preliminary recommendations for the 1994 border governors' conference.* Tijuana, Baja California.

Dhillon, H.S. (1991). A call for action: Promoting health in developing countries. *Health Education Quarterly, 18*(1), 5–15.

Freire, P. (1973). *Education for critical consciousness.* New York: Seabury.

Freudenberg, N., Eng, E., Flay, B., Parcel, G., Rogers, T., & Wallerstein, N. (1995). Strengthening individual and community capacity to prevent disease and promote health: In search of relevant theories and principles. *Health Education Quarterly, 22*(3), 290–306.

Gagnon, A.J. (1991). The training and integration of village health workers. *Bulletin of the Pan American Health Organization, 25*(2), 127–138.

Giblin, P.T. (1989). Effective utilization and evaluation of indigenous health care workers. *Public Health Reports, 104*(4), 361–368.

Ginzberg, E. (1991). Access to health care for Hispanics. *Journal of the American Medical Association, 265*, 238–241.

Glanz, K., Lewis, F.M., & Rimer, B.K. (Eds.). (1990). *Health behavior and health education: Theory, research, and practice.* San Francisco, CA: Jossey-Bass.

Gokcay, G., Bulut, A., & Neyzi, O. (1993). Paraprofessional women as health care facilitators in mother and child health. *Tropical Doctor 23*(4), 79–81.

Gonzales, R., McAlister, A., Ramirez, A.G., Amezcua, C., & Cardenas, C. (1994). Volunteer health promoters in Eagle Pass, Texas. *Border Health Journal, 10*(4), 1–3.

Green, L.W. & Kreuter, M.W. (1991). *Health promotion planning: An educational and environmental approach.* Mountain View, CA: Mayfield Publishing Co.

Hubbard, J.K. (1989). Emergence of the role of the village health worker—A new status in Tarahumara society. *Border Health, 1*(Special Issue), 6–10.

Institute for Border Community Health Education. (1994). Community health workers administer equal dose of education and friendship. *Palabras, 1*(1), 7–8.

LeMaster, P.L. & Connell, C.M. (1994). Health education interventions among Native Americans: A review and analysis. *Health Education Quarterly, 21*(4), 521–538.

Marin, G., Burhansstipanov, L., Connell, C.M., Gielen, A.C., Helitzer-Allen, D., Lorig, K., Morisky, D.E., Tenney, M., & Thomas, S. (1995). A research agenda for health education among underserved populations. *Health Education Quarterly, 22*(3), 346–363.

Meredith, E. (1994). Critical pedagogy and its application to health education: A critical appraisal of the Casa en Casa model. *Health Education Quarterly, 21*(3), 355–367.

National Migrant Resource Program. (1994). *Overview: Traveling lay health advisor program.* Austin, TX: National Migrant Resource Program, Inc.

Ortega, H. (1991). Promoting binational cooperation to improve health along the U.S.-Mexico border. *Carnegie Quarterly, 36*(1–4), 1–8.

Robertson, A. & Minkler, M. (1994). New health promotion movement: A critical examination. *Health Education Quarterly, 21*(3), 295–312.

Romer, D. & Kim, S. (1995). Health interventions for African American and Latino youth: The potential role of mass media. *Health Education Quarterly, 22*(2), 172–189.

Sanders, B. (1994). *National community health advisor act: H.R. 4024: Provides for the establishment of a national program of trained community health advisors to assist states in attaining the Healthy People 2000 goals and objectives.* Press Release, July 26, 1994. Washington, D.C.: United States Congress.

Selwyn, B.J., Loe, H., & Moore, F.I. (1992). The primary health care review approach to binational community based health care evaluation and action along the U.S.-Mexico border. *Border Health, 8*(3), 56–66.

Steckler, A. (1993). Community health education: Principles and problems. *Health Education Quarterly, Supplement 1,* S29–S47.

Steckler, A., Dawson, L., Israel, B., & Eng, E. (1993). Community health development: An overview of the works of Guy W. Steuart. *Health Education Quarterly, Supplement 1,* S3–S20.

United States Department of Health and Human Services (1990). *Healthy People 2000: Priorities for the nation.* Washington, D.C.: United States Department of Health and Human Services, General Accounting Office.

United States-Mexico Border Health Association (1991). *Project Consenso Final Report.* El Paso, TX: Pan American Health Organization, El Paso Field Office.

Villas, P. & Williams, D. (1993). A vertical-horizontal application of PRECEDE-PROCEED: The colonia community experience. *Border Health, 9*(3), 1–8.

Wallerstein, N. (1994). Empowerment education applied to youth. In A.G. Matiella (Ed.), *The multicultural challenge in health education.* Santa Cruz, CA: ETR Associates, 153–176.

Wallerstein, N. & Bernstein, E. (1994). Introduction to community empowerment, participatory education, and health. *Health Education Quarterly, 21*(2), 141–148.

Warrick, L.H., Wood, A.H., Meister, J.S., & de Zapien, J.G. (1992). Evaluation of a peer health worker prenatal outreach and education program for Hispanic farmworker families. *Journal of Community Health, 17*(1), 13–26.

Watkins, E.L., Harlan, C., Eng, E., Gansky, S.A., Gehan, D., & Larson, K. (1994). Assessing the effectiveness of lay health advisors with migrant farmworkers. *Family and Community Health, 16*(4), 71–87.

Williams, J.E. & Flora, J.A. (1995). Health behavior segmentation and campaign planning to reduce cardiovascular disease among Hispanics. *Health Education Quarterly, 22*(1), 36–48.

8   BORDER HEALTH PROBLEMS

A SYSTEMS APPROACH TO SOLUTIONS

John G. Bruhn

THE BORDERLANDS: OPPORTUNITIES AND CHALLENGES

As Mexico and the United States become more interdependent, there is an emergence of a "Mexamerica," a binational, bicultural, and bilingual regional complex that shares opportunities as well as ecology and quality of life (McCarthy, 1983). Air and water pollution, raw sewage and sewage spills, toxic waste disposal and illegal dumping, infectious disease transmission, the environment of the maquiladoras, and health services are some of the more urgent problems facing both countries. These problems continue to grow in scope and complexity because health and ecology are not high profile policy issues. Border issues have not enjoyed high priority with the governments of the United States or Mexico, and therefore, there are few resources for binational efforts to attempt to solve these problems. These problems are further complicated by differences in culture and language (Scrutchfield, 1985).

The La Paz Agreement

In 1983, the presidents of the United States and Mexico signed an executive Agreement to Cooperate in the Solution of Environmental Problems in the Border Area. It was the first formal U.S.-Mexican agreement to address air, land, and water pollution (Ables, 1992). The La Paz Agreement, as it is commonly known, was an attempt to establish a foundation the two countries could build upon to protect and preserve the environment along the border. The Agreement was a document of intent to work together with no enforceable obligations and neither country ever committed funds to implement it. The Agreement authorized the environmental agencies in the two countries, the Environmental Protection Agency (EPA) in the United States, and SEDUE in Mexico, to establish technical advisory groups to address environmental problems along the border. In 1984, three work groups were established to address the topics of water, air, and hazardous waste pollution and communication procedures were established for dealing with these issues. Work groups on contingency planning, cooperative enforcement strategies, and pollution prevention were added later.

The Secretariat of Urban Development and Ecology (SEDUE), the Mexican counterpart to EPA, was to identify problem areas, provide an inventory of hazards, and develop low-cost planning solutions to deal with future hazards. Additionally, they were to encourage voluntary compliance with environmental standards among public and private sectors. In contrast to EPA standards, which have enforceable limits, SEDUE's standards encourage voluntary compliance. Therefore, violation of the La Paz Agreement by SEDUE is not illegal. In addition, although state and local authorities in Mexico have the power to conduct environmental inspections, they are prohibited from doing so because many local jurisdictions have not adopted federal law (Ables, 1992).

The progress made binationally for the border's environmental problems depends to a large extent upon Mexico's economic development and the degree of responsibility the United States is willing to assume for Mexico's waste problems. Since the La Paz Agreement does not carry the weight of a ratified treaty, the United States is unable to force U.S.-owned factories to comply with Mexico's environmental laws. Even a comprehensive plan will not be effective if the two countries fail to enforce their agreements. This argument led the United States to use Mexico's desire to implement NAFTA as leverage to draft and implement the Integrated Border Environment Plan (IBEP) announced in 1992 by President Bush. When the plan was announced, pledged funds approximated a total of $1 billion from Mexico, the United States, private industry, and state governments. The funds were earmarked for a sewage treatment plant for Tijuana and San Diego, a project to clean the New River, which flows from Mexicali, Mexico, to California, and the creation of wastewater and drinking water treatment systems in Texas, among other projects. Critics argue that the plan's provisions are too vague, the plan is underfunded, and immediate border problems are not addressed (Ables, 1992; Kovarik, 1993). The IBEP seems to be little more than the reaffirmation of the La Paz Agreement; many of the goals are voluntary and provide no incentives for compliance by industry.

The enforcement of IBEP includes cooperative customs training, high visibility deterrent enforcement, the development of a tracking system to monitor hazardous waste shipments, and an increase in the enforcement of environmental laws among the maquiladoras where appropriate. The plan lacks details about how these activities will be carried out. The plan states that its guidelines provide an innovative approach to prevention and proposes to establish a work group on prevention. Each country's environmental agency will provide a technical assistance program to train businessmen to minimize waste. Several university-based pollution prevention research centers will be established along the border. These centers will work to develop model projects to be shared with communities. Education of the public about the protection of natural resources and the environment is also proposed.

Ables (1992) points out that, as with the La Paz Agreement, the IBEP neither commits to upholding any specific environmental standards nor contains a mechanism to enforce its provisions. As a result, there are many new proposals from the environmental community.

One proposal is to diminish the authority of the bodies under the La Paz Agreement, replacing them with a United States-Mexico environmental treaty and environmental commission. Another suggestion is to establish a continental North American Environmental Commission with regulatory authority that includes the ability to establish standards and enforce them. Both governments have resisted the establishment of international commissions that would intrude on the sovereignty of each country. Instead, the U.S. and Mexico call for existing work groups under the IBEP to be more aggressive in building sewage treatment plants, tracking hazardous wastes, and providing clean-up facilities. In addition, there are proposals that would provide for cooperation and communication between the two countries and their environmental protection agencies by the establishment of a U.S.-Mexico Border Environmental Health Commission (American Medical Association, 1990). However, it would not be regulatory. Thus, environmental groups are calling for a more integrated environmental plan but, again, none of these commissions would have regulatory or enforcement power (Utton, 1993).

The North American Free Trade Agreement (NAFTA) between the United States, Mexico, and Canada, while providing many new economic opportunities, will exacerbate existing problems, especially in health services. It is projected that as the public social security system in Mexico is restructured and recognizes the right to health, and selective privatization of health services is introduced, that inequalities in health services will increase (Laurell & Ortega, 1992). The U.S. insurance industry and hospital corporations are interested in promoting these changes in order to gain access to the Mexican market. A public-private system would polarize services for the poor majority and make private services accessible only to the 30 percent of the population that can afford them. This will have a significant effect on health services in Mexico, where about 50 percent of the people live below the poverty line. It is also likely that border crossings will increase, and unless infectious diseases are better controlled, increased immigration and migration will widen the spread of some diseases. In addition, some environmental problems may increase with industrial expansion and social problems will increase as the border becomes more affluent. The major point is that NAFTA will make many aspects of our international boundaries invisible and make our interdependence more obvious. Ecological and social problems which affect health and quality of life will become social system problems and will require our collective wisdom and resources to solve them.

A Superordinate Goal: Survival

Recently policy recommendations were presented for managing the El Paso-Ciudad Juárez metropolitan area (Schmidt & Lorey, 1994). By the year 2010, the rapidly growing population of this area is projected to reach 3.3 million. In El Paso-Ciudad Juárez, there is at present no consistent monitoring of either water or air pollution and there are no statistics on basic aspects of economic and social change.

To frame a binational analysis and discuss the management and long-range planning of El Paso-Ciudad Juárez, the 80 members of PROFMEX (the Worldwide Consortium for Research on Mexico) and the 80 members of ANVIES (the Mexican Asociacion Nacional de Universidades y Instituciones de Educacion Superior) organized teams of scholars to cooperate in defining policies for the U.S.-Mexico border region. Projects focused on four topics:

- management of urban services and policy planning in the greater metropolitan area;
- water, hazardous waste, and public policy;
- environmental pollution and health issues;
- public housing, irregular settlements, and the informal sector.

While the population in the El Paso-Ciudad Juárez metropolitan area has grown to about 1.5 million, the social and physical infrastructure supporting the living conditions has not kept pace. Infrastructure bureaucracy has resulted in serious backlogs in public housing, transportation, sewage, potable water, electricity, paved roads, health services, garbage removal, and child care facilities. The expected economic activities stimulated by the NAFTA will further strain an already limited infrastructure.

The two cities depend on a shared underground aquifer (Hueco Bolson) for the majority of potable water. The supply of water from this source has been declining for years. Supplying a growing population will become an increasingly urgent challenge. Environmental concerns have grown as the area is generally covered by a thick pall of smoke and haze from factory emissions, the burning of used tires, and windblown dust.

Government efforts to provide key urban services have only been partially successful. In Ciudad Juárez, maquiladoras generate only token income taxes and because state and municipal authorities in Mexico have no independent tax levying authority to fund public services, infrastructure support on the Mexican side of the border is largely dependent on funds from the Federal Government of Mexico. In contrast, El Paso's lack of public service infrastructure is due to the location of colonias outside the city limits where the county claims it has no resources to resolve public service shortfalls (Schmidt & Lorey, 1994).

Few mechanisms exist at present for the resolution of the urban services and environmental problems in the twin city area. Policy makers on both sides are only beginning to recognize that the costs of not attending to short- and long-range solutions continue to mount.

NAFTA assumes that there will be reciprocity between the counties involved. Reciprocity can evolve into cooperation, but cultures differ in the extent to which they motivate people to behave cooperatively (Boyd & Richerson, 1990). Therefore, a common (superordinate) goal needs to be agreed upon that strongly motivates both countries, but cannot be reached by one country alone without the help of the other. In a situation requiring action to reach a common goal, membership in subgroups loses relevance. A superordinate goal is usually easier to establish in a culture that has an orientation to groups and institutions as opposed to a culture that emphasizes the individual (Triandis, 1991). Harman (1992) points out that there is growing worldwide interest in a social paradigm that emphasizes "wholeness" in dealing with societal illnesses. This view transcends cultures and may be the basis upon which to establish a superordinate goal of improving health and the quality of life along the U.S.-Mexico border.

There is a need to introduce a goal that can transcend cultural differences and is potent enough to gain the attention of both cultures. A superordinate goal that has compelling appeal for both the United States and Mexico is survival. If a state of interdependence between cultures is produced for the attainment of survival, both cultures would seemingly be more inclined to take up ecological and health problems and proceed to plan and execute their solutions jointly.

A Systems Approach: Beyond Partnerships

A systems approach to solving and preventing border health problems has several advantages: (1) it can focus on several problems simultaneously; (2) it provides a holistic perspective for planning and forecasting; (3) it shifts the emphasis from quick-fix solutions to long-term ones; (4) it examines the process and effects of change, and (5) it involves all levels of complexity of a living system. Border health problems are simultaneously local and international; therefore, interventions in one county or at one level within a country will not bring about lasting solutions. The lack of interest and financial resources on the part of the federal governments of both Mexico and the United States have often been blamed for the piecemeal and episodic attention to border health at the federal level. There have been numerous fact-finding and infrastructure development projects. For example, the Pew and Carnegie Foundations and the Pan American Health Organization collaborated to develop and establish institutional networks for interdisciplinary and collaborative research, education, and training along the U.S.-Mexico border in order to improve the health status of women, adolescents, and children (Pan American Health Organization, 1992). Other projects have specific targets for intervention. For example, the cities of El Paso, Ciudad Juárez, and Las Cruces have developed a public health promotion and health education initiative to reduce the high level of preschool-age children who have not been fully immunized against preventable diseases. Another project diagnoses, treats, and thereby reduces the incidence of tuberculosis in Ciudad Juárez and El Paso. A third project, developed with the cooperation of the U.S. Environmental Protection Agency, the Texas Air Control Board, and the El Paso City-County Health District, consisted of studying the generation and movement of inhalable particulates (Nickey, 1994). There is no question that partnerships directed toward studying specific health issues have been successful, especially private foundations partnering with universities and public health agencies (Nightingale & Peck, 1991). However, the nature and scope of border health problems challenge us to go beyond partnerships and professional traditions (See Table 8.1).

Two Countries: One Goal

It is tempting to rely on two extremes of the continuum when considering intervention—either the federal government or the community is usually expected to assume the responsibility. The disadvantages of either extreme are apparent. Initiatives are usually politically motivated, limited in scope, inadequately funded, and there is rarely any accountability regarding the long-term effects of an intervention. Yet, perhaps more importantly, interventions are seldom developed and implemented with the total system in mind, that is, the effect of the intervention on other parts of the system where

TABLE 8.1. Advantages and Disadvantages of Different Approaches to Solving U.S.-Mexico Border Health Problems

Approach	Advantages	Disadvantages
1. Informal Agreements between Communities	informal	changes in people involved may require starting over
	usually a small number of people	does not involve entire community
	usually focused on a specific issue	limited scope
	based on trust, open communication	no formal agreement, timeline, or long-term commitment
	rapid start-up	may run out of resources, interest
	commitment may be political	inability to to continue project or program
2. Small-scale Binational Cooperation	can mobilize teams across communities	need strong leaders willing to commit time and energy
	involves a variety of institutions, agencies, etc.	inter-group conflicts
	problem-specific; mutual goal	teams and commitment may dissipate after problem is solved
	can minimize differences in language and culture	differences in priorities of what needs to be done

(continued on next page)

Approach	Advantages	Disadvantages
	variety of resources pooled	time spent in coordinating and planning financial resources
3. Regionalization of Communities	empower citizenry; network relationships	may be threat to non-involved
	may develop national constituency	may become too broad
	overcomes local intransigence	may mobilize resistance groups
	financial support from a variety of sources	coordination and fund-raising time-consuming
	lasting change can result	dissatisfaction with compromises to achieve results
	can be innovative to meet regional needs	local areas may feel neglected
4. National Policy	usually resources are allocated	resources usually time-limited, insufficient and very focused
	national attention to problems	usually involves agencies, not wide citizenry involvement
	usually a policy of the party in power	usually no continuity and follow-up
	usually directed toward a specific issue or problem	no comprehensive health or ecology policy
	can mobilize a variety of institutions and agencies	often conflict between turf of agencies

(continued on next page)

Approach	Advantages	Disadvantages
	resources directed by government bureaucrats	often resources do not reach local levels
	needs determined by government	local communities often not involved in needs assessment
5. Systems	ability to examine input and output factors in the system	usually impossible to involve a large number of people or "customers" of the system
	can focus on several problems simultaneously	the importance of human values can get lost
	provides a holistic perspective for planning and forecasting	small, pressing problems are part of larger problems which take longer to resolve
	shift in emphasis from short-term or quick-fix solutions to long-term solutions	impatience with the process

the intervention is not intended to have an effect. In attempting to solve one problem we often unknowingly create new ones or worsen others that are not targeted for intervention. A systems approach considers not only input and output, but the process in between.

Figure 8.1 illustrates a social systems structure for solving border health problems. The first step to solving or preventing any border health problem is for the United States and Mexico to reach agreement on a superordinate goal. The goal should have fairly equal importance in both cultures. It is suggested that survival is valued relatively equally in both cultures. But merely surviving is not sufficient. The issue is to minimize self- and societal-induced disease risks, which not only reduce survivability but also the quality of life.

The two countries, if there is a commonly valued goal, can then work toward developing a binational policy on how to increase survivability and enhance the quality of life on both sides of the border. The policy must be endorsed and promoted by the two governments and jointly funded. If only one government promotes and funds efforts, the entire enterprise is doomed, as health issues are not confined to geographical borders nor are they the responsibility of only one country.

It is essential that border health problems be addressed by both the United States and Mexico. While policy and financial resources are the prerogative of the federal governments, the major work toward improving life on the border will be accomplished at the regional and community levels. There is a need for a planning and oversight body that will interface between the federal, regional, and community levels. The proposed Binational Survival Commission should be of reasonable size to be effective, yet representative of community, regional, and federal constituencies. This commission should have monitoring and enforcement powers agreed upon by both Washington and Mexico City. The primary purposes of the commission would be to: (1) establish a plan of action with objectives and priorities for solving and preventing border health problems; (2) suggest the allocation of funds to various priorities; and (3) monitor the progress toward reaching the objectives agreed upon. The commission should be a facilitating mechanism for receiving advice and recommendations from regions and communities that could be used in policy making and resource allocation at the federal level.

Local Coalitions and Regional Impacts

Usually decisions and resources flow downward from the federal level to regional levels to local levels, which usually have little power and influence.

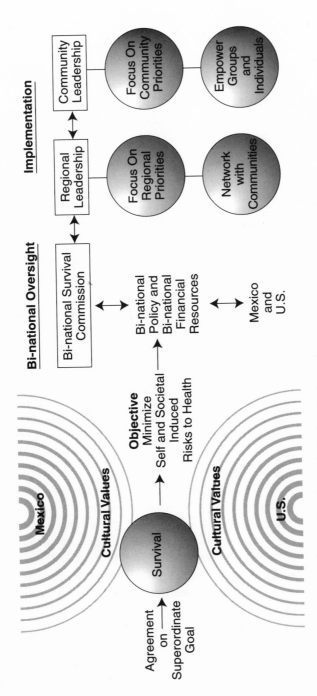

Figure 8.1. Social systems structures for solving U.S.-Mexican border problems.

The superordinate goal of survival and the reduction of risks to health cannot be mandated by government and be accepted. There must be a buy-in from citizens. This will be a formidable challenge, as officials in most U.S.-Mexico border towns attempt to minimize the influence of external policy makers and use informal rather than formal agreements to achieve cooperation (Sloan & West, 1977). Border cities protect their autonomy, but many environmental problems, such as air and water pollution, must involve the federal governments of both the United States and Mexico.

One approach is to build coalitions from local groups experiencing similar problems. Local groups have developed national constituencies and influence through regional coalition building in the U.S., for example, Gray Panthers and Mothers Against Drunk Driving. Through the regionalization of community building, national policy can be developed. This would be a way communities and regions could leverage their concerns with the federal government.

Guidotti and Conway (1987) point out that most border health problems are both local and international and that large-scale government-to-government interactions have generally failed to achieve lasting cooperation on important health issues. One reason is that health problems have largely been identified by government, which has attempted to induce change by mandate. Guidotti and Conway suggest that binational cooperation can be successfully achieved in small-scale local projects. They found that small local projects in the San Diego-Tijuana area were more culturally acceptable than large institutional ones. Small projects were achievable because they were locally conceived, less grandiose, less bureaucratic, and had lower visibility than reverse models often imposed by the government. Another example is the successful partnership between Nogales, Arizona, and Nogales, Sonora, Mexico, called Platicamos Salud, in which a bilingual group of eight trained community women educate other women in prenatal care, immunization, breast feeding, cancer prevention, and other preventive health measures.

While these are excellent examples of problem solving at the community level across cultures, as one community health worker said, "It's hard to talk about hygiene when a family doesn't have water." This illustrates the real meaning of the superordinate goal of survival. In many border communities survival means food, some type of shelter, and water from the nearest available source. Health, personal or environmental, is often not a consideration in survival. Thus, in order to achieve a superordinate goal of survival, both countries will have to put the basic necessities of life as first priority for a majority of the population residing on the U.S.-Mexico border. It is ironic that NAFTA has provided the opportunity for many hospitals in

U.S. border cities to market their services in Mexico to attract Mexican patients to U.S. hospitals and clinics while the essential aspects of survival, let alone health, remain ignored. The challenge to government officials, health care providers, and all citizens is to think and act as if life and health were part of the same system. The 1993–94 Texas State Health Plan states, "The current health system along the border lacks an adequate personal health care delivery system that stresses primary and preventive health care services. Both Mexico and the United States need to recognize and treat the border as a single epidemiological unit for purposes of assessing health problems, planning, and implementing remedial program systems" (p. 155).

Prevention: A Difficult Choice

Preventing disease and reducing or eliminating risks to longevity are logical and common sense goals. They are promoted by public health officials with varying degrees of success. One of the reasons prevention is hard to "sell" is that a culture or an individual may have other priorities that are valued more than, or compete equally with, health. For most cultures and individuals prevention is a choice. Whether one experiences good or poor health is often relegated to chance or fate. In some cultures people have never experienced what would be regarded clinically as good health and their daily attention is focused on obtaining basic subsistence for survival. In affluent cultures, or parts of cultures, on the other hand, prevention is often faddish and episodic and is usually focused on physical fitness. It is often thought of as a luxury, as prevention takes time and resources that could be allocated to non–health-related activities (Figure 8.2).

There are a number of different types and sources of data available that can be used to describe the health status of a population or culture. Most of these data relate to evidence of illness, death, or social pathology, and few relate to positive health (Rogers, 1960). It is noteworthy that most health indicators are measures of negative health. Our tendency is to characterize cultures and individuals as more or less sick by using these measures. Measures to characterize cultures and individuals as well or healthy are sparse.

Measurements used to indicate negative health include mortality data, morbidity data, and social pathology such as alcoholism, drug addiction, crime, mental illness, and so on. Measurements used to indicate positive health include birth and fertility rates and life expectancy. There are also numerous environmental factors that can affect health negatively or positively. These are difficult, if not impossible, to quantify and include physical, biological, and social environmental factors, as well as intrinsic factors such as age, sex, and hereditary characteristics. Because of the diversity and

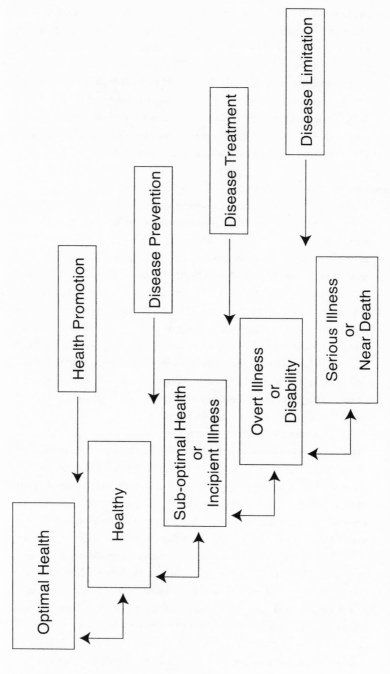

Figure 8.2. A theoretical representation of health status in an individual and options for intervention at a given time.

complexity of all of these indicators it has been impossible to arrive at an index of health status for a population or culture (Rogers, 1960). However, it is possible to illustrate the theoretical relationship between negative and positive indicators of health and the effect of preventive activities (Figure 8.3). This diagram shows that health status is relative and wellness is an ideal, as some degree of illness, or risk for it, always exists even in the healthiest of cultures.

Arsenian and Arsenian (1948) offer a challenging conceptualization of cultures and their degrees of health. They outline conditions requisite for cultures to be "tough" or "easy." Toughness and easiness are characterized as bipolar; easy cultures are the least tension-producing and -sustaining and tough cultures are pathogenic. Indicators of toughness are crime, suicide, neurosis and psychosis, tenseness, and general malaise. The authors argue that a culture defines the paths by which an individual or group satisfy their needs. In some cultures these paths will be easier than others. When a culture's paths make for easy tension reduction in its members, the culture is easy. Conversely, where a culture's paths make for difficult tension reduction, the culture is tough. It is likely that the majority of cultures will fall somewhere within the extremes of this continuum. With respect to characterizing the United States and Mexico according to this scheme, the United States would probably fall somewhat past the middle of the continuum toward the easy end, while Mexico would probably fall somewhat past the middle of the continuum toward the tough end. This would fit with the earlier observations that Mexico, with substantial poverty and environmental risks to health, would find these challenges the most pressing. While preventive activities are important to both tough and easy cultures, it is a difficult choice for both cultures for different reasons. For Mexico, individual survival is conditioned by access to the necessities for living each day; for the United States, individual survival is conditioned by the value the culture gives to health and individual responsibility for maintaining it. In the United States, prevention has not been highly valued or stressed, until recently, by the culture. The majority of U.S. citizens do not engage in preventive activities.

One of the greatest challenges to solving U.S.-Mexico border health problems is to increase the value of health in both cultures. Health must be given high priority and resources by both governments. Only when there is a positive and receptive cultural climate can policies be framed to be developed and implemented by regional and community groups. Perhaps the largest, but not insurmountable, task is to obtain U.S. and Mexican government agreement on issues and policies and their implementation and enforcement.

Pastor and Castaneda (1988) describe the tensions, conflicts, and

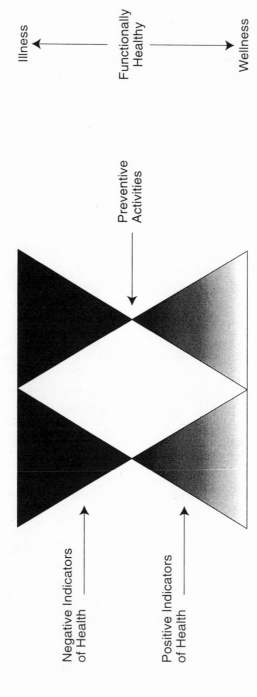

Illness ← Functionally Healthy → Wellness

Preventive Activities

Negative Indicators of Health

Positive Indicators of Health

Figure 8.3. Interrelationship between preventive activities and positive and negative indicators of health.

misperceptions that have always characterized the U.S.-Mexican relationship. These are rooted in history and have changed in the two countries over time. There have been policy mistakes and misconceptions, but this does not mean that nothing can be done to improve the relationship. Survival and the quality of life is a superordinate goal of great and pressing significance to both countries. It is not a question of whether the United States and Mexico will face their common problems jointly, but when. As border health problems continue to worsen, the climate for cooperation is turning more and more to managing crises.

Next Steps

Frenk, Gomez-Dantes, Cruz, Chacon, Hernandez, and Freeman (1994) suggest that there are short-term and long-term steps needed to transform the health care system in Mexico and to provide for the international exchange of health services between Mexico, the United States, and Canada. They propose that, despite the asymmetry of health care resources among the three countries, a new infrastructure can be developed. Specifically, they suggest changes in Mexican health services including:

- modernization of services, including the definition and enforcement of standards that will promote quality and protect consumers,
- licensure and certification of health professionals,
- evaluation of new technologies,
- equity in the system of delivering health services, and
- strengthening of consumer protection of users of health services.

Frenk and his colleagues then propose several long-term measures such as:

- reciprocal recognition of private health insurance among the three countries,
- payment of public and private American and Canadian insurance agencies for services rendered in Mexico,
- establishment in Mexico of low-technology facilities, e.g., hospitals for the chronically ill, convalescence hospitals, and nursing homes, to care for American and Canadian patients
- establishment in the United States and Canada of medical care facilities for the Hispanic populations living in these countries as well as for seasonal workers from Mexico and other Latin American countries, and
- adoption of compatible information systems to speed patient referral, especially in the U.S.-Mexico border area.

Midterm proposals include a study of the feasibility of Mexican financing of health services provided in the United States and Canada when patients' needs so require and the establishment of a tripartite group to analyze ways of strengthening linking mechanisms in health care.

The proposals are ambitious and value-laden. There is a long way to go before health services become more seamless between countries because individual differences have to be overcome within individual countries first. Health is both a value and a commodity. Therefore, any change involving personal or collective health requires risk-taking and tradeoffs. At whatever level, personal or societal, health and health issues are emotional because they involve finances and value systems. The challenge to create matches between the health systems of Mexico, the United States, and Canada is a formidable one, yet if these countries abdicate leadership and permit change to mark a future course, it is likely our mutual problems will become more "unfixable."

REFERENCES

Ables, S. (1992). The integrated plan for the Mexican-U.S. border: A plan to clean up the border or a public relations ploy to promote a free trade agreement? *Arizona Journal of International and Comparative Law, 9,* 487–512.

American Medical Association Council on Scientific Affairs (1990). A permanent U.S.-Mexico border environmental health commission. *Journal of the American Medical Association, 263,* 3319–3321.

Arsenian, J. & Arsenian, J.M. (1948). Tough and easy cultures: A conceptual analysis. *Psychiatry, 11,* 377–385.

Boyd, R. & Richerson, P.J. (1990). Culture and cooperation. In J.J. Mansbridge (Ed.), *Beyond self-interest* (pp. 111–132). Chicago, IL: University of Chicago Press.

Frenk, J., Gomez-Dantes, O., Cruz, C., Chacon, F., Hernandez, P. & Freeman, P. (1994). Consequences of the North American free trade agreement for health services: A perspective from Mexico. *American Journal of Public Health, 84,* 1591–1597.

Guidotti, T.L. & Conway, J.B. (1987). Cooperation in health affairs between adjacent international communities: A successful model. *American Journal of Preventive Medicine, 3,* 287–292.

Harman, W.W. (1992). The emerging "wholeness" worldview and its probable impact on cooperation. In A. Combs (Ed.), *Cooperation: Beyond the age of competition* (pp. 47–57). Philadelphia, PA: Gordon and Breach.

Heller, K. (1990). Social and community intervention. *Annual Review of Psychology, 41,* 141–168.

Kovarik, C. (1993). NAFTA and environmental conditions on the United States-Mexico border. *Kansas Journal of Law and Public Policy, 2,* 61–72.

Laurell, A.S. & Ortega, M.E. (1992). The Free Trade Agreement and the Mexican health sector. *International Journal of Health Services, 22,* 331–337.

McCarthy, K.F. (1983). *Interdependence in the U.S.-Mexican borderlands: An irresistible dynamic or fragmented realty?* Santa Monica, CA: The Rand Corp.

Nickey, L.N. (1994). Personal communication.

Nightingale, E.O. & Peck, M.G. (1991). Partnerships for improving border health. *Western Journal of Medicine, 155,* 303–305.

Pan American Health Organization. (1991). *Primary health care and maternal and* child health technologies for women, adolescents, and children. *Binational project on maternal and child health*. Final Report and Evaluation. El Paso, TX: El Paso Field Office, PAHO.

Pastor, R.A. & Castaneda, J.G. (1988). *Limits to friendship: The United States and Mexico*. New York: Vintage.

Rogers, E.S. (1960). *Human ecology and health*. New York: Macmillan.

Schmidt, S. & Lorey, D. (1994). Policy recommendations for managing the El Paso-Ciudad Juárez metropolitan area. El Paso Community Foundation and Center for InterAmerican and Border Studies. El Paso, TX: University of Texas at El Paso.

Scrutchfield, F.D. (1985). The United States-Mexico border. *The Pharos*, Spring, 9–11.

Sloan, J.W. & West, J.P. (1977). The role of informal policy making in U.S.-Mexico border cities. *Social Science Quarterly, 58*, 270–282.

Texas Statewide Health Coordinating Council (1992), *1993–94 Texas State Health Plan*. Austin, TX.

Triandis, H.C. (1991). Cross-cultural differences in assertiveness/competition vs. group loyalty/cooperation. In R.A. Hinde & J. Groebel (Eds.), *Cooperation and prosocial behavior* (pp. 78–88). Cambridge: Cambridge University Press.

Utton, A.E. (1993). Protecting the environment in the U.S.-Mexico border region. *U.S.-Mexico Law Journal, 1*, 211–214.

Contributors

MICHAEL D. BARNES, PH.D.
New Mexico State University,
Las Cruces

JEFFREY E. BRANDON, PH.D.
New Mexico State University,
Las Cruces

JOHN G. BRUHN, PH.D.
Pennsylvania State University,
Harrisburg

ROBERT W. BUCKINGHAM,
  D.P.H.
New Mexico State University,
Las Cruces

FRANK CRESPIN, M.D., M.P.H.
New Mexico Department
of Health, Las Cruces

JO FAIRBANKS, PH.D.
New Mexico State University,
Las Cruces

CELINDA LEVY, PH.D.
New Mexico State University,
Las Cruces

CARLETON H. MORRISON, JR.,
  J.D., L.L.M.
Morrison and Associates, Inc.
Fallbrook, California

DANIEL M. REYNA, M.P.H.
New Mexico Department
of Health, Las Cruces

KITTY RICHARDS, M.S.
New Mexico Department
of Health, Las Cruces

ALLISON M. WESLEY, B.S.
School of Medicine,
University of Minnesota,
Minneapolis

INDEX

Families USA Foundation, 47, 48
Farm worker population, demographics, 81
Fecal coliform, 127
Federal Qualified Health Centers, 76
Federally Qualified Community/Migrant
        Health Centers, 76, 82, 85
Fertility, 6–7, 185
Folk diseases in South Texas, 20
Folk medicine, 16, 20, 26
    beliefs, 15
    criteria for health, 16
    Mexican, 15
    practices, 15
    utilization, 20
        patterns of, 20
FTA. See Free Trade Agreement
Free trade, 10
Free Trade Agreement. See North American
        Free Trade Agreement
Friendship networks and ties, 4, 5
FQHC. See Federally Qualified Health
        Centers

Gallbladder disease, xvi, 44
Gastrointestinal diseases, 45, 118, 120, 126
    among children in the border states, 127
General Ecological and Environmental
        Regulation Law, 10
Geographic Information System database,
        145–146
    environmental health, and, 143–144
Good Neighbor Environmental Board, 64,
        136
    findings, 136
    recommendations, 60, 64–65, 136–137
Gray Panthers, 192
Groundwater resources, transboundary, 127
Growth patterns, 6

Harmony and balance, 14–15
Hazardous and toxic waste, 84, 130–131,
        183
    disposal, 181
Hazardous chemical exposure, 120
Health
    beliefs, 30
        culturally based, 16
        desire of Anglo physicians to con-
            vert to Anglo beliefs, 16
        knowledge and understanding of
            health professionals, 16
    concepts of, 14–26, 30, 31
    criteria for, 16
    culture, interplay with, 14
    definition, 13, 14, 73, 198

educators, 171
environmental. See Environmental health
environmental studies on, 138
events, sentinel, 144–145
hazards, 9
Hispanic, ix
indicators, positive and negative, 193,
        195
    interrelationship with preventive
        activities, 196
insurance, xvi
issues, 41–43. See also Border, U.S.-
        Mexico, health issues
meaning and expression, 13–36
perceived, 15–18
public. See Public health
responsibility for, 16
services, 181. See also Health services
        utilization
    international exchange of, 197–198
socioeconomic factors, 73, 74
status, 195
    children's, relationship of parental
        perceptions with actual, 17
    individual, options for intervention,
        194
subculture of the migrant, 26–28
values, 30, 195
Health behavior
    border, 14
    ethnic differences in attitudes about, 78
    interventions to modify, 23–24
        value of family involvement, 23
Health care, xvi
    access to, 38, 43, 50, 51
    barriers to, 73–74
    delivery system shortfalls, 74–75
    facility shortages, 74, 75–76
    financing services, 85
    funding, 75
    Mexico's national system, xvi
    obstetrical, 50, 51
    provider(s)
        distribution, educational strategies
            to improve, 82–84
        shortages, 74, 75–76
    reciprocal financing system, 85
    subcultures, 13
    uncompensated, 50, 85
    utilization patterns, 20. See also Health
        services utilization
Health education, 164
    interventions
        culturally appropriate, 165, 176
        group specific, 166

Housing, 8, 51
substandard, 79, 84, 125
HPSA. *See* Health Professional Shortage
Areas
HRSA. *See* Health Resources and Services
Administration
Human abuse, xvi
Human immunodeficiency virus infection,
46–47, 87–116
death rate, 45
of Hispanics along border, 88–116
heterosexual infection, 89
Hispanic border youth, 96–98
increase in the U.S., rate of, 110
male to female transmission, 90–91
prevention
outreach efforts, 91, 96
programs, 96. See *also* AIDS prevention programs
risk, 66, 89, 94
transmission modes among border Hispanics, 90–91, 110–111
Hypertension, xvi, 44, 80

IBEP. *See* Integrated Border Environmental
Plan
IBWC. *See* International Boundary and Water Commission
Illegal dumping, 181
Illegal immigrants, xiii
Illegal immigration, xiv, 11, 65
social consequences in California, 11
Illness. *See also* Disease
categories of, 18–21
causative factors, cultural differences, 78
chronic, morbidity rates of Hispanics,
29
folk-defined, 19
self-treatment, 48
treatment, appropriate, cultural differences, 78
Immigrant status, 118
Immigration, 10–11
illegal, xiv
Mexico to the U.S. from, 4
Immigration and Naturalization Services,
xiv, 52
Immunization, 45
Index of Health Status, 195
Infant mortality, 7, 41–42
birth weight–specific fetal and neonatal
rates, 41–42
causes, 41
Institute for Border Community Health
Education, 174

Integrated Border Environmental Plan, 61,
62, 63, 182, 183
enforcement, 182
Integration/adaptation, 54
Interdisciplinary grants, 82
International Boundary and Water Commis-
sion, 61, 122, 157
Intravenous drug users, 91

Job opportunities in the labor market, 4
Juarez, 4, 6, 8, 39, 48, 63, 84, 128, 129,
133, 134, 150, 151, 186
Juarez-El Paso border, 4
JUNTOS UNIDOS, 41, 59

Kellogg Foundation, ix
Kinship ties, 4, 5

La Clinica de Familia, 76
La Clinica de la Raza, Oakland, CA, 172
La Paz Agreement, 61, 122, 144, 181–183
Land use management, 146
Laredo, 6, 121
Las Cruces, 39, 186
Latin America in, cause of HIV infection, 94
Lay health advisors, 83
Lead exposure, 120
Lead poisoning, 150
Life expectancy, 7, 193
increasing, 122
Lower Rio Grande Valley Regional Develop-
ment Council, 167
Lupus, 140

Magic, 19
Maquila(doras), 8–9, 10, 60, 84, 128, 132–
135, 156
American-owned, 133
contamination of border area, 134–135
definition, 78
enforcement of environmental laws, 182
enviromental problems caused by, 134–
135, 181
impact on environmental health, 10
impact on population increase, 132,
149
Mexican, 132
occupational health concerns, 134–135
program, 158
working conditions, 134
Maquila(dora) industry, 29, 38, 66, 78,
132–135, 149
growth, 132
plant conditions, effect on workers, 79
problems related to, 79

size, 79
workers, 29, 79, 132–133
satisfaction of, 79
Mal ojo, 19
Matamoras, 8
Maternal and child health, 167
grants, 82, 83
issues, 41–43
programs, 43
recommendations, 43
Maverick County, 8
Mediation of hot and cold, 18–19
Medicaid, xvi, 76, 77
Medical services
demand for, 76–77
Mexican, utilization by U.S. citizens, 47
utilization, 47. *See also* Health services utilization
Medicare, 76, 77
Mental health
interpersonal relations and, 21–23
issues, 51–53
women's, effect of immigration, 55
Mesothelioma, 145
Methemoglobinemia, 145
Mexican(s)
birth outcomes, effects of U.S. residency of mothers, 42
folk beliefs, 18
folk medicine, 15
homosexuality, attitudes toward, 96
immigrant labor force, 3
labor, 3, 9
mental health problems, 21–23
migration, ix, 22, 53–54
use of U.S. health services, 49
women, common disorders of, 80
workers, 133
wages, 78
Mexican-Americans, ix, 14
death and disability in children, causes, 80
diabetes prevalence rate, 80
health behavior, 23
health professionals, 32
health status, 23
health values, 23
homosexuality, attitudes toward, 96
infant mortality rates, 41–42
low birth weight infants, 41
mental health problems, 22
patients, 15
population in Texas, 32
health professionals serving, 32

ratio of primary care physicians to, 32
reality, external, perceptions of, 21
renal disease, end stage, rates of, 80
research findings, contradictory, reasons for, 28, 30
retinopathy, diabetic, rates of, 80
therapists and, barriers between, 22
utilization of health services, 17, 20–21
differences from Anglo-American, 27
utilization of mental health services, 23
values, 23
women
disorders, common, 80
exploitation and sexual harassment, 79
health beliefs, 18
workers, wages, 79
Mexican Household Survey, 58
Mexican Institute of Psychiatry, 58
Mexican National Institute of Ecology, 149
Mexico
access to health care, 73, 74, 75
AIDS cases, male, female and children's, 94–95
AIDS problem, contributing factors, 95
AIDS-related deaths along border, 88
border cities, 9
drug use, 58
environmental laws, 151, 182
environmental standards, 84
fertility rates, 3
Health and Welfare Ministry, 74
health services, 74
proposed changes, 197–198
use by U.S. residents, 47–49
health system, 145
HIV transmission, 94
immunization rates for children, 84
minimum wage, 51
mortality, declining, 3
national health care system, xvi, 74
plants and workers, increase in, 132
population growth, 3
population of border states, 7
poverty, 3
quality of health care, 75
social security system, 74
women's roles, 55
Mexico AIDS Case Registry, 94
Migrant farmwork camps and water pollution, 125–126
Migrant farmworkers, 124
lifestyle, 118